EXPLORERS, SOLDIERS
AND STATESMEN

COLUMBUS AT THE COURT OF ISABELLA.

EXPLORERS, SOLDIERS AND STATESMEN
A HISTORY OF CANADA THROUGH BIOGRAPHY

BY

WILLIAM JOHN KARR

Essay Index Reprint Series

originally published by
J. M. DENT & SONS LTD.

BOOKS FOR LIBRARIES PRESS
FREEPORT, NEW YORK

First Published 1938
Reprinted 1970

STANDARD BOOK NUMBER:
8369-1577-1

LIBRARY OF CONGRESS CATALOG CARD NUMBER:
79-108640

PRINTED IN THE UNITED STATES OF AMERICA

CONTENTS

		PAGE
	PREFACE	ix
I.	CHRISTOPHER COLUMBUS	1
	The Discoverer of a New World	
II.	JOHN CABOT	8
	The Italian Mariner of Bristol	
III.	JACQUES CARTIER	12
	The Discoverer of the St. Lawrence	
IV.	SAMUEL DE CHAMPLAIN	21
	The Founder of New France	
V.	HENRY HUDSON	30
	An English Adventurer in the North	
VI.	FATHER JEAN BRÉBEUF	35
	The Jesuit Martyr	
VII.	ADAM DAULAC	41
	The Hero of the Long Sault	
VIII.	JEAN TALON	46
	The Great Intendant	
IX.	PIERRE RADISSON	51
	Coureur de Bois par Excellence	
X.	FATHER JACQUES MARQUETTE	56
	The Missionary Explorer	
XI.	LA SALLE	60
	The Greatest of French Explorers	
XII.	COUNT FRONTENAC	67
	The Fighting Governor	

CONTENTS

		PAGE
XIII.	MADELEINE DE VERCHÈRES	74
	The Heroine of Lower Canada	
XIV.	LA VÉRENDRYE	78
	The Pathfinder of the Prairies	
XV.	MARQUIS DE MONTCALM	85
	The Defender of French Canada	
XVI.	GENERAL JAMES WOLFE	92
	The British Hero of Quebec	
XVII.	GENERAL JAMES MURRAY	101
	The First Governor of British Canada	
XVIII.	PONTIAC	106
	The Indian Conspirator	
XIX.	SIR GUY CARLETON	112
	The Father of British Canada	
XX.	JOSEPH BRANT	120
	The Mohawk Ally of Britain	
XXI.	CAPTAIN JAMES COOK	125
	The Explorer of the Pacific	
XXII.	SAMUEL HEARNE	131
	The Traveller of the Barren Lands	
XXIII.	SIR ALEXANDER MACKENZIE . . .	137
	The Conqueror of the Rockies	
XXIV.	CAPTAIN GEORGE VANCOUVER . . .	142
	The Geographer of the Pacific Coast	
XXV.	DAVID THOMPSON	145
	The Surveyor of the Great West	
XXVI.	COLONEL JOHN GRAVES SIMCOE . .	152
	The Founder of Upper Canada	
XXVII.	SIR ISAAC BROCK	159
	The Military Hero of 1812	

CONTENTS

		PAGE
XXVIII.	TECUMSEH	166
	The War Chief of the Shawnees	
XXIX.	LAURA SECORD	172
	The Heroine of Beaver Dams	
XXX.	THE EARL OF SELKIRK	176
	The Colonizer of the West	
XXXI.	SIR JOHN FRANKLIN	183
	The Discoverer of the North-West Passage	
XXXII.	WILLIAM LYON MACKENZIE	189
	The Enemy of the Family Compact	
XXXIII.	LOUIS JOSEPH PAPINEAU	195
	The Tribune of Lower Canada	
XXXIV.	LORD SYDENHAM	201
	The Diplomatist of the Union	
XXXV.	ROBERT BALDWIN	209
	The Great Reformer	
XXXVI.	SIR LOUIS LAFONTAINE	214
	French-Canadian Statesman and Jurist	
XXXVII.	BISHOP STRACHAN	218
	Educator, Churchman, and Statesman	
XXXVIII.	DR. EGERTON RYERSON	223
	The Founder of a Great School System	
XXXIX.	SIR JAMES DOUGLAS	228
	The Founder of British Columbia	
XL.	SIR JOHN A. MACDONALD	235
	The Master Builder	
XLI.	JOSEPH HOWE	248
	The Orator-Statesman of Nova Scotia	
XLII.	SIR GEORGES ÉTIENNE CARTIER	254
	Quebec's Apostle of Confederation	

CONTENTS

		PAGE
XLIII.	HON. GEORGE BROWN	258
	Journalist and Reformer	
XLIV.	HON. ALEXANDER MACKENZIE	262
	The Stone-mason who became Prime Minister	
XLV.	SIR CHARLES TUPPER	268
	The Fighter from Nova Scotia	
XLVI.	SIR LEONARD TILLEY	274
	The Favourite Son of New Brunswick	
XLVII.	THOMAS D'ARCY McGEE	278
	The Irish-Canadian Patriot	
XLVIII.	LORD STRATHCONA	285
	Trader, Railway Builder, and Statesman	
XLIX.	SIR OLIVER MOWAT	292
	Ontario's Great Reform Premier	
L.	SIR WILFRID LAURIER	296
	The Silver-tongued Chieftain of Liberalism	
LI.	SIR JAMES WHITNEY	307
	Ontario's Great Conservative Premier	
LII.	SIR ROBERT BORDEN	314
	Canada's War Premier	
	INDEX	327

PREFACE

ONE of the inherent characteristics of human beings is an interest in personality. It is because of this characteristic that biography is the best medium through which to approach the study of history. The dry, dull facts of social and political changes are coloured, illuminated, and given an interest through their intimate association with the great men and women of the past.

The pages of Canadian history are rich in picturesque and striking figures about whom cluster the great events in the evolution of our national institutions. Through the stories of the lives of these notable men and women, one may obtain, in the most interesting of all ways, a clear and comprehensive grasp of the history of their times. The story of the early settlement of Canada is but a narrative of the stirring exploits of Cartier, Champlain, Talon, and other French heroes; the history of the Conquest is the story of the military feats of Wolfe and Montcalm; the coming of the Loyalists is bound up with the careers of Carleton and Simcoe; the development of responsible government is centred about the struggles of Mackenzie, Papineau, Baldwin, and Howe; the opening of the Great West is linked up with the labours of La Vérendrye, Thompson, Selkirk, and Strathcona; the greatest of all Canadian accomplishments, the confederation of the Provinces, will ever be connected with the names of Macdonald, Cartier, Brown, Mowat, and Tupper. Indeed, it is but stating a truism to say that there is no outstanding event in our history that is not inseparably associated with the name of some national figure.

Not only do the stories of their careers give a picturesqueness and a romance to our history, but they also set before us ideals of the highest type. Who can read the tales of their achievements for the good of Canada without being inspired with admiration, and who can admire without a desire to be worthy of the heritage which we owe to their labours? The self-sacrifice of a Brébeuf, the determination of a La Salle, the heroism of a Brock, the persistence of a Baldwin, the enthusiasm of a Ryerson, the vision of a Macdonald, the moral earnestness of a Brown, the integrity of a Mackenzie, the fervour of a McGee, the fearlessness of a Tupper, the inspiration of a Laurier, the straightforwardness of a Whitney, have almost become proverbs among us, and the influence of the example and work of such men upon our character, both as individuals and as a nation, cannot be estimated.

With a firm belief in these truths, the author has attempted to transfer to the most important events in Canadian history some of the glamour that surrounds the careers of our great men and women, and at the same time to give a glimpse of the motives which inspired them in the service of our country. He freely admits that in his selection of characters he has been compelled to omit many that have earned a place of honour in our history. But he hopes that in the sketches of those he has selected he may be able to give the reader an added interest in the history of Canada and some impression of the moral ideals which they have bequeathed to Canadians.

W. J. K.

ILLUSTRATIONS

COLUMBUS AT THE COURT OF ISABELLA	*Frontispiece*	
AT PORT ROYAL	Facing page	2
PIONEER STAGE COACH	,, ,,	181
QUEBEC: THE FORTRESS CLIFF	,, ,,	196
		PAGE
CHRISTOPHER COLUMBUS		2
JOHN AND SEBASTIAN CABOT		9
JACQUES CARTIER		13
CARTIER'S VOYAGES		15
SAMUEL DE CHAMPLAIN		22
CHAMPLAIN'S JOURNEYS		23
FORT OF SAMUEL DE CHAMPLAIN		26
HENRY HUDSON		31
BUST OF FATHER BRÉBEUF		36
ADAM DAULAC		42
JEAN TALON		47
PIERRE RADISSON		52
FATHER JACQUES MARQUETTE		57
LA SALLE		61
ROUTES OF MARQUETTE, JOLIET, AND LA SALLE		63
COUNT FRONTENAC		68
MADELEINE DE VERCHÈRES		75
LA VÉRENDRYE		79
EXPLORATIONS OF RADISSON AND LA VÉRENDRYE		81
MARQUIS DE MONTCALM		86
GENERAL JAMES WOLFE		93
SIEGE OF QUEBEC, 1759		97
GENERAL JAMES MURRAY		102
ENGLISH MAN-OF-WAR		103
SIR GUY CARLETON		113

ILLUSTRATIONS

	PAGE
JOSEPH BRANT	121
CAPTAIN COOK	126
ROUTES OF WESTERN EXPLORERS	127
SAMUEL HEARNE	132
ROUTES OF HEARNE, MACKENZIE, AND FRANKLIN	134
SIR ALEXANDER MACKENZIE	138
CAPTAIN GEORGE VANCOUVER	143
MIGRATION OF UNITED EMPIRE LOYALISTS	153
COLONEL JOHN GRAVES SIMCOE	155
SIR ISAAC BROCK	160
TECUMSEH	167
LAURA SECORD'S COTTAGE	172
LAURA SECORD	174
LORD SELKIRK	177
SIR JOHN FRANKLIN	184
ABANDONING THE "EREBUS" AND "TERROR"	187
WILLIAM LYON MACKENZIE	190
LOUIS JOSEPH PAPINEAU	196
LORD SYDENHAM	202
NEW BRUNSWICK—MAINE BOUNDARY	205
ROBERT BALDWIN	210
SIR LOUIS LAFONTAINE	215
BISHOP STRACHAN	219
DR. EGERTON RYERSON	224
SIR JAMES DOUGLAS	229
SIR JOHN A. MACDONALD	236
JOSEPH HOWE	249
SIR GEORGES ÉTIENNE CARTIER	255
HON. GEORGE BROWN	259
HON. ALEXANDER MACKENZIE	263
SIR CHARLES TUPPER	269
THE C.P.R. PIERCES THE ROCKIES	272
SIR LEONARD TILLEY	275
THOMAS D'ARCY MCGEE	279
LORD STRATHCONA	286
SIR OLIVER MOWAT	293
SIR WILFRID LAURIER	297
ALASKA BOUNDARY	301
SIR JAMES P. WHITNEY	308
SIR ROBERT BORDEN	315

EXPLORERS, SOLDIERS AND STATESMEN

I

CHRISTOPHER COLUMBUS

THE DISCOVERER OF A NEW WORLD

NEARLY five hundred years ago, there lived in the city of Genoa, in Italy, a boy who was later to become a famous discoverer. His name was Christopher Columbus. Genoa was then, as it is now, a great seaport town. Its seamen had sailed to far-off lands over every sea that was then known in quest of trade. As a young lad Columbus was greatly interested in the sea. He was often to be found among the ships in the harbour in earnest conversation with the sailors. He listened with intense eagerness to the tales of strange lands and peoples which the sailors were ever willing to pour into the ears of an attentive listener. It is not surprising, therefore, that this boy should make up his mind that when he grew up he would be a seaman. He would then sail to these far-away places, and would perhaps find lands never before visited by Europeans.

Before this time European traders had begun to visit India and China, those eastern countries of marvellous wealth, and had brought back rare silks, spices, jewels, and perfumes. These merchants had gone by difficult overland routes, across deserts and mountains—long and hazardous journeys requiring many months of toil and hardship. No ocean route to the East was yet known. We must remember that the Suez Canal, joining the Mediterranean with the Red Sea, did not then exist, and that the route to the East around the southern end of Africa had not yet been discovered. Navigators began to speculate upon the possibility of finding a sea route to the East, so that trade with these fabulously rich countries might be easier.

This problem took hold of Columbus, and aroused in him the ambition to be the discoverer of a possible waterway to the Orient. He had by this time made several voyages in Genoese ships, but he saw that being merely a sailor would not help him to gain his end. He realized that he must become a master mariner and sail ships of his own. But to do this it would be necessary to have a wider knowledge than he already had. He appealed to his father to help him to get a university education. His father, though very poor, agreed, and the young man went for a short time to a university. It is said that he applied himself with such energy and industry that in a few months he had learned as much as other students ordinarily do in several years. However that may be, we know that he gained a knowledge of the sciences that were then known, that he was greatly interested in the study of geography, and that he became expert in the making of maps and charts.

CHRISTOPHER COLUMBUS
(The De Orchi Portrait)
Public Archives of Canada

While at the university Columbus was much impressed by the contention of one of the professors that the earth is spherical in form. It is hard for us now to understand how

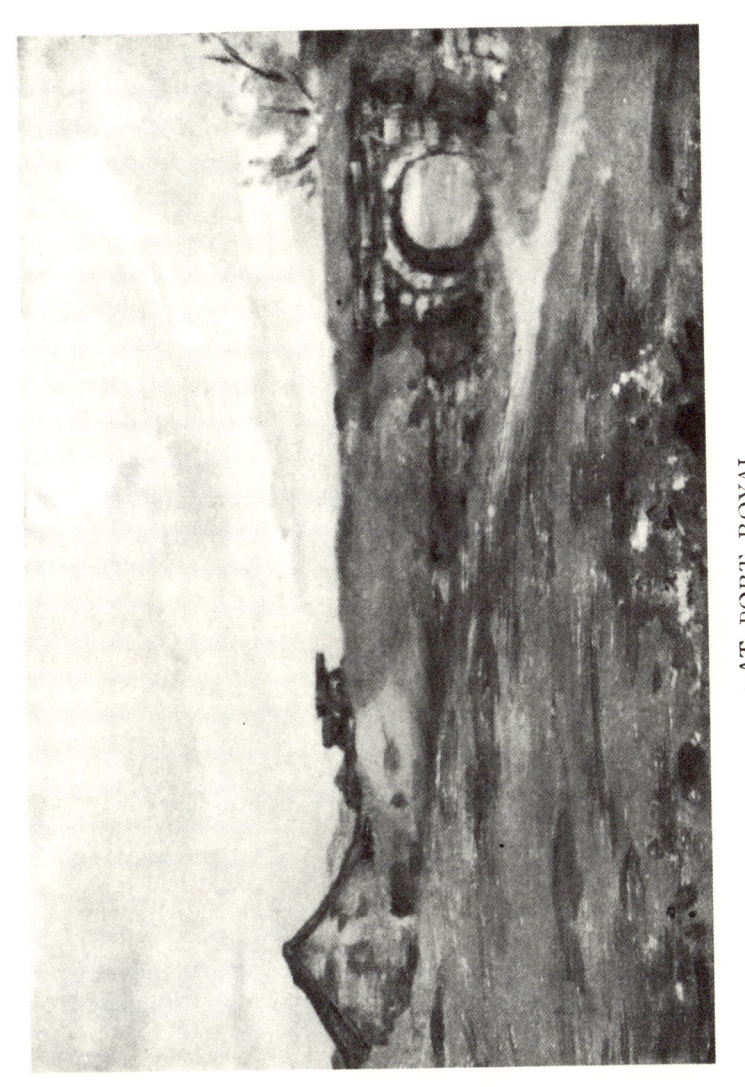

AT PORT ROYAL.

DIFFICULTIES

people could hold any other belief as to its shape, but the fact is that in those times the great majority thought the earth flat. Sailors were filled with foolish fears of what might become of them if they ventured too near the edge of the world. Columbus, however, became convinced that the earth is a great globe, and he therefore believed that by sailing westward it would be possible to reach China and India, those wonderful lands that European traders desired so strongly to reach. But Columbus made the mistake of thinking the earth to be much smaller than it really is. He believed that China could not be more than four thousand miles west of Europe. He did not know that the great continent of America and the vast Pacific Ocean lay between. However, there grew up in his mind the great plan of reaching those eastern countries of untold riches by sailing westward.

To carry out such a daring project Columbus saw that he must have several well-equipped vessels. Where to obtain these was the question. It was hopeless to expect them from Genoa, where he first made the attempt. He went next to the King of Portugal, whose sailors were famous throughout Europe for the discoveries they had made and the wealth they had brought to the country. The king listened with interest to the plan of Columbus, and referred it to his admirals for advice. They treated Columbus with scorn, and ridiculed his scheme as the dream of a madman. Seeing the hopelessness of any help from this quarter, Columbus at length quitted Portugal and went to Spain.

For some time he tried in vain to get the assistance of rich and powerful Spaniards. At length a nobleman was persuaded to write on his behalf to Queen Isabella, who with her husband, King Ferdinand, was joint ruler of Spain. They were at that time the most powerful sovereigns of Europe. Columbus was invited to proceed to the royal court at Cordova, where he unfolded his great plan before the queen. She was much impressed. Unfortunately, affairs in Spain were at that time so unsettled that she could not immediately give him the assistance he needed. For six years Columbus remained in Spain, hoping that the queen would soon be able to send him forth on his great mission. He was often penniless and hungry; he was treated with contempt by the courtiers of the royal palace; he was ridiculed even by the children in the streets. A less steadfast man than Columbus would have given up the project in despair.

At last the long and weary years of waiting came to an end. Early in the year 1492 Queen Isabella was able to provide Columbus with three vessels, the *Pinta*, the *Santa Maria*, and the *Nina*, for his great enterprise. But misfortune threatened the undertaking from the very beginning. There was difficulty in securing enough sailors to man the ships, for nearly everybody thought the scheme foolhardy, and few had the courage to face the perils of the unknown seas. At last eighty-eight men, many of them criminals released from Spanish prisons for the purpose, were persuaded to embark upon the voyage.

The vessels set sail from Palos, in the south of Spain, on August 3, 1492. Three days out at sea, the *Pinta* lost her rudder, and had to be put into one of the Canary Islands to be refitted. It was not till September 6th that everything was again in readiness for the voyage. Having been told that a number of Portuguese vessels were on the lookout to capture him and compel his return, Columbus sailed his fleet out of the harbour in haste, and luckily escaped. Thus began an historic voyage, one of the most difficult and dangerous ever undertaken by a sailor, and one of the most momentous in its consequences for the nations of the world.

Scarcely had the last trace of land faded on the eastern horizon when feelings of uneasiness began to appear among the crews. The mystery of the unknown filled their hearts with vague fears. Every unusual happening became to them a foreboding of evil.

"Did you see that star fall into the sea?" said one sailor. "That is a sign of some dreadful thing to come."

"And these north-east winds are blowing us farther and farther from Spain," said another. "We shall never be able to sail back against them."

FEARFUL SAILORS

As the days wore on and no signs of land were seen, the fears of the crews turned first into disobedience and then into open rebellion. In the midst of all these difficulties Columbus showed the greatest patience and cheerfulness. He tried to inspire the men with his own confidence in the outcome of the voyage.

"We shall surely come to land soon," he said. "India or China cannot be far away. Let us not stop when we are so near the goal. Let us sail on. Think of the honour and fame that will be ours when we find a new road to the East."

But the sailors grew daily more mutinous, and whispered among themselves: "The commander is a madman. Let us throw him into the sea. We can then seize the ships and go back to our families and friends."

"Return to Spain! Return to Spain!" was the incessant cry of the crews.

"Give me three days more," demanded Columbus. "If signs of land do not appear within that time, I will yield to your wishes and turn back."

Fortunately, proofs of the nearness of land were soon afterwards seen. The sailors observed flocks of field birds. Then they picked up a branch with berries on it, a piece of board, and a carved stick. There could no longer be any doubt that the ships were nearing the land for which the sailors had so long and anxiously looked. The grave danger in which Columbus had stood for many weeks at last disappeared. Late at night on the 11th of October he was keeping an anxious watch on deck. Peering eagerly into the darkness, he fancied that he saw a light glimmering in the distance.

"Do I see a light ahead, or do my eyes deceive me?" he asked an officer at hand.

"It is surely a light," said the officer after a pause.

"Thank God!" exclaimed Columbus fervently. "The long and hazardous voyage is over!"

At dawn on the following morning, to the great relief of the crew, land was plainly visible. Before noon Columbus, clad in the scarlet uniform of an admiral and bearing the royal standard of Spain, landed, and took solemn possession of the land in the name of the Spanish sovereigns. There is some uncertainty to-day as to the place he landed, but it is generally supposed that it was Watling Island, the most easterly of the Bahama group. The natives thronged around Columbus and his men with every mark of astonishment.

"We shall call this island San Salvador," said Columbus, "for God has been gracious in saving our lives through all the dangers of the sea. And we shall call these people Indians, for we must be near the eastern coast of India."

Thus, through a mistaken idea of the discoverer of the North American continent, the natives acquired an inappropriate name which has clung to them ever since.

The delight of the sailors in standing once more upon solid earth was unbounded. They gathered around their commander, applauding his wisdom and begging pardon for their rebellion. Those who had been most troublesome during the voyage were now loudest in their praises and warmest in their devotion. In the moment of triumph Columbus could afford to be generous, and he freely forgave them for the trouble they had caused.

The remainder of the year was devoted to the exploration of the neighbouring islands in the hope of reaching the mainland of India. Early in 1493 the *Pinta* and the *Nina* were made ready for the return voyage to Spain, the *Santa Maria* having in the meantime been wrecked. The two vessels became separated during the voyage, but by a strange chance both reached Palos about the same time.

Columbus proceeded at once to Barcelona, where the royal court was. At the news of his coming a procession was formed, and he entered the city in triumph. He made his report to the king and queen and received the royal thanks. For his great services he was given the title of Don, and had other great honours showered upon him.

It would be pleasant if we could leave Columbus thus, a national hero, secure in the favour of his sovereigns and in the honour of the people to whom he had brought renown. But, sadly enough, the later years of his life were filled with troubles. He made three other voyages to the New World, and attempted to form a colony on one of the islands of the West Indies. He failed as a governor, and was actually sent by his enemies back to Spain a prisoner in chains. Through the influence of the queen, however, his honours were restored, and he regained popular favour for a time. On his return from his last voyage in 1502, his steadfast friend, Queen Isabella, was dead, and jealous enemies soon brought about his downfall. The nation for which he had won so much renown permitted him to be neglected and to sink into poverty. Broken-hearted and friendless, Columbus died at Valladolid in 1506.

II

JOHN CABOT

THE ITALIAN MARINER OF BRISTOL

ANOTHER man who dreamed of great discoveries in the western seas was John Cabot. He was born in Genoa four years later than Columbus. They may have known each other as boys; it is quite possible, indeed, that they listened to the same tales of the sea from the same sailors. At any rate, they were filled with the same aspiration to find a new avenue of trade with the East by way of the Atlantic Ocean.

At the age of eleven Cabot went with his father to Venice, a city equally famous with Genoa for its seafaring people and its foreign trade. There is no clear record of how Cabot spent his early years, but we know that somehow he became a geographer as well as a practical seaman. He visited Mecca, in Arabia, which was then the great market for the exchange of goods between the East and the West. Cabot learned that the spices, perfumes, silks, and precious stones which were sold in Mecca to European traders came from eastern Asia, carried thither over great distances by caravans. The idea came to him that these goods might more easily be brought to Europe from the west across the Atlantic. Thus the same great purpose came to Cabot as had come to Columbus, to find a western route to China, Japan, and India.

For some time before Columbus made his great discovery, Cabot had been in England, engaged in sea-going trade from the port of Bristol, which was then the great rival of London as a seaport. The story of the exploits of Columbus fired his imagination, and presently he applied to King Henry VII

A CAREFUL KING

for leave to make a similar voyage of discovery. The king had a few years before refused to consider a request for assistance made to him on behalf of Columbus, and it is quite possible that he regretted his mistake. He was now quite willing to give encouragement to Cabot in the undertaking he proposed. But, being a most miserly king, Henry refused to put any money into the venture, and he merely gave Cabot permission to fit out his expedition at his own cost. He agreed, however, that the goods brought back should be admitted free of duty, but stipulated that one-fifth of the profits should be paid into the king's treasury. Cabot was to take all the risks, but the king was to share in the rewards.

Accordingly, early in 1497 Cabot fitted out a small vessel, the *Matthew*, and secured a crew of eighteen men. In May, with his son Sebastian, a youth of twenty-one, he embarked upon the voyage westward.

Public Archives of Canada
JOHN AND SEBASTIAN CABOT

The little ship was tossed about by the storms and the variable winds, but the commander was not troubled by a mutinous crew as Columbus had been during his memorable voyage. Cabot's men knew that there was land ahead of them and had no superstitious terror of unknown dangers.

After a voyage of fifty-one days, land was sighted. Going

ashore, Cabot took possession of the country in the name of His Majesty Henry VII of England. The land was found to be fertile and well wooded, and the weather at this summer season was delightful. It is fairly certain that the spot where the sailors landed was what is now called Cape Breton Island, the northern part of the present Province of Nova Scotia. John Cabot was thus the first European to land in Canada, and may therefore fairly be called its discoverer.

Sailing through the waters south of Newfoundland, Cabot was amazed at the vast numbers of codfish to be found there. These were so numerous that all the sailors needed to catch them was a basket weighted with a stone and lowered over the side of the vessel. Cabot was the first to see the possibilities of the cod-fishing industry on the banks of Newfoundland.

By August the expedition had returned to Bristol. Cabot's report of the voyage was so glowing that he aroused great enthusiasm in the city. Whenever he appeared in the streets he was followed by crowds of admirers. We are told that he dressed in silk every day and lived in princely style. King Henry VII was generous enough to make a gift of £10 "to him who found the new isle," and to make extravagant promises of support in future expeditions. Cabot believed that he had discovered the north-east coast of Asia, and declared that on his next voyage he would reach Japan and bring back the rich products of the East. On the strength of this prospect, the king conferred on Cabot a pension of £20 a year, to be paid, not out of the royal purse, but out of the duties on goods collected at the port of Bristol.

Early in the following year, 1498. Cabot was ready with two ships, manned by three hundred men, for a second voyage. The king had opened the doors of the prisons to a large number of convicts, and these formed the greater part of the crews. This time Cabot directed the vessels in a more northerly course. Why he did this has never been very clear, unless it was that he had some idea of finding Japan and China by sailing around the northern shore of the land he had touched on his former voyage. If this is true, Cabot was the first man to think of a "North-West Passage"—an idea that was to be fatal to so many seamen during the next

UNFULFILLED HOPES

three centuries. Whatever may have been Cabot's purpose, he sailed his ships north-westward, skirting the coast of Greenland, entering Davis Strait, and landing on Baffin Island. They passed huge icebergs and sailed through immense fields of ice, the crews meanwhile suffering intensely from the cold. Mutiny broke out among the seamen, and Cabot was compelled to direct his course southward.

On the southward voyage he skirted the forbidding coast of Labrador. He thought the Strait of Belle Isle merely one of the many bays of the coast, and Newfoundland a part of the mainland. He touched again at Nova Scotia, and continued his southerly course along the coast of what is now the United States. The cold of the Arctic currents gave place to the warmth of the Gulf Stream, and the barren and rocky coasts of Labrador were succeeded by the wooded and sandy beaches of the Carolinas. But nowhere could Cabot find the rich and populous island of Japan. He had to turn homeward with his great mission unfulfilled.

Of what happened to Cabot afterwards, we know very little. It is certain only that he reached Bristol, and that he lived long enough to draw at least one payment of the pension arranged by the king.

III

JACQUES CARTIER

THE DISCOVERER OF THE ST. LAWRENCE

THE seaport of St. Malo, on the northern coast of France in the old province of Brittany, has for centuries been the home of hardy fishermen and daring seamen. A boy born and brought up in St. Malo could scarcely fail to become interested in the seafaring life. Four centuries ago, when new lands were being rapidly discovered across the western seas, we can imagine the stir and excitement about the wharves of this seaport town. We can picture in our minds the busy scene—the fishing-boats coming and going; the ships being provisioned for distant voyages; the groups of sailors here and there in lively conversation; the small boys near at hand with faces aglow, drinking in the tales of far-off lands. We may be almost sure that among these lads was one who later became the greatest of all the mariners of St. Malo—Jacques Cartier.

Like many another boy of St. Malo, Jacques Cartier quite naturally determined to follow the adventurous life of the sea. We know little of his boyhood and youth beyond the fact that he early became a seaman and soon advanced to the post of pilot. It is probable that among his early voyages he went at one time as far as Brazil. We find him, at forty years of age, a master pilot in the service of His Majesty Francis I, King of France.

By this time people had become convinced that the great new continent of America lay between Europe and Asia on the west, and it now became the ambition of sailors to find a way around or through the new continent to Asia. It seems strange to us in this day, with our better knowledge

DISAPPOINTING SHORES

of the size of the earth and the wealth of America, that this continent should have been regarded only as a barrier to trade with the East.

In April, 1534, Jacques Cartier was sent by the King of France with two vessels and sixty-one men to find a north-west route to the East. The expedition made a quick voyage in favourable weather across the Atlantic, and reached the shores of Newfoundland just twenty days after starting. The passage through the Strait of Belle Isle was delayed for several days by storms and gales. Cartier skirted the coast of Quebec opposite Newfoundland for some distance, but found the country so barren and forbidding that he said, "This is surely the land that God gave to Cain." From time to time he caught sight of painted Indians dressed in skins paddling in bark canoes among the bays and islands of the coast.

Public Archives of Canada
JACQUES CARTIER

He directed his course southward along the western coast of Newfoundland, and touched at the Magdalen Islands and Prince Edward Island. He was much delighted with the appearance of the latter, which he believed to be part of the mainland of the continent. Coasting northward along the New Brunswick shore, he came at length to a large open body of water, which he at first thought must be the passage to the East that he was seeking. He was much disappointed to find, upon exploring it, that it was merely a land-locked bay. On account of the hot weather that he met at this time, Cartier called the bay *Chaleur*, this name being the French word for *heat*. On the north shore of the bay he met a large number of Indians, who surrounded the ships in their canoes. Though at first he feared that they might be hostile, he was soon convinced by their gestures that they were friendly. They gladly exchanged furs for the knives and iron tools that the French offered them.

Proceeding northward, Cartier landed at Gaspé Bay, where he met with another large party of friendly Indians. Here he set up with solemn ceremony a large wooden cross thirty feet high, bearing the emblem of his country, the *fleur-de-lis*, and the inscription, "Long live the King of France." The Indians were much puzzled.

"Does this mean that these people are taking possession of our lands?" they asked among themselves.

Before the French sailed away the chief and his two sons came on board one of the vessels to protest that the country belonged to his nation.

"The Indians need have no fears," replied Cartier. "The cross has been erected just to mark the entrance of the harbour."

The chief was loaded with gifts, and went ashore highly pleased, leaving his two sons to accompany the French to their land across the seas.

Cartier next visited the Island of Anticosti. Standing at its western end, he looked at the broad estuary that washes its shores. As far as the eye could see in the direction of the setting sun stretched an unbroken expanse of water.

"This surely is the passage to the East for which we have been looking," exclaimed Cartier.

"But it is getting late in the year," said one of the sailors.

"The stormy season is approaching, and France is far away," urged another.

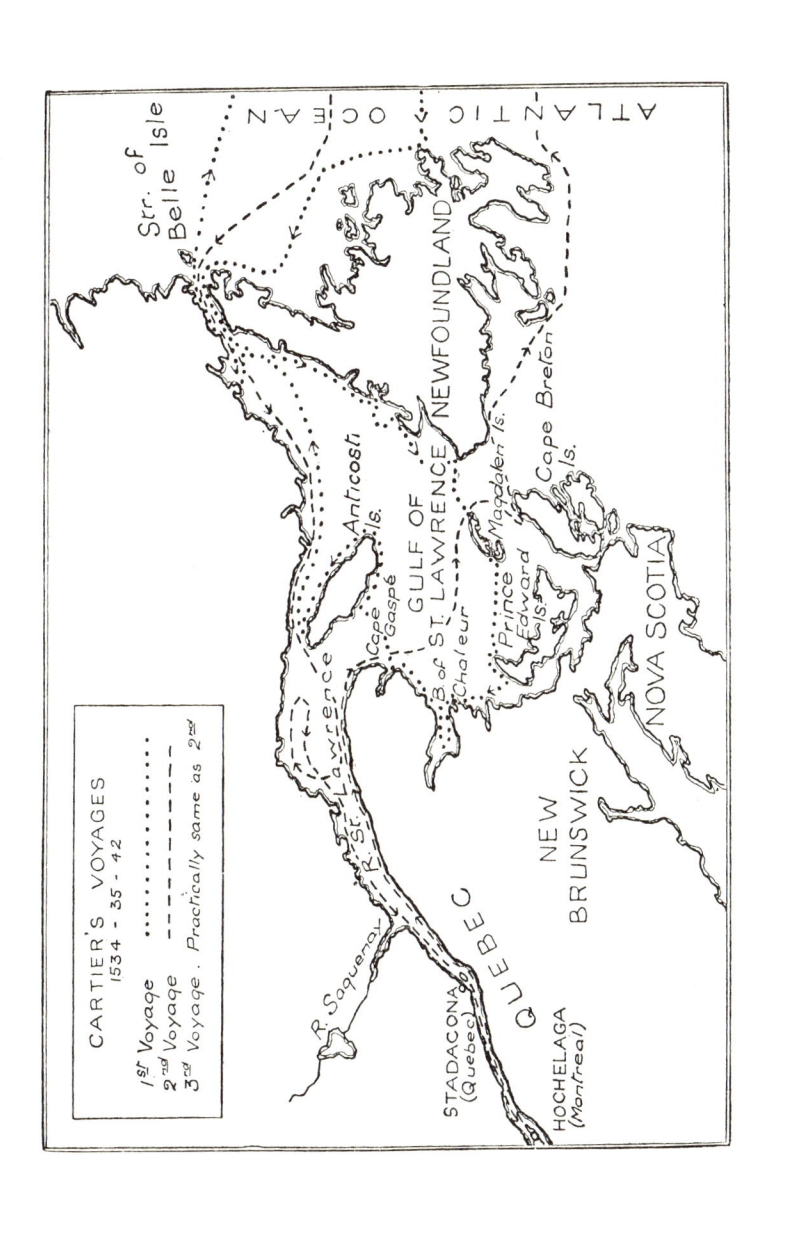

"That is true," replied Cartier. "We shall have to postpone the exploration of the passage till our return next year."

Cartier's report of his explorations aroused great interest in France. King Francis I was highly pleased and offered generous assistance in the equipment of another expedition. Three ships, the *Grande Hermine*, *Petite Hermine*, and *Emerillon*, manned by one hundred and sixty men and provisioned for a year, were ready in May, 1535, for the second venture.

This time the voyage was not so fortunate, for the winds were unfavourable and storms were frequent. The ships became separated during a heavy gale. Early in July Cartier, in the *Grande Hermine*, sailed through the Strait of Belle Isle and landed on the Quebec shore to await the coming of the other ships. At length, towards the end of the month, they appeared. After repairs had been made, the fleet proceeded up the St. Lawrence, which Cartier at that time fondly hoped would lead him at last to Asia.

The two Indians whom Cartier had brought back as guides soon found themselves amid familiar surroundings.

"The waters through which we are sailing," they told him, "narrow into a great river farther on."

"The freshness of the water seems to show that what they say is true," said Cartier to his men. "The water is not salt like the ocean."

"If this is just a river," he continued, "it cannot be a passage between two seas, as we had hoped, and so it cannot be the road to China. However, we shall sail on. Perhaps we may find new sources of wealth for France."

Presently Cartier reached the Island of Orleans, where he met a number of Indians. The savages were astonished to find that the two Indian guides belonged to their tribe and spoke their language. Thereupon they swarmed about the French with every mark of friendliness, brought them corn and pumpkins, and received with great delight the trinkets which Cartier distributed. Their chief, Donnacona, invited him to visit his village of Stadacona, which was situated on the north bank of the St. Lawrence where the city of Quebec now stands. Cartier found the village to be merely

STADACONA AND HOCHELAGA 17

a collection of rude wigwams. He moored his two larger vessels at the mouth of the St. Charles River near at hand, but kept the *Emerillon* in readiness for a further voyage.

Having learned from the Indian guides that there was another village, named Hochelaga, many miles up the St. Lawrence, Cartier determined to visit it also. Donnacona tried to persuade him not to go. The chief feared that there might not be any more gifts for him if he allowed the French to get away from his village.

"Hochelaga is not worth visiting, and there are great dangers on the way," he said to Cartier.

Then he tried by a curious device to frighten him into giving up the plan. A canoe shot out from the bushes into the river and approached Cartier's vessel. It contained three Indians, dressed in the most outlandish fashion, with black paint on their faces, huge horns on their heads, and skins of animals on their bodies. They made long speeches, apparently warning Cartier not to go to Hochelaga.

"They are evil spirits," explained Donnacona impressively. "If you disobey them, terrible things will happen. The spirits say that the white men must not go farther up the river."

"Such foolish threats cannot frighten us," said Cartier with amusement. "We are going to Hochelaga."

He took with him his smallest vessel and fifty men, leaving the rest of the crew at Stadacona with instructions to make preparations for wintering there.

Cartier reached the Island of Montreal at the beginning of October, and was received by the Indians there with great friendliness. He found the village of Hochelaga to be composed of about fifty large oblong buildings, each divided into many rooms and occupied by several families. The Indians believed the Frenchmen to be supernatural beings, and they brought their sick and lame for Cartier to heal. He read for them the Gospel of St. John, and, though they understood not a word of it, he believed that something of its meaning penetrated to their darkened souls. Before leaving the island Cartier, with some of the Indians as guides, climbed to the top of the mountain that lay near the village. From here he obtained a magnificent view of the surrounding country—the turbulent Lachine rapids, the yellow waters of the Ottawa, the blue Laurentian hills, and on all sides the trees arrayed in their brilliant autumn colours. Cartier was told by the guides that beyond the rapids he might sail for many weeks, and up the Ottawa he might find stores of gold and silver.

By the middle of October Cartier was back at Stadacona, the voyage to Hochelaga having occupied only three weeks. He found that the men he had left behind had made good use of the time. They had built a strong fort on the bank of the St. Charles for protection against a possible attack by the Indians, and about its walls had mounted the cannon taken from the vessels. Cartier was never fully convinced that the Indians were as friendly as they appeared.

Soon the northern winter was upon them, and the ships were frozen fast in the ice of the river. Accustomed as they were to the milder climate of France, the men suffered severely from cold. To make matters worse, many of them were attacked by scurvy, a dreadful disease caused from lack of proper food. Huddled together in the narrow holds of the vessels, chilled by the cold, without doctors or nurses to relieve their pain or priests to give them religious comfort, in constant fear of an Indian attack, the French met the terrible situation with true courage. Cartier, whose iron frame and robust health withstood the attacks of the disease, kept the Indians in ignorance of the sore straits of his men. The sailors who died, twenty-five in number, were buried in the snow on the farther sides of the vessels. Whenever the Indians appeared in sight, Cartier caused a vigorous hammering to be made on the ships to give the impression that the French were too busy with their tasks on board to appear on shore. At last, by accident, Cartier learned the remedy used by the Indians for the cure of scurvy. This was a drink made by boiling in water the leaves and bark of a tree, probably the white spruce. When this was given to the victims of the disease, they recovered so quickly that it seemed almost a miracle.

At last the long and dreadful winter passed. By the middle

INDIAN CAPTIVES

of April, 1536, the ice of the river had broken and the ships were loosed. Cartier started preparations for the return to France. But before he could get away he noticed a large number of strange Indians in the village. Believing that Donnacona was getting ready to wipe out the French, Cartier formed a daring plan. He invited the chief and eleven other Indians to the vessels to celebrate his departure, and when they came on board he made them prisoners. The rage of the Indians, thus deprived of their leaders, was great. Fortunately, Donnacona, soothed by fresh gifts and the promise of a speedy return, decided to go to France without further protest. He appeared on deck and quieted his enraged tribesmen. The French, having distributed many gifts among the Indians, were then allowed to depart in peace. They reached the harbour of St. Malo in safety in July, 1536.

For some time the King of France was so busy with other matters that he could give no assistance in the further exploration of the New World. In 1540, convinced of the wealth of Canada by the stories of Cartier and the Indian captives, he decided to establish a colony. He assigned the task to a French nobleman, the Sieur de Roberval. Jacques Cartier was to accompany Roberval as captain-general. Each was given a large sum of money to fit out vessels and secure the necessary supplies for the colony. Prisons were emptied of convicts to provide a sufficient number of colonists. Cartier was ready first. In May, 1541, he set sail with five vessels, leaving Roberval to follow later.

Reaching Stadacona in August, Cartier had first to explain to the Indians what had become of the prisoners who had been carried off five years before. Though Donnacona and his fellow-captives had all died, Cartier told the Indians that only the chief was dead, and that the others were now great lords in France and had decided to remain there. The Indians accepted the explanation, and the new chief, who was now sure of his position, showed the greatest friendliness towards the French.

A few miles above Stadacona, on the north bank of the river, at a point affording good anchorage for the ships,

Cartier built a strong fort. He called it Charlesbourg Royal. Near the fort they discovered quantities of bright stones which they took to be diamonds, and near the water's edge they found thin leaves of what they believed to be gold. When examined later in France, the bright stones turned out to be only rock crystals; and though the gold was genuine, the supply was afterwards found to be very small.

In the spring of 1542 Cartier decided to abandon the colony and return to France. He met Roberval in the harbour of St. John's in Newfoundland, and, though commanded to return to Canada, he stole away in the night. Cartier believed that the attempt to found a colony was doomed to failure, and disliked the idea of serving as an inferior officer under Roberval.

Roberval, with three vessels and two hundred colonists, reached Charlesbourg Royal in the early summer. The fort was strengthened, and good buildings were put up to live in. But food ran short, and disease broke out, carrying off about fifty of the colonists. They passed a winter of suffering, perhaps greater even than that of Cartier's men seven years before. Next year Cartier was sent out to assist in bringing the colonists back to France. And thus ends the first romantic and yet tragic chapter in the history of Canada.

Of the last fifteen years of Jacques Carter's life there is little record. He was given a title of honour by the king for the great services he had rendered. He lived in retirement in his native city until his death in 1557. We who live in Canada to-day may well pay tribute to the courageous mariner of St. Malo, whose explorations gave the world the first definite knowledge of this country.

IV

SAMUEL DE CHAMPLAIN

THE FOUNDER OF NEW FRANCE

No name is more highly honoured in the history of Canada than that of Samuel de Champlain. He is rightly regarded as the founder of this country, because it was under his leadership and guidance that the first permanent settlement was made.

He was born in a little village on the west coast of France. His father was a mariner, and without doubt the young Samuel received early lessons in seamanship. But before he became a sailor he fought as a soldier in the civil war that was being waged in France at that time. When he was freed from fighting at the age of thirty-one, he became captain of a Spanish vessel trading in the West Indies. He wrote an interesting book describing his experiences in Spanish America and the customs of the natives there. In this book Champlain made the remarkable suggestion that a canal should be dug across the isthmus of Panama, a work that was not carried out till more than three centuries later. Returning to France, he was given the official title of geographer to the king.

For sixty years after Cartier's bitter experiences, little attention had been given to Canada. It was regarded as "a land of barbarians, bears, and beavers," with a soil so barren and a climate so severe as to make the formation of a colony impossible. French fishermen came to the banks of Newfoundland for the rich catches of cod, and French traders visited the St. Lawrence for the valuable furs obtained from the Indians. But no attempt to plant a colony had been made.

22 SAMUEL DE CHAMPLAIN

It was in 1603 that the great work of Champlain's life began. In that year he joined a French merchant in an expedition to the St. Lawrence. It was agreed that, while the merchant bartered with the Indians for furs, the geographer should explore the country and study the native customs. Champlain traced the Saguenay and the Richelieu Rivers for some distance from their mouths, and visited the Lachine rapids, but added little to the information that Cartier had secured many years before. After this voyage he wrote another book, in which he described the character and habits of the Indians.

Public Archives of Canada
SAMUEL DE CHAMPLAIN

During the next three years Champlain was occupied in an effort to establish a colony in Acadia. The leading spirits in the venture were two French gentlemen, De Monts and Poutrincourt, who were given a monopoly of the fur-trade. In 1604 the party landed on the east coast of Nova Scotia not far from where the city of Halifax now stands. Champlain was sent to find a suitable harbour along the coast for the establishment of a colony. He skirted the Atlantic coast southward as far as Long Island, exploring the islands and the mouths of rivers as he went. The place selected for the settlement was the Island of St. Croix, at the mouth of the river of the same name, which now forms part of the New Brunswick boundary. The following winter was exceedingly severe, and the colonists suffered terribly from lack of warm dwellings, good water, and proper food. Scurvy broke out, and before the winter was

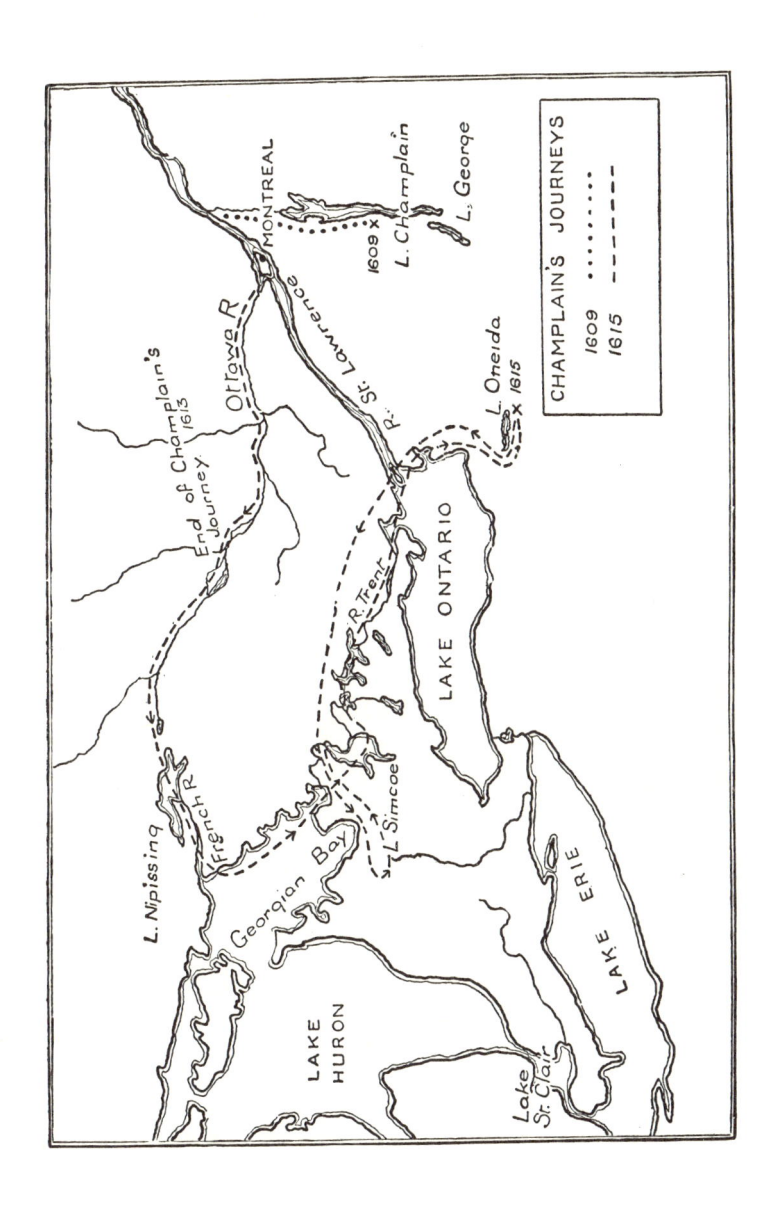

over more than a third of the party had died. It was a repetition of the experience of Cartier's companions at Stadacona in 1536.

As was to be expected, the survivors of this terrible winter set out in the spring to find a better place to live. This time the choice fell upon a harbour on the opposite coast of the Bay of Fundy, now known as Annapolis Basin. Here the colony of Port Royal was set up. The next winter was mild; and as the French had better shelter, food, and water, they suffered little from scurvy. In the following summer Poutrincourt arrived from France with more settlers, and things looked bright for the colony.

Poutrincourt then undertook another exploring expedition southward. He unwisely insisted upon covering the same ground as Champlain had gone over two years before, so that little additional knowledge of the country was gained. The Indians along the coast were unfriendly and had little to offer in trade. As the French were looking for furs, this part of the continent did not therefore attract them. It is interesting to speculate upon what might have been the course of North American history if the French had chosen to plant a colony upon the Atlantic coast, along which they sailed at this time. They missed a chance which never came to them again, for the English began settlements along this coast a few years later.

The succeeding winter was very comfortably spent by the settlers at Port Royal. To ward off the dreaded scurvy and to keep the people contented, Champlain saw that they must have abundant food and pleasant entertainment. So he organized a society called the Order of Good Cheer. Each member of the society in turn was required to furnish food and entertainment for the other members for one day. For several days before his turn came, this man had to bestir himself to find game in the forest and fish in the stream to provide a good dinner for his fellow-members. The banquet was served with much pomp and ceremony. The neighbouring Indians were often invited to share in the festivities, and thus a bond of friendship was forged between them and the white men. Champlain's

FOUNDING OF QUEBEC

plan kept the colonists well fed and cheerful, and they passed a comfortable winter, free from hardship and disease.

The colony seemed to have a promising future, but its hopes were dashed when in 1607 De Monts had to surrender his monopoly of the fur-trade in Acadia. In consequence the colony at Port Royal had to be abandoned, and the settlers returned to France.

And now we reach the most important milestone in Champlain's life, and one of the most important events in the history of Canada. In 1608, with a few colonists, he returned to the St. Lawrence, determined to form a settlement on its shores. He selected for the site of his colony the lofty northern bank where the majestic river begins to expand into its broad estuary. Here had stood the ancient Indian village of Stadacona, though all traces of the village of Cartier's time had now disappeared. At this spot he erected a large building to serve as storehouse, fort, and living quarters. Thus the city of Quebec was founded, and the first permanent Canadian settlement was established. On the day that the flag of France was unfurled over the St. Lawrence in 1608 by Samuel de Champlain, the history of Canada really begins.

The new colony had difficulties from the start. One of the men turned traitor and induced several others to enter a conspiracy to kill Champlain. Luckily the plot was discovered, and the ringleader was hanged. The first winter was a repetition of that at St. Croix upon an even more dreadful scale, for twenty of the twenty-eight in the party died of scurvy. The wonder is that Champlain did not give up in despair the effort to form a colony, but he clung to his purpose with steadfast courage.

Two great aims directed Champlain's efforts during the rest of his life. The first was the exploration of the country and the discovery of a route to the East, and the second was the conversion of the Indians to Christianity. To accomplish the first of these aims he saw that he must obtain the aid of the Indians who knew the country. To accomplish the second aim he gave every assistance to the priests of the

SAMUEL DE CHAMPLAIN

Récollet and the Jesuit Orders, who came to Canada at his suggestion.

The Indians on their part were not slow to take advantage of Champlain's desire to explore the country. As the price of their assistance, the Hurons and Algonquins demanded that he should aid them in war upon their enemies, the Iroquois. Champlain's eagerness as an explorer thus led him into a mistake for which the French colonists of later times had to pay dearly. In 1609 he was persuaded by the Algonquins to join them in a raid upon the Iroquois. This gave him an opportunity of tracing the Richelieu River to its source and of exploring the great lake which now bears his name. Near the south end of the lake, with two French and sixty Algonquin companions, he had an encounter with two hundred Iroquois. The latter would have made short work of the fight had not Champlain fired his musket and killed two of their chiefs. The Iroquois had never before seen fire-arms and were seized with panic. The sight of the strange white man, who seemed to command the thunder and lightning, filled them with deadly fear. They turned and fled, pursued by the Algonquins, who killed many of them and made several prisoners. Champlain was unable to control his savage allies in their hour of victory, and was forced to look on in silence while they, in Indian fashion, inflicted horrible tortures upon their captives. This ill-advised attack laid the foundation of the Iroquois enmity toward the French, which later brought much trouble and bloodshed to the colony.

Champlain was induced to make a voyage up the Ottawa River in search of the western sea that would lead to the

FORT OF SAMUEL DE CHAMPLAIN

East. Nicolas Vignau, a Frenchman who had spent some time trading with the Indians in the region of the Ottawa, told Champlain that the sea could be reached by way of the river. What Vignau's purpose was in inventing such a tale has never been clear. Champlain, in high hope, set out in canoes up the Ottawa, passed the Long Sault and Chaudière rapids with difficulty, and pressed on as far as the Island of Allumette. Here it became evident that Vignau's story was false, and in disappointment Champlain returned to Quebec. Vignau was compelled to make a public confession that he had lied.

In 1615 Champlain was persuaded by the Hurons to carry out a long-standing promise to assist them in an attack upon the Iroquois. In preparation for this he made an historic journey around the eastern portion of the Province of Ontario. He proceeded up the Ottawa and the Mattawa, and by portage reached Lake Nipissing. Thence, through the French River, he came to Georgian Bay, along the shore of which he paddled to the southern end. He thus reached the territory of the Hurons. When the war party was in readiness, it proceeded by way of Lake Simcoe and the Trent River to Lake Ontario.

From the eastern end of this lake the party struck across the country towards Oneida Lake, near which it came upon a palisade fort of the Iroquois. The attack was badly planned and badly carried out. The Iroquois had, in the interval since Champlain's previous raid upon them, learned something about muskets, and were not this time terrified by the firing. The Hurons were beaten and compelled to retreat, carrying their wounded with them. Champlain himself received two severe wounds and was unable to walk. He was bound in a basket to the back of one of the savages, and suffered great agony while being carried back to Lake Ontario.

When he reached this point he expected to proceed to Quebec, but the Indians made him understand that they wished him to go home with them. "We need the aid of the great white chief," they said, "to plan another attack upon our enemy." Champlain accepted a situation which he could not avoid, and spent the winter with the Hurons. During this time he explored the country south of Georgian Bay, and reached the shore of Lake Huron at the Bruce peninsula. He returned to Quebec the following spring. This expedition ended Champlain's efforts in exploration.

Meanwhile the colony at Quebec had made little progress. In the twenty years following its foundation, it had never numbered more than one hundred souls. This was due in part to constant quarrels among the fur companies. At last, in 1627, Champlain persuaded Cardinal Richelieu, the French prime minister, to put the fur-trade entirely in the hands of an organization known as the Company of One Hundred Associates. In return for a monopoly of the trade for fifteen years, the Company was to bring out three hundred colonists each year to Canada. Champlain was made governor of the colony.

Next year war broke out between France and England. An English fleet under David Kirke appeared before Quebec and demanded its surrender. From Champlain's reply Kirke suspected that he could take the fort more easily by starving the defenders than by force of arms. So, after capturing the cattle and destroying the crops, he withdrew down the river to await the supply ships from France that were bringing to the colony the season's supply of food and building materials. The ships were captured and sent to England. Quebec suffered another winter of famine, and when, in 1629, Kirke returned there was nothing for Champlain to do but to surrender. Thus ended the first of the memorable sieges of the great Canadian fortress. Champlain was sent as a prisoner to England.

When the war closed in 1632 Quebec was given back to the French. Champlain, now an old man, was sent out as governor once more. The last years of his life were spent mainly in promoting the fur-trade and in assisting the Jesuit missionaries in their efforts to christianize the Indians. He died on Christmas Day, 1635, after giving twenty-seven years of devoted service to Canada.

The name of the kindly and chivalrous Champlain is perpetuated by many monuments erected to his memory by the Canadian people. One of the most striking has been placed in the city of Ottawa at Nepean Point, a towering bluff jutting out into the river of which he was the earliest explorer. On this lofty eminence the noble statue of Canada's first governor stands with uplifted arm, facing the setting sun, as if surveying the glorious panorama of mountain, stream, and cataract, and pointing forward with confident expectation to the exploration and occupation of the great western land under the banner of old France.

V

HENRY HUDSON

AN ENGLISH ADVENTURER IN THE NORTH

No other explorer is so well commemorated in the geographical names of the North American continent as Henry Hudson. His name has been given to a great bay in the north, as large as the Mediterranean; to a large strait connecting this bay with the Atlantic; and to a great river, important in the commerce of the United States. In two memorable voyages in the early part of the seventeenth century, Hudson discovered these three large bodies of water. The story of his tragic expedition to the great northern bay forms one of the saddest tales in the annals of Canada.

Of the early life of Hudson, nothing definite is known except that he was a seaman in England in the stirring days of Queen Elizabeth. The hope of discovering the North-West Passage to the East, which had been the dream of many explorers before his time, and was to be the dream of many others after him, took strong hold upon Hudson. In 1607, in a small ship fitted out by a London trading company, with a crew of ten men and a boy, he set out to find the mythical route to the East by sailing across the North Pole! He proceeded north-westward and coasted along the eastern shores of Greenland until the ice barrier would permit him to go no farther. Turning eastward, he reached Spitzbergen, and then returned to England. Next year the same company sent him north-eastward, hoping that he would find a short route to China in that direction. But after sailing for some time through the icefields of the Arctic north of Siberia, Hudson found that the route was

EARLY VOYAGES 31

impossible. These two failures convinced the company of the uselessness of further search.

In 1609 Hudson received a request from the Dutch East India Company to take charge of an expedition to look for the North-West Passage. In a little vessel, the *Half Moon*, manned by twenty Dutch sailors, he sailed from Amsterdam. This time he followed a course farther south, and came to what is now the harbour of New York. Here a large river, up which the tide rushes for many miles, looked as if it might be the long-sought passage to the East. Up this river the *Half Moon* sailed for many miles, until Hudson was convinced that his hopes were groundless. This river is now called the Hudson, one of the great rivers of the United States, famous alike for its beauty and its commerce. It is an interesting fact that, while Hudson was proceeding up this river from the south, Champlain was coming up the Richelieu from the north, and at one time the two explorers could not have been more than fifty or sixty miles apart.

Public Archives of Canada
HENRY HUDSON

Undaunted by three failures in his quest, Hudson set sail from England early in the spring of the next year, 1610, in the *Discovery*, a little vessel provided by a company of London merchants. The crew, collected from the London slums, were from the start difficult to manage. On this occasion Hudson directed his course north of Newfoundland and Labrador, and entered what is now known as Hudson Strait. He encountered great fields of ice, and the treacherous currents made the passage of the strait very difficult and dangerous. The crew, unused to the cold and unprepared with proper clothing to withstand it, complained loudly.

"The boat will be crushed by these tremendous masses of ice," some of the sailors said, "and we shall all be lost."

"Or the swift currents will dash us on the rocks," said others.

"We shall be frozen to death in this awful cold; we ought to turn back before it is too late," they urged.

"We must go forward," was the unvariable answer of the resolute commander.

The demand to return to England grew louder day by day. Hudson refused to listen. In the face of discontent and expostulation, he remained steadfast and determined. After six weeks of struggle with ice and adverse currents, the ship came to the end of the strait where the southern shore turns off abruptly to the south. It had entered the great bay that cuts Canada almost in two from the north.

"Surely this is the great western sea for which we have been seeking," said Hudson hopefully. "If this be true, on the other side lie China and Japan. We have doubtless found the road to the East."

"But the season is advancing," objected one sailor.

"If we go farther we shall have to spend the winter in these northern seas," said another.

"The ship is not provisioned for a long voyage," protested a third.

"Nevertheless we shall sail on," said Hudson with determination. "It would be shameful to come so near the goal and yet not reach it."

So the vessel continued to sail southward along the rockbound coast, and the crew grew daily more mutinous. As winter drew on, storms became frequent and the waters of the bay were thown into huge waves which tossed the little vessel about like a chip. When the shallower waters of James Bay were reached, the storms were more violent and the waves still higher. Arriving at the south-west corner of James Bay, Hudson saw the shore stretching away again to the northward. He realized that his hopes were vain.

A MUTINOUS CREW

"This cannot be the sea that leads to China, as we thought," he said with intense disappointment. "We have merely discovered a great inlet from the Arctic on the north shore of America."

Hudson's fourth attempt to find the North-West Passage had failed!

It was now December, and the ice had begun to form in the bay. In a few days the *Discovery* was frozen in. The crew landed and very unwillingly built some rude huts of rocks and trees to serve as winter quarters. There was abundance of game, and Hudson tried to get the men to hunt in order to lay in a supply of food. But hunt they would not, possibly because they did not know how, but more probably because they were obstinate and rebellious. So they passed a terrible winter, suffering from hunger, cold, and disease, constantly quarrelling among themselves and complaining against the commander.

When the ice broke the following June, Hudson began to prepare the *Discovery* for the homeward voyage. The supply of food was all but exhausted. A horrible revenge for the sufferings and injuries which they had endured and which they attributed to the obstinacy of Hudson was now planned by the mutineers.

"If half the crew were left behind," they whispered among themselves, "there would be double the quantity of food for the rest of us."

In the darkness of the night the conspirators completed their dreadful plot.

"We shall leave for England on the morrow," said the ringleader. "Hudson and his young son shall stay here. Eight of the crew who have been faithful to him shall remain, too. It would be a pity to part such good friends."

"We will let them have some food—a very little," said another conspirator.

"Also a gun, a few knives and spears, and some kettles and pots," added another. "They can keep themselves alive for a while at least."

"In the morning," said the leader, "we shall seize the ten

and set them adrift in one of the ship's boats. Thus we shall even up old scores."

The plot was carried out precisely as it had been arranged by the mutineers. When morning came, Hudson, his young son, and eight others who were faithful to him were seized and thrust into one of the ship's boats. A few weapons, tools, and utensils were thrown in, and the boat was cast off. The sails of the *Discovery* were then hoisted, and, with a derisive farewell, the mutineers sailed away. What happened to them afterwards is soon told. The ringleader and several companions were killed in a fight with Eskimos; others died of starvation and disease; only four famished men were left when the vessel reached England, and they were at once thrown into prison. It was from admissions made by these men that the dreadful details of the ill-starred expedition were made known to the world.

What became of Hudson and his companions, nobody knows. It is hardly likely that so resolute a man would calmly submit to starvation without putting forth a great effort to avoid it. It is generally thought that the party met their death at the hands of Eskimos or Indians. Hudson's expedition was the first great tragedy associated with the quest of the North-West Passage.

VI

FATHER JEAN BRÉBEUF

THE JESUIT MARTYR

There were so many different tribes of Indians living in Canada in Champlain's time that it would be hard to learn all their names and the regions where they lived. It is important, however, to remember at least three tribes that had a good deal to do with the early history of Canada. They were the Algonquins, the Hurons, and the Iroquois.

The Algonquins were the least intelligent of the three. They had no settled homes, but wandered from place to place in that vast region stretching from Lake Superior, north of the Ottawa and the St. Lawrence, to the Atlantic Ocean. They lived entirely by hunting and fishing, and, owing to the severity of the climate and the lack of sufficient food and shelter, they led lives of great hardship and suffering during the long winters of this region.

The Hurons and Iroquois were close relatives, but a deadly enmity had somehow arisen between them, and they were continually at war with each other. Both of these tribes, besides hunting and fishing, tilled the soil to some extent, and added to their food supplies by raising grain and vegetables. They had settled homes, and lived in villages scattered here and there in a comparatively small territory. From these villages the hunters went out in parties, often for hundreds of miles in all directions through the wilderness, in search of game, fish, and furs. The Hurons inhabited that portion of the present county of Simcoe lying between Nottawasaga Bay and Lake Simcoe, while the Iroquois lived in the central part of what is now New York State.

FATHER JEAN BRÉBEUF

The Indian villages were surrounded, by way of protection in war, by a palisade, a wall of logs placed upright in the ground and firmly fastened together. The houses were made of two rows of saplings, bent together at the top to form an arch, and covered with bark. They were often two hundred feet long, and were occupied by from six to twelve families. Fires were built on the ground, and the smoke escaped through holes in the roof. The homes were very filthy and uncomfortable.

The Indians had dark skins, straight black hair, small eyes, high cheekbones, and prominent noses. Their bodies were strong and supple from living much in the open air, walking through the forests, and paddling on the lakes and rivers. They had wonderful powers of endurance, and bore suffering and even torture without any outward sign. They were ferocious and pitiless in warfare, and inflicted the most horrible cruelties upon captives taken in battle. Their religion was mere superstition. They believed that spirits inhabited the sun, moon, and stars, and the lakes, rivers, and waterfalls, and that these objects demanded their worship. They believed in a life after death, but heaven was to them a place of perpetual hunting, unlimited game, inexhaustible food, and continuous comfort. They were much under the influence of their "medicine-men," who professed ability to communicate with the spirits, to foretell coming events, and to cure disease by strange ceremonies.

One of the plans dear to the heart of Champlain was to

BUST OF FATHER BRÉBEUF
Preserved in the Hôtel Dieu, Quebec

MISSION TO HURONS

send missionaries among these benighted people to convert them to the Christian faith. Near his home in France was a monastery of the Récollet friars, and Champlain succeeded in interesting them in the project. Through his influence several Récollet priests were sent to Canada and set up a monastery near Quebec. One of them, Father le Caron, accompanied Champlain's party in 1615 in the historic journey to Huronia. He was joyfully received by the Hurons, but could make no impression on them by his teaching. He went back to Quebec with Champlain, but returned to Huronia some years later. Again he met with no success, and in despair gave up the effort. The conquest of the Hurons for Christianity was not to be made by the gentle, brown-robed Récollets.

Later Champlain succeeded in having several priests of the Jesuit Order sent to Canada. The story of the labours of these men on behalf of the Indians forms one of the most glorious and yet most tragic pages of Canadian history. And bright in the roll of Christian martyrs shine the names of Fathers Brébeuf, Lalemant, Daniel, and Jogues. Like many another Christian missionary since, they left comfortable homes in their native land to go out among savages; to spend years separated from their friends; to endure discomfort, cold, privation, and want; to be insulted, to be ill-treated, and often to suffer death in its cruellest form, in order to spread abroad the gospel of Christ. In twenty-five years, twenty-five priests were at work among the Hurons and Iroquois, and of these six were put to a cruel death.

Foremost among these Jesuit missionaries stands Father Jean de Brébeuf. Strong, tall, erect, with a deep voice and piercing eye, he was, in the black robe of his Order, a commanding figure among the Indians. He reached Huronia in 1626 with a party of Huron traders over the route taken by Champlain and Le Caron in 1615. He set to work to master the Huron language, to compile a dictionary, and to translate the Catechism. Though his preaching had little effect upon the savages, they came to regard him as their friend. At the end of three years he decided to go to Quebec to arrange for more assistance, but assured the Indians that he would soon return. While he was at Quebec the fort was captured by Kirke, and Brébeuf was one of the prisoners of war sent to England, though he was soon allowed to proceed to France.

On the restoration of Canada to the French, Brébeuf made preparations to resume his missionary work. Accompanied by Father Daniel, he returned to Huronia, and was received with great joy by the Indians. He was later joined by Father Gabriel Lalemant. It is quite probable that the Indians regarded the missionaries merely as medicine-men of extraordinary powers who would be able to assist them in repelling attacks by the Iroquois.

For some time the preaching of the missionaries seemed to have little effect. "The Christian religion is good for the French," said the Indians, "but we are another people with different customs, and it is not for us." The missionaries had strong opponents in the medicine-men, who feared that they would lose their power over the Indians. When misfortunes came, the medicine-men blamed the missionaries. Once when a drought threatened the crops, the red cross on the chapel was said to be the cause. Brébeuf had the cross painted white, but still the drought continued. He then suggested that the Indians should appeal to God for rain; and, as if by miracle, a sudden storm came on, drenched the parched earth, and saved the crops. Smallpox often attacked the villages, and the priests were accused of casting an evil spell over the people. It was difficult to make headway against the foolish superstition of the savages.

Nevertheless the work went on for many years. Brébeuf and his fellow-missionaries continued steadfast at their tasks amidst the greatest discouragements. They built chapels and schools at several villages. They lived with the Indians, helped them in every possible way, taught them at every opportunity, and strove to change their heathen habits. Even the Indians could not but admire their devotion, self-sacrifice, and endurance. Gradually success came. One by one the more intelligent Hurons were converted to the Christian faith. At length there were twelve mission stations,

MARTYRDOM

seven chapels, and several hundred Huron converts who had given up their pagan practices.

But this success, won at such a cost, was doomed to quick destruction. The Iroquois were constantly on the warpath. They watched the routes of trade. They killed or captured the luckless Huron traders on the way to and from Quebec, and looted their goods. A band of Iroquois warriors descended suddenly upon the Huron village of St. Joseph, where Father Daniel had laboured successfully for years. The helpless inhabitants were nearly all killed. Father Daniel was tortured and tied to a stake in a cabin, which was then set on fire by the savages. Two years later St. Ignace and St. Louis were attacked, and their inhabitants ruthlessly slain. At the latter place Fathers Brébeuf and Lalemant were subjected to the most inhuman tortures. Brébeuf was tied to a stake and boiling water was poured on his head in mockery of baptism. Red-hot axes were hung about his shoulders. A belt of tar and resin was placed about his waist and set on fire. In the midst of his sufferings he uttered no word of complaint or pain, but continually called upon God to forgive his enemies. At last in fury they fell upon him with their axes and cut him to pieces. Lalemant, gentler in nature and weaker in body, suffered even more terrible tortures, and died only after fourteen hours of agony.

The Hurons who survived these attacks were in a panic. Many of them fled to neighbouring tribes of Indians and some even to the Iroquois, by whom they were adopted. The rest gathered together on Christian Island, where a strong stone fort was built under the direction of the remaining priests. But there was no time to secure a sufficient food supply, and in the winter that followed half of the Indians died of starvation or disease. In the spring of 1650 the survivors, thirteen priests, sixty Frenchmen, and three hundred Hurons, journeyed to Quebec, and Huronia was deserted. The Indians settled on lands near Quebec, and their descendants are still to be found at the little village of Lorette.

The Jesuits even made an attempt to convert the savage

Iroquois to Christianity. One of their priests, Father Isaac Jogues, was captured by a party of Iroquois warriors while on his way to the Huron mission stations, and was carried up the Richelieu River and Lake Champlain to the Iroquois settlements. He was kept a prisoner for a year, and at intervals in the meantime was inhumanly tortured. His hands were mutilated, his fingers being either cut off or broken. He was aided to escape by the Dutch, who were neighbours of the Iroquois on the east. A few years later he was sent by the governor of Canada as a messenger of peace to the Iroquois. He was received with apparent friendliness. When the treaty of peace was concluded, Jogues set out for Quebec. He promised the Indians that he would return, and left as a pledge a locked box containing his priestly vestments and consecrated vessels. During his absence a plague of grasshoppers and an epidemic of smallpox came upon the Indians, who believed that the locked box left by the priest was the cause. When Father Jogues returned he found the feeling of the savages strongly against him. He was charged as a sorcerer, and was put to cruel tortures once more. One evening he received an invitation to a feast given by one of the chiefs. He knew what the invitation meant, and set out prepared to meet his death. On the way an Iroquois warrior sprang upon him from behind and killed him with a tomahawk.

The early Jesuit missions to the Indians were an apparent failure. Though a large number of the Hurons had been christianized, they were almost exterminated by their bloodthirsty enemies. A few hundred Christian converts among the Huron survivors at Quebec were the only visible result of the labours of the Jesuit fathers. But the glory of the Jesuit missions consists, not in the number of Indians converted, but in the example of heroism, sacrifice, and endurance which the missionaries gave to the world.

VII

ADAM DAULAC

THE HERO OF THE LONG SAULT

AMONG the deeds of heroism with which the early history of Canada abounds, none stands out in greater glory than that of Adam Daulac and his sixteen French companions at the Long Sault rapids in the Ottawa River.

The Iroquois, having destroyed the Hurons and many of their missionaries, soon turned their attention to the French settlements at Montreal and Quebec. Their deadly hatred found vent in frequent attacks upon the settlers, many of whom were killed or carried off for future torture. Life was very insecure in Canada in those days. The farmers carried their muskets with them to their work in the fields, and the priests went about their duties with swords at their sides, for they never knew when a lurking Indian might spring upon them. It was no unusual thing for a settler to return to his home at night to find his wife and children slain or carried off by the bloodthirsty savages. We who live in peaceful times do not know what it means to go about in hourly peril of our lives, and we would do well to remember the fortitude and bravery of the men and women who in those early days laid the foundation of our country.

In the year 1660 the Iroquois determined to wipe out the French settlements completely. A large number of their warriors had spent the winter hunting in the forests of the Ottawa and waylaying the French and Huron traders on their way to the settlements. These Iroquois were to be joined in the early spring by a large number of others who were to come down the Richelieu to the St. Lawrence. The combined forces were then to make an attack upon Quebec

ADAM DAULAC

and Montreal, the inhabitants were to be massacred, and the country was thus to be rid of the hated French.

Adam Daulac, or Dollard, a young man of twenty-five, was at this time in command of the garrison at Montreal. He persuaded sixteen young Frenchmen to join him in an attack upon the Iroquois in an effort to save the colony. He proposed to ascend the Ottawa with his party and waylay the savages on their way down the river. The plan was a daring one, and the young Frenchmen knew that it probably meant death for them if they attempted to carry it out. Nevertheless they willingly consented to make the effort.

After receiving the sacraments of the Church and bidding their friends a solemn farewell, they set out in several canoes well stocked with food and arms. They were not very expert boatmen, and they lost considerable time in passing the rapids of the lower Ottawa. After several days they reached the foot of the turbulent and dangerous rapids of the Long Sault, and decided to go no farther. They knew that the Iroquois were sure to pass the spot, and it offered a favourable battle-ground. A rude fort of stumps and logs, which had

Public Archives of Canada
ADAM DAULAC

AN HEROIC DEFENCE

been built by Indians some time before, stood on the bank of the river. The Frenchmen proceeded to strengthen this in anticipation of an early battle. Presently a party of forty Hurons and four Algonquins joined them, and Daulac found himself at the head of a company of sixty men. A close watch was kept for the appearance of the Iroquois on their way down the river.

In a few days the scouts reported that two canoes containing five Iroquois were coming down the rapids. Daulac posted his best marksmen among the bushes on the river bank with instructions not to let any of the enemy escape. When the Indians appeared they were met by a volley so hastily fired that one or two of them escaped. This was unfortunate, for the Indians who got away at once carried the news of the attack to the two hundred Iroquois who were encamped a short distance up the river. So the French lost the chance of making a surprise attack when the main body of the enemy appeared.

The French had not long to wait for the onset. The Iroquois came down the rapids, and, quickly landing from their canoes, made a vigorous attack upon the fort. But they were soon driven back by the fire of the French, leaving many of their warriors dead on the ground. The Iroquois then proceeded to build a fort of their own near at hand, and in the interval the French made their defences stronger. They planted a row of stakes inside the wall of the fort and filled the space between with earth and stones, leaving twenty loopholes, each of which was to be guarded by three men. Before they had finished, the enemy were upon them again in a new form of attack. The Iroquois had smashed the birch canoes of the French, and, setting fire to the pieces, they tried to burn the walls of the fort. But again they were driven back by the fire of the French.

The Iroquois now saw the impossibility of overcoming the defenders of the fort with their present numbers. So they sent for reinforcements to their tribesmen who were gathered at the mouth of the Richelieu. In the meantime, from the cover of trees and logs, they kept up a continuous fire night and day upon the French.

Inside the fort the defenders began to suffer severely. They had no food except some hominy, or crushed Indian corn. They obtained a scanty supply of muddy water from a hole they had dug in the ground. They were unable to rest because of the incessant attack of the enemy. These conditions began to tell upon the courage of their Indian allies. Among those attacking the fort were several adopted Hurons, who shouted invitations to their former tribesmen within the fort to leave the French. They were promised kindly treatment by the Iroquois as a reward of their desertion. To the dismay of the French, these Huron allies one by one climbed the walls of the fort and went over to the enemy, until only the chief remained. The four Algonquins, however, remained loyal. Five days passed, during which Daulac and his companions suffered the tortures of hunger, thirst, and want of sleep, but without any thought of surrender.

When the five hundred warriors from the Richelieu arrived, the combined forces of the enemy rushed upon the fort, sure of an easy victory. But from every loophole there came a steady fire, and the savages fell back. For three days more the heroic defenders kept the assailants at bay. The Iroquois were at one time on the point of giving up the fight and going home. But the more determined among them declared that it would be a disgrace to their nation for so large a body of warriors to admit defeat by such a handful of Frenchmen. They resolved upon a final attack. Under cover of large shields made of split logs lashed together, the whole band advanced, and when they reached the walls of the fort they hacked with their axes to tear an opening. Daulac had made a sort of bomb charged with powder and bullets to burst among the savages outside the fort; but in trying to throw it over the wall he unfortunately let it fall within the fort. It immediately exploded, and brought death or injury to several of the Frenchmen. In the confusion the Iroquois seized the loopholes and fired upon the few remaining defenders. The walls were quickly broken through, and the savages swarmed into the fort. In the hand-to-hand encounter the Frenchmen fought furiously with knives and

DISHEARTENED FOES

spears, but were at last overcome by sheer force of numbers. Daulac was struck dead, and in a moment all resistance was over.

Among the dead bodies the Iroquois found four Frenchmen still alive. Three were almost dead, and they were burned on the spot, while the fourth was carried off for further tortures. The Huron deserters, despite the promises of the Iroquois, were doomed to a similar fate. Five of them, however, escaped, and carried to the colony at Montreal the story of the magnificent defence of the fort at the Long Sault.

Daulac and his companions did not die in vain. Their valiant fight against overwhelming odds so discouraged the Iroquois that they gave up for that year the project of attacking the French settlements. And so the colony in Canada for a time rested in peace.

VIII

JEAN TALON

THE GREAT INTENDANT

No man did more in the early days of Canada to promote her material welfare than Jean Talon. He spent only about five years in the colony, and yet in that brief period he brought about a wonderful improvement in its condition.

It will be remembered that in Champlain's time a fur-trading organization, known as the Company of One Hundred Associates, had been entrusted with the direction of the affairs of Canada. This Company had undertaken in return for the monopoly of the fur-trade, to bring out three hundred settlers each year. After the first year or so it made no pretence of carrying out its arrangement. The colony was dying for lack of settlers, for lack of sufficient food and tools, and for lack of soldiers as a defence against the bloodthirsty Iroquois.

To save the colony Louis XIV cancelled the charter of the Company and placed the government of Canada in the hands of a Sovereign Council. There were ten members of this body, but the chief officers were the governor, the intendant, and the bishop. The Council was given charge of the settlement of the colony, its defence, its trade, its roads, and its educational and religious welfare. It was an absolute body, in the appointment of which the colonists themselves had nothing to say. Fortunately, the members were for the most part good men, who were sincerely devoted to the welfare of the colony. On the whole, the Sovereign Council gave the people the kind of government they needed in those pioneer days.

A LESSON TO THE IROQUOIS 47

The intendant was the chief business man of the Council. He looked after the raising of money and made arrangements for bringing out colonists and settling them on the land. The first and greatest intendant was Jean Talon. He was a native of the Province of Champagne in France, and as a young man had studied law. His ability had attracted the attention of the king, who had become convinced that Talon was the man to send to Canada to manage its business affairs under the new plan of government. Talon arrived in Canada as intendant in 1665.

In the fifty-seven years that had elapsed since the founding of the colony by Champlain, the population had grown only to about three thousand. If the colony was to make reasonable progress, the first thing for the new government to do was to make the lives and property of the colonists safe from the marauding Iroquois. This task was undertaken by the Marquis de Tracy, who had come out as lieutenant-general at the head of the famous Carignan regiment.

Public Archives of Canada
JEAN TALON

Tracy led his regiment in an expedition to give the Indians a much-needed lesson. After a most toilsome journey up the Richelieu and through forests and swamps, the army reached the Iroquois territory. The Indians had intended to put up a stubborn resistance, but when they saw the strength of the French forces they made a hasty retreat. Tracy completely destroyed three Iroquois villages and their great stores of food. The savages were thus taught that distance and a difficult country to cross were no barrier to the French when bent on punishment. The Indians were thoroughly cowed for the time being, and sent messengers to Quebec to sue for peace. Tracy demanded that several Iroquois families should be brought to Quebec and held as hostages. Thus a peace, which continued for eighteen years, was established with the Iroquois.

This period of freedom from attack gave Talon an opportunity for carrying out his great plans for the colony. He had settlers brought out from France to be placed on the land. A farm was given to each settler, a house was erected for his family, and flour was provided until a crop was reaped.

Talon's method of laying out the grants of land was peculiar. Instead of dividing the land into rectangular farms, he had it laid out in triangles, each farm being narrow at the front and wide at the rear. The houses were built at the narrow end, so that they were grouped together in a little village. Three villages were thus established near Quebec. This arrangement was good for protection and social intercourse. Talon realized the necessity of concentrating the people as a means of defence against savage enemies and as a means of avoiding that loneliness from which pioneers in a new land often suffer.

Each settler was paid for clearing the first two acres of his farm, and in return was required within three or four years to clear two acres on another farm to be given to an incoming settler. Soldiers were encouraged to take up lands, and many of them became good farmers.

To make homes for the unmarried men, young women were brought out from France under the care of nuns. When a ship arrived with these young women, the young men gathered at the wharf to make their selection of wives. Strange as it may seem, the marriages arranged in this haphazard way nearly always turned out happily. The results of Talon's colonization schemes were seen in the doubling of the population within a period of three years after his arrival in Canada.

Talon also turned his attention to developing other industries as well as farming. The timber was well suited to shipbuilding. Fishing in the St. Lawrence yielded a rich return. It was not long before one or two ships a year went

THE SEIGNEURIAL SYSTEM

to the West Indies laden with fish, planks, staves, masts, barley, and flour, which the people of these islands needed. This marked a decided advance in Canada's foreign trade.

Talon's methods of encouraging production were sometimes novel. For instance, hemp was needed in the colony to make coarse cloth. Hemp seed was brought from France and sown. The following year the seed was gathered and distributed among the settlers. Then Talon seized all the thread in the colony, and the people could secure thread only in exchange for hemp. Thus a sufficient supply of hemp was secured.

Talon encouraged home manufactures by requiring the women to learn to spin and weave wool and the men to tan leather. Spinning-wheels and looms were secured from France. Talon was able to report to the king on one occasion: "I am now clothed from head to foot with home-made articles."

Talon was the organizer, if not the founder, of the seigneurial system of holding land in Canada. This resembled in its main features the Feudal System which prevailed in parts of Europe for many centuries. The seigneur was usually a man of high birth and good education, who had taken an important part in the development of the colony, often as an officer in the army or as a member of the Sovereign Council. In return for his services he was given a large grant of land, called a seigneury. The grant was conferred upon the seigneur with some ceremony. He knelt before the governor, swearing allegiance to the king, and pledging his services in war. If the seigneur sold his land, he had to give one-fifth of the money he received to the king.

The seigneur divided his land among his tenants, the *habitants*, who were pledged to pay rent either in money or in the form of a part of the produce they raised. If the tenant sold his land he was expected to pay one-twelfth of the price to the seigneur.

This method of land tenure prevailed in French Canada for nearly two hundred years. Talon established over sixty seigneuries, and at a later time there were as many as three hundred. The seigneurs formed the aristocracy of Canada in the early days.

A question which gave the Sovereign Council a good deal of trouble was the sale of liquor to the Indians. The fur-traders had begun to give brandy in exchange for furs. The effect on the Indians of "fire-water," as they called it, was disastrous. It led to violent disorders and serious crimes. An Indian drunk with fire-water was like a wild beast, crazed and murderous.

Talon at first was in favour of the prohibition of the sale of liquor to the Indians, but gradually changed his mind about it. He saw that the English traders of the Atlantic coast gave liquor in exchange for furs, and he believed that if the French refused to do so the fur-trade would be lost. Moreover, the colony would lose the friendship of the Indians, who would ally themselves with the English against the French. Bishop Laval, as a member of the Council and the director of religious affairs, vigorously maintained that the moral good of the Indians should not be sacrificed for the material welfare of the colony. Through Talon's influence the prohibition of the sale of liquor was removed, though severe penalties for drunkenness were established. The question was the cause of much ill-feeling between the intendant and the bishop. The strictness of the laws to-day against the sale of liquor to the Indians is an acknowledgment that on this question Laval was right and Talon wrong.

After spending three years in the colony, Talon returned to France, but it was soon felt that he was needed in Canada. He was sent back, and again threw himself earnestly into the service of the colony. But his health was not good, and he found the climate too severe. The governor was unfriendly because he believed that Talon assumed too much authority in the government. In 1672 Talon asked to be relieved of his office. He returned to France for good, but his advice was often sought when affairs in Canada were discussed by the king's ministers.

Talon will be remembered because he saved the French colony in Canada at a critical period in its history, and by his wise measures started it off for the first time towards prosperity.

IX

PIERRE RADISSON

COUREUR DE BOIS PAR EXCELLENCE

ONE of the great difficulties that the French had in forming a colony in Canada lay in the lure of the wilds. There was a fascination about life in the forest for the virile young men who came out from France. The life was adventurous and exciting, and the trade in furs with the Indians was profitable. So it came about that many young Frenchmen forsook the civilized life of the colony and went into the wilderness to live with the savages. They adopted Indian customs, and hunted, fished, traded, and made war in Indian fashion. They were called *coureurs de bois*, runners of the woods. The governors of Canada did what they could to check this roving tendency of the French youths by forbidding them to engage in the fur-trade without a license, and by fining them heavily when they violated this rule. Nevertheless the colony lost many of its most vigorous and daring young men who adopted the wild life of the woods.

One of the most picturesque of these early *coureurs de bois* was Pierre Radisson. When a young man, not yet twenty years of age, he was one day captured by a band of Iroquois lurking in the forest near Three Rivers. He was taken on the long journey to the Iroquois territory, and, after the Iroquois custom, was doomed to torture. A favourite method of beginning this in the case of captured French youths was to make them run the gauntlet between two rows of Indians, armed with sticks to strike the victims as they passed along. But so quick and agile was Radisson that he was able to escape the clubs of the Indians without being struck. This so won the admiration of the chief that he adopted Radisson into his family, and the youth was thus spared further torture. Soon afterwards he made his escape. He had almost reached Three Rivers when he again fell into the hands of some roving Iroquois and was carried back. Once more his torture began, but again the friendly chief intervened. To escape the taunts of the Indians, Radisson now stained his body, adopted their dress and habits, and made himself very useful to them. But contact with the Dutch at Albany, with whom the Iroquois sometimes traded, made the young Frenchman long for civilization again. One day he set off for Albany, running so rapidly that he threw off all pursuers. The Dutch protected him, and he was soon able to take ship for France.

It was not long, however, before Radisson was back at Three Rivers. The "call of the West" was now strong upon him. With his brother-in-law, Groseilliers, he pushed westward beyond Lake Superior.

Public Archives of Canada
PIERRE RADISSON

Finding furs abundant there, they returned to Quebec to make application to the governor for a license to trade in the West. But the terms demanded were so heavy that they were rejected with scorn. The two adventurers slipped away without a license, and were soon at Lake Superior among the Crees and Sioux. They acquired a great influence over these fickle Indians by their daring and resource. How they managed to preserve their lives among the savages, to endure the severe cold of the winters, to keep a sufficient supply of food, and to save their store of furs, forms a very remarkable story. They even pressed on northward during the winter, and it is believed that they reached the shores of Hudson Bay, which, it will be remem-

A ROMANTIC TRADE

bered, had been discovered by Hudson fifty years before. Radisson and Groseilliers were probably the first white men to reach the Bay by land.

In the spring the adventurers induced a large number of Indians to go to Montreal to trade. A fleet of three hundred canoes, laden with furs of great value, started from Lake Superior, and proceeded through Lake Huron and across to the River Ottawa. Their arrival in Montreal aroused much interest among the merchants, and showed them the possibilities of a profitable fur-trade in the Far West. But when Radisson and Groseilliers went to Quebec, they were met by a blustering governor, who declared that they had broken the law in trading without a license and must therefore be punished. He took for taxes and fines the greater part of the furs that they had secured, and left the two traders only about one-tenth of the quantity for themselves. The greed and unfairness of the governor thus put an end to the activities of the two men in developing a profitable fur-trade for the colony.

In anger and disgust Radisson and Groseilliers betook themselves to the English in the Atlantic States and thence to England. London was then just recovering from the effects of the Great Plague of 1665, and Charles II was living in seclusion at Windsor. Radisson managed to secure the ear of the king, and we can imagine how the tales of the adventurer, which doubtless lost nothing in the telling, would beguile the tedious hours of the Merry Monarch. The king recommended Radisson to his royal cousin, Prince Rupert, who had turned his attention from war to science and exploration. The result was that Radisson and Groseilliers were fitted out with two ships to trade in Hudson Bay. Groseilliers in the *Nonsuch* reached the Bay, but Radisson in the *Eaglet* was forced by storms to turn back. When Groseilliers returned the following spring with a rich cargo of furs, he convinced his English friends that there were splendid possibilities for the fur-trade at Hudson Bay.

Accordingly, in 1670, a company was formed, consisting of Prince Rupert and seventeen others, known as "The Governor and Company of Adventurers of England trading into Hudson Bay." King Charles II gave the Company a charter, conveying the sole right to trade in all the lands watered by the streams flowing into the Bay and the sole right to rule in these lands. It was a domain of a million square miles that the king lightly gave away. Whether he had a right to do it did not trouble Charles. It is probable that he considered the discovery by Hudson, sixty years previously, as sufficient to justify the claim of England to the territory surrounding the Bay. Thus, through the influence of two Frenchmen, was founded a famous organization, known to-day as the Hudson's Bay Company, which has played an important part in the development of the Dominion. The Company is still active, having trading posts distributed over all the north and west of Canada, and having large retail stores in many western cities.

As may be imagined, the French were not inclined to leave the vast region about the Bay in the undisputed possession of the English. They claimed the territory as part of Canada, and thus ushered in a period of forty years of fighting for possession. Radisson and Groseilliers quarrelled with the chief official at the Bay and abruptly left the service of the Company. They went to Quebec, and later to France. For several years they served in the French Navy, but at length the severe discipline began to pall on them, and they longed for the free life of the western woods. Radisson returned to Canada and persuaded Frontenac, the governor at that time, to form a French company for trading in the north. Thus was formed the Company of the North, which was for many years a thorn in the flesh of the English Company. Radisson proceeded to the Bay, and, though he had only a small number of men, he deceived the English as to his strength and took possession of two English ships with rich cargoes of furs. These with his prisoners he took to Quebec. Contrary to Radisson's expectations, the new governor, La Barre, who had succeeded Frontenac, severely reprimanded him for his action, and sent the captured cargo and prisoners to the English at Boston.

Radisson left for Paris, and soon slipped across to London. He found the change of allegiance from one of the rival

SERVICE TO CANADA

countries to the other surprisingly easy. He was again taken into the service of the Hudson's Bay Company, a proof of its belief in him in spite of his desertion in the past. He continued to serve the Company, presumably faithfully, for several years. He married an English wife, the daughter of one of the leading members of the Company, and this fact doubtless made his fidelity to the organization more secure. During his later years he seems to have fallen into poverty and to have lived more or less upon the charity of the Company for which he had done so much.

Radisson deserves to be remembered in Canadian history for two reasons: first, because he is a type of the restless, roving trader who did so much to unravel the mysteries of the vast interior of Canada; and secondly, because he is responsible, Frenchman though he was, for the establishment in Canada of a great English institution, the Hudson's Bay Company.

X

FATHER JACQUES MARQUETTE

THE MISSIONARY EXPLORER

A JESUIT priest who deserves attention, not only because of his work as a missionary among the Indians, but also because of his work as an explorer, was Father Jacques Marquette. He had heard the "call of the West," and had taken charge of the Jesuit mission at Sault Ste. Marie. Later he went to St. Esprit, a trading-post on the south-west shore of Lake Superior, and set up a mission there. The Indians at this point were mainly Hurons who had come to this far western post to be out of danger of the Iroquois. They had retained much of the teaching of the missionaries at Huronia; so the new mission promised to be successful.

From the western Indians, the Illinois and the Sioux, who came to trade at St. Esprit, Marquette heard stories of the great river of the West, the Mississippi. The river had been discovered more than a hundred years before by De Soto, the Spaniard, but no European had traced it for any considerable distance. Even the Indians did not know where it emptied. Marquette thought that it might flow into the Pacific. If so, it would form the great passage to the East which explorers had been unsuccessfully seeking for nearly two hundred years. Marquette made up his mind to reach the Mississippi and explore it to its mouth. But before he could set out on his quest a war began between the Hurons and the Sioux, in which the latter won. Marquette had to abandon St. Esprit. He went to Michilimackinac, where Lake Michigan joins Lake Huron, and established the mission of St. Ignace.

A GREAT PROJECT 57

About this time Talon, the great intendant, who took a keen interest in exploration, determined to find out the truth of the Indian tales of the great river of the West. He commissioned Louis Joliet, a French fur-trader at Quebec, to find and explore the Mississippi. Father Marquette was requested to accompany him.

Accordingly, in the spring of 1673, Marquette and Joliet with five companions set out from St. Ignace. They paddled along the west coast of Lake Michigan to Green Bay. Here the Indians tried to dissuade them from their purpose, telling them tales of savage Indian tribes who would be sure to put them to death. If they escaped the Indians, they would fall a prey to the evil spirits of the forests. If, perchance, they avoided the evil spirits, they would surely be destroyed by the monsters which dwelt in the river. And, in addition to all these dangers, the heat of the country through which the river passed was too great to be endured. Heedless of the warnings of these Indians, the explorers proceeded up the Fox River, where other friendly Indians showed them where to make a portage to the Wisconsin River. Paddling down this stream, they came at length to the object of their quest, the great Mississippi.

Public Archives of Canada
FATHER JACQUES MARQUETTE

For some days they drifted down the river with the current. At night they anchored the boats midstream, fearing an attack by Indians. For a time they met no human beings, but saw many animals, deer, elk, and great herds of buffalo. They came at length to a village of the Illinois Indians, where Marquette preached the gospel in the Algonquin tongue to a great assembly. The Indians told the explorers stories of savages to be met farther down the river, but Marquette and Joliet were not to be turned aside. The Indians gave them a calumet, a large peace-pipe with stone bowl and reed stem, which would ensure their safety among some of the tribes that they would meet later.

After passing the mouth of the Illinois, the explorers came to a place where the banks of the river are steep and rocky, and on the face of the rocks they saw pictures of strange monsters that had apparently been painted there by Indians. These pictures probably accounted for the tales of savages and demons to which they had so often listened. Presently they came to the point where the Missouri pours its turbulent waters into the Mississippi, and Marquette resolved that at a later time he would ascend this river. Near the mouth of the Ohio the explorers came upon another Illinois village where the Indians wore European clothing and carried knives and hatchets, probably obtained from the Spaniards. They were told by these Indians that the mouth of the river could be reached by a ten days' journey. This was incorrect, for at this point it was at least a thousand miles distant.

Near the mouth of the Arkansas they were met by a hostile band of Indians, and were in great danger of falling victims to the arrows of the savages. Marquette stood up boldly in the bow of his boat and held up the calumet given to him previously. This gave safety for the moment, but a few miles farther down another hostile band was encountered. Marquette and Joliet now decided that the danger from the savages was too great to proceed farther. Besides, it was possible that they might fall into the hands of Spaniards, which would be equally dangerous. They had gone far enough to be sure that the Mississippi did not flow into the Pacific. From its southerly course it was evident that the river must empty into the Atlantic, probably through the Gulf of Mexico. And so, reluctantly, the explorers turned back on the 17th of July, having spent just a month paddling down the great river.

RETURN JOURNEY

On the return journey Marquette and Joliet were told by some Indians of a route back to Lake Michigan shorter than the one they had followed on the way down. The route lay through the Illinois River and by portage to the Chicago River. The explorers reached Green Bay in September, having travelled a total distance of 2,500 miles. Marquette had been attacked by fever on the homeward route, and was now unable to proceed farther. Joliet continued his journey to Quebec; but, unfortunately, while passing through the Lachine rapids his boat was upset and all his charts and records were lost. However, he was able from memory to give a fairly accurate account of the expedition.

In the following spring Marquette had so far recovered from his illness as to be able to return to the Illinois Indians to found a mission. He was received with the utmost friendliness. But the fever returned, and, though he fought heroically against it, he saw that he must give up the work and return to Quebec. He preached his farewell message to a great audience of three thousand Indians, who sorrowfully saw him depart.

The homeward journey became a race with death. Marquette's strength decreased daily. He was carried as far as Lake Michigan, and there it was plain that his earthly journey must end. He died, and was buried on the shore of the lake. He was only thirty-eight years of age.

XI

LA SALLE

THE GREATEST OF FRENCH EXPLORERS

ONE of the most remarkable men that came to Canada in the early days of her history was Robert Cavelier, Sieur de La Salle. Few men have ever undertaken more arduous tasks, or undergone severer hardships, or endured keener disappointments than this intrepid Frenchman. He met a multitude of difficulties without complaint or discouragement, and fearlessly and resolutely set himself to overcome them. We owe to La Salle a great geographical discovery, but, far more important than that, we have in him a shining example of undaunted determination in the face of obstacles almost insuperable.

La Salle belonged to a wealthy family in Rouen. At the age of twenty-three his adventurous spirit led him to Canada, where his brother was already a missionary. He secured a grant of land on the St. Lawrence a few miles above Montreal and set up a trading-post. From the Indians who came here to exchange their furs, La Salle heard of the Ohio River, and concluded that it flowed into the Pacific. He believed that if he could find this river he would thereby discover the route to China and the East, which had been the ambition of Cartier, Champlain, and other French explorers before him. La Salle talked so much of China that his neighbours in derision called his estate *La Chine*, the French word for China. The name Lachine is still given to the rapids in the river just above Montreal.

La Salle sold his estate in order to get funds to equip an expedition to search for the Ohio. He went up the St. Lawrence, skirted the southern shores of Lake Ontario,

VISION OF A WESTERN EMPIRE 61

passed the mouth of Niagara, and reached the head of the lake where Hamilton now stands. Thence he proceeded southward overland, and after a toilsome journey he at length reached the Ohio. He paddled down the river to a point where the present city of Louisville is located. Here he was deserted by his men and was forced to give up the project of tracing the river to its mouth. He found his way back to Lake Erie, and at length to Montreal.

The story of the partial exploration of the Mississippi by Marquette and Joliet convinced La Salle that neither this river nor the Ohio flowed into the Pacific. He therefore had to revise his earlier plans. He was now filled with the eager desire to complete the work that Marquette and Joliet had begun, and to lay the foundation of a great French empire in the West.

With this great scheme in mind La Salle made two visits to France to enlist the sympathy and aid of Louis XIV. The king listened with interest to La Salle's story and gave him a grant of land at the eastern end of Lake Ontario, together with the privilege of exploring the West and securing it for the French—at his own expense.

Public Archives of Canada

LA SALLE

On his return to Canada La Salle decided to set up a trading-post on his newly acquired estate. With the assistance of Frontenac, the governor, with whom he had secretly entered into partnership for the fur-trade, he re-built Fort Cataraqui and, in honour of his patron, re-named it Fort Frontenac. He expected that the Indians in this part of the country would bring their furs to Fort Frontenac instead of disposing of them to the English traders as they had hitherto done. Had La Salle chosen to be merely a fur-trader he might have become rich, for all the conditions here were favourable. He spent a few years clearing his lands, establishing the settlers, developing the fur-trade with the Indians, and training his men for the expedition he had in view.

In 1678 he embarked upon his great adventure, the exploration of the Mississippi and the establishment of a new French empire in the West. He had borrowed a large sum of money to equip the expedition. He proceeded from Fort Frontenac up Lake Ontario to the Niagara River. Reaching the Falls, he found that he could go no farther with his boats, and set his men to build a ship on the bank of the river some distance above the cataract. The *Griffon*, as he called the new vessel, was not completed till the following year, and in the meantime La Salle had to return to Fort Frontenac to settle difficulties there. In August, 1679, the *Griffon* sailed out of the Niagara River into Lake Erie, and within a month it had reached Green Bay in Lake Michigan. It was the first sailing-vessel to traverse these lakes. Those who are familiar with the huge steam freighters that to-day in great numbers ply up and down this route may in imagination contrast them with the *Griffon*, the little sailing-craft of two and a half centuries ago, and reflect upon the great changes that have occurred within that period. Where there were then unbroken forests lining the shores of the Great Lakes, there are now well-cultivated farms and comfortable homes. Where there were then only a few scattered Indian villages, there are now populous towns and cities with tall buildings, smoking factories, and millions of industrious inhabitants. The present happy conditions have been made possible through the heroic labours of explorers like La Salle and the pioneer settlers who followed in their wake.

La Salle had collected a large and valuable cargo of furs during the voyage up the lakes. He now decided to send the *Griffon* back with this cargo to Niagara, and with the money it brought to pay his debts. Accordingly he despatched the boat in charge of a few trusted followers. The *Griffon* was

ROUTES OF MARQUETTE JOLIET AND LA SALLE

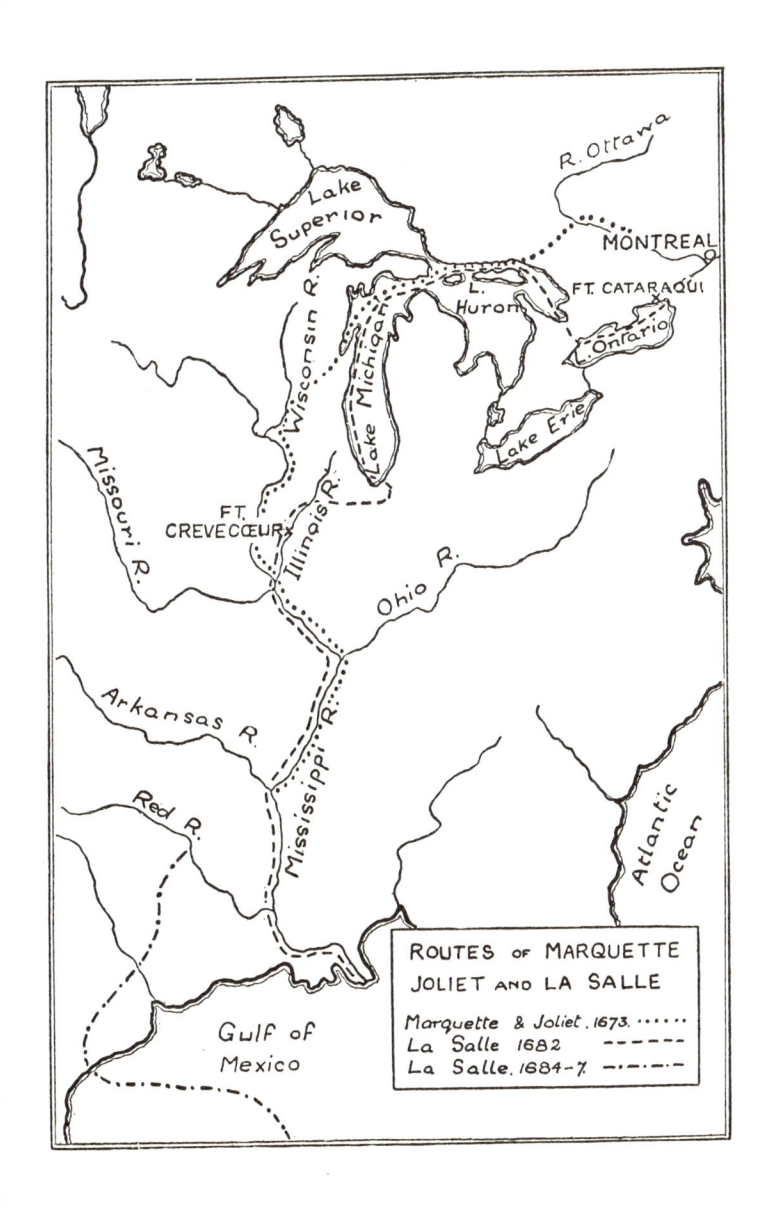

Marquette & Joliet, 1673 ....
La Salle 1682 — — — —
La Salle, 1684-7 —·—·—

never heard of again. La Salle believed that the men had looted the furs and sunk the ship. It seems more probable, however, that it went down in a storm with all its crew. Its loss was a great blow to La Salle.

In the meantime La Salle, with about thirty men, proceeded to the southern end of Lake Michigan. After a difficult portage, during which he was lost in a snowstorm for twenty-four hours, he reached the Illinois River. The food ran short, and the company were saved from starvation, once by finding a buffalo stuck fast in the mud, and later by coming upon a deserted Indian village where supplies of corn had been left behind. La Salle now had trouble with his men. Several of them deserted and others plotted against his life. Poison was placed in his food, but by good luck he discovered it in time. The Indians too became unfriendly. For protection against attack and for shelter during the winter, he built a strong fort on the bank of the Illinois, which he called Crèvecœur (Heartbreak). Seldom has a place been more suitably named. Early in the following spring La Salle determined to return to Fort Frontenac to secure supplies for the company. He left the fort in charge of his faithful lieutenant and friend, Henry de Tonty, and fifteen men. With four men he started to walk the distance of over a thousand miles to Canada.

This journey was one of the most toilsome and dangerous ever undertaken by an explorer. The way lay through a region with many hostile Indian tribes. The snow and ice of winter had not yet disappeared. La Salle and his companions had to march through pathless forests, to wade waist-deep through swamps, and to ford streams swollen by the spring thaws, carrying their blankets, kettles, axes, and guns. They had to sleep at night in the open, sheltered only by the trees. They were often hungry, for they had to depend upon their guns for food, and game was scarce. We who can to-day pass through this same region on a luxurious railway train in three days, or over good roads in a motor-car in about a week, can have only a slight idea of the hardships endured by the explorer on this memorable expedition.

PLANS THAT MISCARRIED

After a journey of sixty-five days, La Salle reached Fort Frontenac, only to find that his creditors had seized his property and that the supplies sent to him from France had been lost. To crown all this, news presently came from Tonty that the men left behind at Crèvecœur had torn down the fort, and, after destroying all the supplies they could not carry off, had deserted.

A less resolute man than La Salle would have given up in despair. But he was still undaunted, and before the end of the following summer he was ready to start westward again with twenty-five men. This time he took a shorter route by way of Lake Simcoe and Georgian Bay, reaching the Illinois in November. He could find no trace of Tonty, but pushed on down the river to the point where it enters the Mississippi. He was unwilling, however, to proceed farther without a search for Tonty. With difficulty he retraced his route, but his friend could not be found. He spent the winter on the shore of Lake Michigan, and in the spring determined again to return to Canada. By a fortunate chance he came upon Tonty at Michilimackinac, and together they proceeded to Fort Frontenac.

Late in the next summer La Salle and Tonty were again on the way westward with thirty men, one hundred Indians, and a good equipment. They followed the route through Lake Simcoe and Georgian Bay, as La Salle had previously done, and reached the Mississippi by way of the Chicago and the Illinois Rivers. From February till April, 1682, they floated down the great river to its mouth. No difficulties barred the way. They had abundance of food. The Indians were friendly. At the mouth of the river La Salle set up a cross bearing the emblem of France and the name of his king, Louis XIV. In honour of the king La Salle named the country through which he had passed Louisiana, the name still borne by the state surrounding the mouth of the river. Thus one of the great dreams of La Salle's life was realized.

One further daring scheme La Salle tried to carry out. He went to France to get the permission of Louis to establish a fort at the mouth of the Mississippi, to seize the Spanish posts in the neighbourhood, and to plant a French colony.

The king consented, and, with four vessels, La Salle sailed from La Rochelle for the Gulf of Mexico. Unfortunately, he could not find the mouth of the Mississippi. After several weeks the expedition landed in what is now the State of Texas, about three hundred miles west of the Mississippi. The colony was doomed to failure from the beginning. The men were unfaithful to their leader and plotted against his life. For nearly a year he sought in vain for the elusive river, and made fruitless attempts to reach the Illinois. One morning he was shot to death by one of his men, and his body was left unburied on the open plain.

In this sad way ended the career of one of the greatest explorers of America. He was only forty-three years of age, but he had crowded into his brief life a host of marvellous achievements. Had he been a more successful leader of men, he might perhaps have accomplished more than he did for his country. But however this may be, his determination of purpose, his courage in adversity, his endurance of hardship, his supreme desire to advance the interests of France, are worthy of all admiration, and have given his name a high place in the history of Canada.

XII

COUNT FRONTENAC

THE FIGHTING GOVERNOR

LOUIS DE BUADE, Count Frontenac, was the most outstanding of the French governors of Canada. He administered the affairs of the colony during two periods: first between 1672 and 1682, and later from 1689 until his death in 1698. During the first period he kept the Indians from invading the colony and encouraged the exploration of the country. But he quarrelled constantly with his colleagues in the Council, and was recalled to France by the king. In the interval between his first and his second administration, the Iroquois threatened to destroy the colony, and Frontenac was sent back to avert the disaster. His second administration was marked by almost continuous warfare with the Iroquois and with the English settlers in the New England States. Such in brief outline was Frontenac's career in Canada. But his story is so romantic and picturesque that it is worth telling in more detail.

Frontenac belonged to the French nobility. At an early age he became a soldier and won glory in the French wars in Europe. His rise in the army was rapid. At twenty-three years of age he was a colonel; at twenty-six he was a general. He was regarded as one of the most brilliant military officers in France. In the intervals between campaigns he spent most of his time at the gay court that surrounded Louis XIV. His extravagance was so great that he soon squandered his estate and was in need of money. It is probable that the king made him governor of Canada not merely because he was an able man, but mainly because he needed a salary to live on. It is hard to explain on any other ground why a

COUNT FRONTENAC

man of Frontenac's character and habits should accept an office so far removed from the camps and courts of Europe.

Frontenac was fifty-two years of age when, in 1672, he received the appointment to the governorship of Canada. On his arrival in the colony he was at once struck with the commanding position of Quebec, and began to dream of the day when the city would be the capital of a great empire with himself as viceroy. Here in the New World he would plant a court that would rival in splendour the royal court of Versailles. With a pomp that was quite out of harmony with the simple conditions of the colony at that time he called a sort of parliament, consisting of the three estates, the clergy, the nobility, and the commons. It was rather hard to get representatives of the nobility in Canada, but Frontenac called the seigneurs as members of that order. To this assembly the new governor made a speech, giving the members much fatherly advice about serving the king and working for the welfare of the colony. Frontenac dearly loved display, and this affair was merely a method of providing a spectacle for the people to mark the beginning of his governorship. The king, however, soon gave the governor to understand that he wanted no such things as parliaments in Canada. He would govern the colony to suit himself, without advice from the colonists. The governor must henceforth take orders from the king.

Public Archives of Canada
COUNT FRONTENAC

Frontenac's extravagance soon made it necessary for him

AN IMPRESSIVE MEETING

to add to his salary as governor by engaging in the fur-trade. He formed an alliance with La Salle for this purpose. La Salle was to develop the trade and Frontenac was to share in the profits. They believed that Cataraqui, at the eastern end of Lake Ontario, where the city of Kingston now stands, would be an excellent place to establish a trading-post. Frontenac decided that he would build a fort at this point, and would at the same time meet and impress the Iroquois with the power of the new governor. La Salle was sent to summon the Iroquois to the meeting-place.

Knowing the Indian love of display, Frontenac prepared for the assembled Iroquois a fine spectacle to mark his arrival at Cataraqui. First in the procession appeared four squadrons of canoes filled with Indians. Then came two large boats, brightly painted and armed with cannon. Frontenac himself followed in state in a boat rowed by soldiers. A squadron of canoes, bearing a well-equipped company of soldiers, brought up the rear. Next day the Iroquois were invited into Frontenac's presence. Sheltered by a canopy of canvas, clothed in his most brilliant uniform, and surrounded by his soldiers, he made a pompous speech to the Indians. He made them understand that he wished to be friendly with them, but that he would severely punish them if they showed any sign of hostility towards the French. Nothing was neglected to make the occasion very impressive. The Iroquois had not forgotten the stern lesson they had been given a few years before by Tracy. They now concluded that Frontenac was even more powerful than Tracy, and that it would be dangerous to provoke his enmity. By his firmness, his good-humour, and his ability to provide a good show, Frontenac gained a power over the Iroquois which kept them friendly towards the French for ten years longer.

In 1675 two men arrived in Quebec who proved to be thorns in the flesh of Frontenac for the next seven years. These were Laval, who was now returning to Canada as the first bishop of Quebec, and Duchesneau, the intendant appointed to succeed Talon. Up to this time Frontenac had had a monopoly of the honours at Quebec; now he had to share these honours with two other officials. He was soon in the midst of serious quarrels with both.

With Laval the trouble arose over the sale of liquor to the Indians. Frontenac took the same position as Talon had taken, that this sale helped the fur-trade, and that if it were prohibited the Indians would take their furs to the English. "Better that the Indians should have French brandy and Christianity at Quebec than English rum and heresy at Albany," said Frontenac. Laval, on the other hand, maintained that the liquor was destroying the Indians, soul and body, and that matters of trade should not overshadow the moral welfare of the natives.

Frontenac's quarrel with the intendant, Duchesneau, arose over the trivial question as to which should preside over the meetings of the Council. Other causes of dispute rapidly developed. Duchesneau sided with Laval against the governor. The quarrels became so violent that friends of the rival parties actually fought in the public streets. At length the complaints to the king were so bitter and so frequent that he recalled both the governor and the intendant to France in 1682. He might have recalled the bishop, too, if he had had the power. The wonder is that the king endured the quarrels so long.

Frontenac's immediate successor, La Barre, was a weak governor, and failed entirely to overawe the Iroquois. He called a meeting at Fort Frontenac, but when the Indians refused to go there he weakly consented to meet them on the south shore of Lake Ontario. Here he made bold threats of what he would do if they showed themselves unfriendly, but the Iroquois saw that this was mere bluster. He was soon recalled to France, a failure as governor.

It was left to La Barre's successor, Denonville, to commit an act of folly that started a deadly war, which extended over several years and brought calamity upon the French. At a meeting with friendly Iroquois at Fort Frontenac, Denonville had two hundred of them treacherously seized. Fifty were sent to France to work as galley-slaves, and many of the others were put to torture. Denonville followed up

SIEGE OF QUEBEC

this outrage by leading a party of French soldiers into the territory of the Senecas, one of the Iroquois tribes. He destroyed a village with its food supply, and killed a number of Indians. Denonville's actions were entirely without justification, and it is little wonder that they aroused the fury of the Indians.

In revenge for the governor's perfidy, the Iroquois one night in 1689 fell upon the sleeping village of Lachine, near Montreal, massacred a hundred of the inhabitants, and carried off more than a hundred others for torture. This atrocity threw the French into a panic. Denonville was recalled, and Frontenac was sent out again to save the colony from destruction.

Though he was now in his seventieth year, Frontenac threw himself with all his energy into the task of reviving the courage of the despairing colonists. France and England were at this time at war, and, rightly or wrongly, he blamed the New Englanders for inciting the Iroquois to attack the French. He organized expeditions to attack the English settlements at the south at three points simultaneously. The English settlements were destroyed and the people were ruthlessly butchered. The Indian allies of the French committed the most dreadful atrocities.

The English were not slow to retaliate. A naval expedition was fitted out to attack Quebec. Sir William Phips, with thirty-four ships and 2,300 men, sailed up the St. Lawrence in 1690, and appeared before Quebec, confident of its surrender without resistance. A lieutenant was sent ashore under a flag of truce to demand the instant capitulation of the fort. Again Frontenac staged a spectacle. The messenger was blindfolded and led to the Council chamber, where Frontenac and his officers had assembled with military pomp. When the bandage was removed from his eyes, the lieutenant was astonished at the unexpected magnificence of the scene before him. Frontenac was seated on a throne, arrayed in the brilliant robes of a colonial governor and surrounded by his officers in their most resplendent uniforms.

"What proposals do you bring from the commander of the British fleet?" demanded the governor haughtily.

"Security to the prisoners if the surrender of the fort is instantly and quietly made," replied the messenger.

"And what if I refuse to surrender?" sternly asked the governor.

"Immediate bombardment by the warships," answered the Englishman, "and the transportation of the prisoners to Boston."

"My reply is easily and quickly given," said Frontenac with emphasis. "Go back and tell Sir William Phips that the answer of the governor of Canada will come from the mouths of his cannon in the citadel of Quebec."

The messenger's report of the forcible reply of the governor was rather disturbing to the English. However, some of the troops were landed and a skirmish took place. The English, fighting on unfamiliar ground, were driven back, leaving several cannon behind. The bombardment from the ships was ineffective, and Phips decided to withdraw his fleet. The bold attitude taken by Frontenac and his spirited defence of the fort won an easy victory for the French, and did much to restore confidence in the colony.

The Iroquois were a more serious menace. Frontenac had brought back from France the Indians seized by Denonville, and had sent them to their tribesmen to act as peacemakers. But this was futile. The Iroquois were bent on the destruction of the colony. For several years they harried the French incessantly. There were no open battles, but the Indians stalked the French as they did the deer. Trappers were killed in the forests, farmers were shot in the fields, defenceless women and children were butchered in their homes.

At last Frontenac resolved to stop this sniping warfare in a decisive way. Though he was now in his seventy-seventh year, he led in person an army of two thousand men into the Iroquois country. The march was a most difficult one, but Frontenac stood the hardships as well as much younger men. He inspired the admiration and stirred the courage of the whole company. The Onondagas, hearing of the approach of the French, burned their villages and escaped. The French destroyed the crops in the fields. Frontenac then turned to the Oneidas and destroyed their settlements and crops.

SERVICE TO THE COLONY

This attack had a good moral effect on the Iroquois. So long as Frontenac lived they were fearful of provoking his wrath. The Treaty of Ryswick in 1697 made peace between the French and English, and the Iroquois thus lost the active support of the English.

Frontenac died in 1698, and was sincerely mourned by the colonists. Though they recognized his faults, his haughtiness, boastfulness, and extravagance, yet they saw beneath them a bravery, steadfastness, and daring which commanded their admiration. Frontenac will be remembered in Canadian history as "The Fighting Governor," who saved the colony when it was on the verge of disaster.

XIII

MADELEINE DE VERCHÈRES

THE HEROINE OF LOWER CANADA

THE stirring story of Madeleine de Verchères deserves a place beside the heroic tale of Adam Daulac in the annals of French Canada. Her story illustrates two things: first, the ever-present danger of murderous attack by the Iroquois in which the French colonists were placed in the early days; and second, the determination and heroism which this danger inspired in even the young people of that time.

The incident with which the name of Madeleine de Verchères is associated occurred during the second administration of Frontenac in the year 1692. It will be remembered that this was the period during which the Indian attacks on the French were most frequent and violent. Madeleine was the daughter of the seigneur of Verchères, whose estate was situated on the south shore of the St. Lawrence about twenty miles below Montreal. The fort at Verchères was a stone structure, with the usual bastions and loopholes. It was surrounded by a palisade of logs, and was connected by a covered way with a strong blockhouse where the ammunition was kept.

Madeleine was at the time only fourteen years of age. Her father was spending some time on military duty at Quebec, and her mother was on a visit at Montreal. On the morning of the 22nd of October the settlers were at work in the fields as usual, and the fort was occupied by Madeleine, her two small brothers, two soldiers, an old man, and some women and children. Madeleine was at the landing-place at the bank of the river when she heard sounds of firing in the fields. A man shouted the alarm that the Iroquois

A COURAGEOUS MAID

were coming. She ran with all speed for the fort amid a shower of bullets, and reached the gate unharmed. She closed and locked the gate in the face of the baffled savages.

Madeleine immediately set about preparing the fort for defence. Going to the blockhouse, she found the two soldiers in a panic of fear. One of them held a burning match in his hand.

"What are you doing here?" she asked sternly.

"We are going to light the powder and blow up the fort," they replied.

"What cowards you are!" she said with scorn. "And you pretend to be soldiers!"

"Better die that way than die of torture at the hands of the savages," they returned.

"There are women and children here. You propose to murder them all instead of defending them. Who could have thought this of Frenchmen!" There was contempt in her tone.

The soldiers were silent in the face of the

Public Archives of Canada
MADELEINE DE VERCHÈRES

scornful accusation of the young girl. Out of very shame they turned to assist her. She placed guns in the hands of her young brothers and the old man, and gave orders to fire from the loopholes whenever an Indian appeared.

In the meantime the Indians, who numbered forty or fifty, gave the defenders of the fort a breathing-spell, and turned their attention to chasing and killing the people in the fields. While this was going on, a settler named Fontaine with his family arrived at the landing-place.

"These people will be killed if we do not get them into

the fort immediately," said Madeleine. "Who will volunteer to bring them in?"

She looked significantly at the soldiers, thinking that perhaps she had aroused some spark of courage in their cowardly hearts.

"To attempt that would mean certain death," said one. "There are Indians watching behind every tree."

"I have no wish to be a mark for an Iroquois bullet," said the other.

"Since your courage is not equal to the attempt," she said with resolution, "I will go myself."

So with her gun in her hand she herself marched boldly down to the landing-place in full view of the savages. Thinking probably that she must be strongly guarded from the fort, the Indians allowed her to conduct the family to safety.

Madeleine placed the women and children in the blockhouse for greater safety.

"The blockhouse is stronger than the fort," she said. "You, Fontaine, will go there and guard the women and children with your life."

"But I should rather stay in the fort and help you to hold it," protested the settler.

"No, that will not do," she replied with decision. "Someone must protect the blockhouse, and you are the one on whom I can best depend. The Indians cannot possibly take it if it is fairly defended. Under no condition must you surrender it, even though I am cut to pieces or burned before your eyes."

Then turning to her two small brothers and the old man, she said: "Let us remember that we are fighting for our country, our homes, and our religion. Are you willing to help me defend them even at the sacrifice of your lives?"

"We are ready," they said, and took their places at the loopholes with quiet determination.

During the night a violent storm arose. Madeleine feared that under cover of the noise and darkness the savages would make a strong attempt to get into the fort. She exhorted her companions to maintain a close and steady watch. All night long, above the sound of the wind and

RELIEF

rain, the savages could hear the call, "All's well!" from the fort and the blockhouse. This stratagem led them to think that the place was full of soldiers. They decided that it would be dangerous to make an attack upon a fort that was evidently so well protected. Had they known the weakness of the defenders, they could easily have overcome their feeble resistance, and Madeleine would either have met her death or have been carried off for torture.

For two days Madeleine and her companions dared neither to eat nor to sleep, so closely were they compelled to keep watch upon their enemies. For several days longer they remained on careful guard, with the Indians always lurking about them. At length word of the plight of the fort was somehow conveyed to Quebec, perhaps by one of the settlers who had escaped the attack in the fields. An officer with forty soldiers arrived at Verchères in the night. They approached the fort cautiously, fearing that the Indians might be in possession.

"Who goes there?" rang out the sharp challenge of the sentry at the loophole.

"A French lieutenant with reinforcements," was the reply.

When the gate was opened and the officer entered, Madeleine advanced to meet him.

"Sir, I surrender my arms to you," she said.

"They seem to be in excellent hands already," replied the officer gallantly.

"Nevertheless I am glad to transfer the defence of the fort to you," said Madeleine. "My soldiers have not been off their posts for a week, and we could not have held out much longer."

When the Indians learned of the reinforcements they hastily withdrew. One can imagine their rage and disappointment when they heard that they had been baffled by the pluck and strategy of a fourteen-year-old girl.

Madeleine de Verchères will always be remembered as one of the heroines of Canadian history. Her name is still commemorated in the titles that are given to many women's organizations throughout the country.

XIV

LA VÉRENDRYE

THE PATHFINDER OF THE PRAIRIES

THE most famous of the "native-born" explorers of Canada was Pierre Gaultier de La Vérendrye. To him and his sons is due the credit of exploring and opening up for trade the great western plains. Two hundred years ago the vast prairie belt of Canada and the United States was inhabited by wandering tribes of Indians who had never seen a white man. To-day this area is peopled by many millions of inhabitants of European descent, living in prosperous cities or towns, or on fertile farms and ranches. The Vérendryes, father and sons, were the first white men to reach those expansive plains lying between the Missouri and Red Rivers on the east and the Rocky Mountains on the west.

La Vérendrye was born at Three Rivers during Frontenac's second administration. As was usual among the young men of Canada at that period, he served as a soldier, and took part in some of the raids on the English settlements on the New England coast. At the age of twenty-one he went to France to fight in the War of the Spanish Succession. He was severely wounded at the battle of Malplaquet and was left for dead on the field. He recovered, however, and at the end of the war was soon back in Canada. For some years he was engaged in the fur-trade.

La Vérendrye used to take great interest in the stories of the Far West told by the Indians who came to his trading-post. Knowing the Indian tendency to magnify the wonders of far-off places, he, of course, used to discount their stories very considerably. But one tale impressed him particularly.

MONEY DIFFICULTIES

An old Indian told him that far in the west there was a great river that flowed into the sea. The desire to find this route to the western sea thus took possession of La Vérendrye as it had seized Cartier, Champlain, Marquette, La Salle, and many others before. But to fit out an expedition to search for this western route required a great deal of money, and La Vérendrye was not a rich man. He succeeded at last in interesting the governor at Quebec, who tried to secure assistance for him from King Louis XIV of France. Louis, however, would not give any assistance in money, but agreed to give La Vérendrye a monopoly of the fur-trade of the West, out of the profits of which the expenses of the expedition might be paid. Now the monopoly of the fur-trade was of little use unless he could borrow money on the strength of it. After much difficulty, La Vérendrye persuaded some merchants of Montreal to finance the expedition in return for all the furs that he might gather. Thus La Vérendrye made an ill-advised bargain that caused him considerable difficulty later on. It showed, however, that he was seeking only the glory of exploration and not wealth from a profitable trade.

Public Archives of Canada
LA VÉRENDRYE

Accordingly, in 1731, with a large party of boatmen, hunters, and soldiers, and with canoes well stocked with provisions and goods for barter, La Vérendrye embarked

LA VÉRENDRYE

upon his expedition. He took along with him three of his sons, Jean, Pierre, and François. The party followed the usual route as far as Michilimackinac—up the Ottawa, across Lake Nipissing, down the French River, and across Lake Huron. Thence they paddled along the desolate and dangerous north shore of Lake Superior as far as Grand Portage at the mouth of Pigeon River. Here a number of his men mutinied, fearing to go farther lest they should never return. It was arranged, however, that La Vérendrye and most of the men should spend the winter at Kaministiquia, where the present city of Fort William stands, while a small party would ascend the Pigeon River and establish a fort.

The following May the men returned with a rich collection of furs, which were at once sent to Michilimackinac to be despatched to La Vérendrye's creditors at Montreal. The men reported that they had built a fort on Rainy Lake. Thither the expedition proceeded, but it took a month to reach the new post over difficult streams and portages. Pushing on down Rainy River, the party reached the Lake of the Woods, on a little peninsula of which they built another fort. During the winter Jean, the eldest son of La Vérendrye, led a small party on snow-shoes down the Winnipeg River to Lake Winnipeg. This great body of water was so expansive that for a moment the men believed that they had reached the western sea. This hope was, however, dispelled when it was found that the water was fresh. At the mouth of the river still another fort was erected. Thus La Vérendrye had established a chain of trading-posts between Lake Superior and Lake Winnipeg.

The explorer's creditors now refused to advance any more money, and he had to go to Montreal. They complained that he was devoting too much attention to exploration and too little to the fur-trade. However, his glowing pictures of the prospects of trade were so convincing that they at length decided to furnish the needed assistance. Before leaving for the west again he arranged that his fourth son, Louis, should go out the following spring, and in the meantime should study chart-making in order that he might be useful in the exploration.

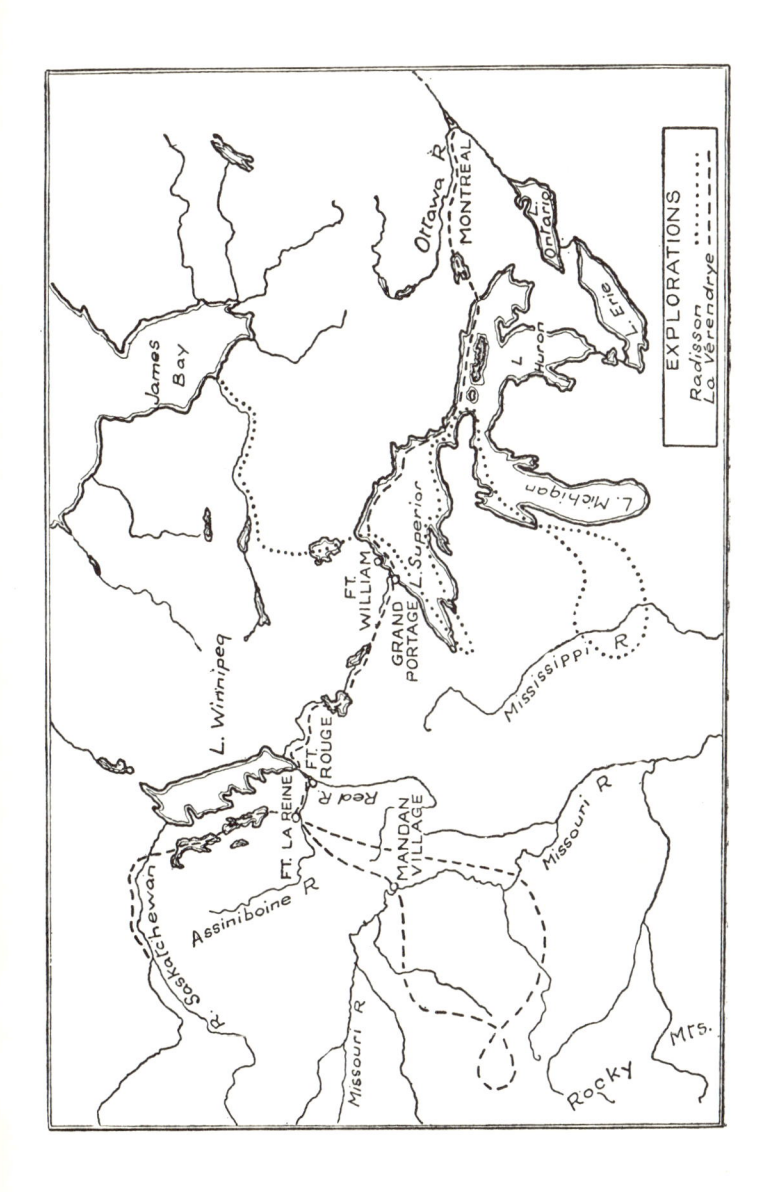

LA VÉRENDRYE

La Vérendrye hurried westward, and when he reached the Lake of the Woods he found that the men at the post were at the point of starvation. He at once despatched his son Jean with a party of over twenty men to Lake Superior to meet the supplies that were coming from Montreal and to hurry them forward. On the shore of the Lake of the Woods the whole party was massacred by the Sioux. The death of his son was a great blow to La Vérendrye. The friendly Crees tried to persuade him to join them in a war of revenge against the Sioux for the murder of the French, but La Vérendrye refused to consent. He knew that such a step would precipitate a general war among the Indian tribes. His trading-posts would probably be destroyed, and his enterprise would thus be ruined, while no good would be accomplished.

From time to time La Vérendrye had heard from the Crees tales of a wonderful tribe of Indians called the Mandans, who lived away to the southward. He concluded that they must be a very superior people, and, in the hope of securing assistance in his search for the route to the sea, he determined to visit them. Leaving Pierre in charge of the post at the Lake of the Woods, he took with him his other sons, François and Louis, and a number of his men. They proceeded down the Winnipeg River to Lake Winnipeg, and thence up the Red River to the junction of the Assiniboine. Here he established Fort Rouge, on the site of the present city of Winnipeg. Thence he went up the Assiniboine to where Portage la Prairie now stands, and erected another trading-post. From here La Vérendrye started south with twenty men in search of the Mandans. As they had no horses at that time, they had to walk, carrying their supplies on their backs. Soon they came to a village of the Assiniboine Indians, whom they asked for information concerning the Mandans. Instead of offering a few guides as the Frenchmen had expected, the whole village went along to direct them. Strangely enough, the journey was made in a very orderly manner—the Indian scouts ahead to look out for enemies; the hunters next to shoot buffalo for food; the women, children, and dogs behind to carry the burdens. When

PRAIRIE INDIANS 83

this interesting expedition reached the Mandan territory, the visitors were received with friendliness, but naturally the Mandans were somewhat alarmed at the prospect of providing food for so many Assiniboines. After several days of feasting, the Mandans got rid of their unwelcome guests by reporting that the Sioux were on the warpath. The chief took La Vérendrye aside and explained that the report was merely a ruse to frighten away the Assiniboines. The French were, however, invited to remain.

La Vérendrye found that the Mandans were not the wonderful race that had been described to him, and that they were much like the other Indian tribes. He realized once more that Indian tales must be heavily discounted. As his main reason for visiting the Mandans was to find the route to the western sea, he was much disappointed when he found that they could tell him nothing about it. He saw that the river he had reached, the Missouri, flowed eastward, and that therefore it could not be the passage to the sea that he sought. He decided to return to the post on the Assiniboine. He became ill on the way, and the journey across the frozen prairie in the month of December was made under most trying conditions. La Vérendrye had never before endured such severe hardships.

In 1739 François La Vérendrye made an expedition of exploration to the north and west. He built two forts, one on Lake Manitoba, and the other near the mouth of the Saskatchewan. The purpose of these forts was to secure the trade of the western Indians, who had hitherto been carrying their furs to the posts of the Hudson's Bay Company. François made his way up the Saskatchewan as far as the junction of the north and south branches. He made inquiry of the Indians as to the source of this great river, and was told that it came from the mountains a great way up, and that beyond these was the great western sea. He decided that a journey thither by this route was too difficult to undertake at this time.

Pierre and François returned to the Mandan country in the hope of assistance in reaching the great river which led to the Pacific. They went south-westward, and had many adventures with various tribes of Indians. From one of these they secured horses, and thereafter the journey was easier and faster. On January 1, 1743, they came in sight of the Rocky Mountains, somewhere in the territory that now forms the State of Wyoming. A few days later they reached the foot of the mountains. Their guides refused to go farther, fearing attack by their enemies, and the explorers were reluctantly forced to turn back. When they reached the Missouri, the brothers buried at a spot on the bank a lead tablet bearing the arms of the French king. One hundred and seventy years later, in 1913, this tablet was by a strange chance unearthed by a young girl at Pierre, North Dakota. The young men eventually reached the Assiniboine post, having been absent more than a year.

Soon after this La Vérendrye was summoned to Montreal. His enemies there complained to the governor that he was making too much money out of the fur-trade, and was not promoting the exploration as he should. After much difficulty, La Vérendrye convinced the governor and the king that the charges were false. He regained his privileges of exploration and prepared to return to the west; but, before he was able to start, death overtook him. His sons expected to continue the work where their father had laid it down, but this the governor would not allow. From that time their names disappeared from the pages of history.

XV

MARQUIS DE MONTCALM

THE DEFENDER OF FRENCH CANADA

Louis Joseph, Marquis de Montcalm, the great general who commanded the French forces when Canada was finally won by the British, was born in 1712 at Candiac, the estate of his ancestors, in the south of France. The Montcalms had been soldiers from the time of the Crusades, and the family name had always stood high in the military annals of France. It is not surprising that Louis Joseph early decided to become a soldier. While still at school, at an age when boys usually think very little about the future, he wrote to his father: "First, I want to be a man of honour, brave, and a good Christian. Secondly, I want to read moderately; to know as much Latin and Greek as other men; also arithmetic, history, geography, literature, and some art and science. Thirdly, I want to be obedient to you and my dear mother. Fourthly, I want to be able to manage a horse and to handle a sword as well as ever I can." As a result of keeping these aims before his mind, he became a very well-read man, a classical scholar, a master of French, and an excellent horseman and swordsman.

At the age of fifteen he was an ensign in his father's regiment and saw fighting in Germany. Eight years later his father died, and he became head of the family. For the next twenty years he spent as much time on his estate as he could spare from his military duties. He fought during the War of the Austrian Succession and won rapid promotion in the French Army. His skill as a military leader was recognized in his appointment as commander of the French forces in America, with the rank of major-general.

MARQUIS DE MONTCALM

Two years before Montcalm's arrival in Canada, serious trouble had developed between the French and English colonists. The French claimed the valley of the Ohio and the Mississippi, and maintained that the English had no right to trade beyond the Alleghany Mountains. This meant that the English would be confined in that narrow strip of land between the Alleghanies and the Atlantic, a plan to which the English would not, of course, agree. The French built Fort Du Quesne, where to-day the city of Pittsburg stands, to mark their claim to possession of the Ohio Valley. General Braddock, with an army of British regulars, was badly defeated in an attempt to take this fort in 1755. This defeat was counterbalanced by a victory at Fort George, which the French commander surrendered, thus giving the British a foothold on Lake Champlain. Next year war was formally declared between France and England —the famous Seven Years' War, which was carried on in three continents, Europe, America, and Asia.

Public Archives of Canada
MARQUIS DE MONTCALM

When Montcalm arrived in Canada he found conditions most unfavourable for carrying on a war. The affairs of the colony were badly managed by Vaudreuil, the governor, and Bigot, the intendant. The former, though honest and well-meaning, was vain, boastful, and incompetent. As governor he had authority to direct the army, and Montcalm was therefore under his orders. Having been born in the colony, Vaudreuil thought he knew more than Montcalm about the management of a war there. He became jealous, too, of the general's success and his growing popularity with the soldiers and Indians.

Bigot was a clever rascal, who was systematically robbing the colony and enriching himself. As the business man of the government he was expected to see that food and war supplies were properly distributed to the colonists and soldiers. These supplies were sent from France on the request of the intendant. When they arrived he sold them at high prices and pocketed the money. Bigot and his friends lived in idleness and luxury, while the people were half-starved because they could not pay the exorbitant prices demanded for food. At the same time the army was poorly equipped and poorly fed because of Bigot's criminal neglect.

Thus, on the one hand, Montcalm had to endure petty annoyances from a bungling governor, who put all sorts of difficulties in his way; and, on the other hand, to submit to having his army ill-fed and ill-equipped by a thieving intendant. "What a country!" he wrote, "where knaves grow rich and honest men are ruined!"

In spite of these conditions, Montcalm was singularly successful during the first three years of the war. He saw clearly that the first thing to do was to destroy the forts established by the English in the area claimed by the French. One of these was Oswego, at the eastern end of Lake Ontario. With a considerable force he went up the St. Lawrence to Fort Frontenac, crossed Lake Ontario, and turned his guns on Oswego. The British commander was killed, and the fort surrendered with little resistance. Montcalm had difficulty in preventing his Indian allies from scalping the prisoners, but by means of promises of gifts he succeeded in restraining them. There was great rejoicing in the colony over the victory. Montcalm was hailed as a hero, but Vaudreuil coolly took all the credit for planning the attack.

The second post to be reduced was Fort William Henry on Lake George. Montcalm went up the Richelieu with a large force to lay siege. Smallpox was raging in the fort, and, after holding out for a few days, the British commander saw the uselessness of resisting a greatly superior force. He ran up the white flag, and it was agreed that the defenders should go out with the honours of war.

Before Montcalm could stop them, some of the Indians burst into the fort and scalped the sick. Next morning a still more dreadful act of savagery was committed. As the disarmed soldiers, with the women and children, were leaving the fort in a long, straggling line, the Indians fell upon them with their tomahawks and scalping knives. Montcalm and his officers did all that could be done to prevent the slaughter, some of the Frenchmen being actually wounded in their effort, but to little avail. The Indians massacred about a hundred of the defenceless British. The savages were indirectly punished later, for the scalps that they carried back to their homes spread the contagion of smallpox among the tribes, and many died as a result.

That Montcalm was disgusted with the conduct of his Indian allies was well known. He would rather have got along without them, but they were useful in bush warfare, and he felt that it was better to have them as friends than as enemies. A passage from a letter to his mother shortly after his arrival in Canada gives a hint of his opinion of the Indians. He wrote: "The men always carry to war, along with their tomahawk and gun, a mirror to daub their faces with various colours, and arrange feathers on their heads and rings in their ears and noses. You would take them for so many masqueraders or devils. They make war with astounding cruelty, sparing neither men, women, nor children, and take off your scalp very neatly—an operation which generally kills you."

The year 1758 saw the tide of war gradually turn against the French. Pitt, Earl of Chatham, the great English secretary of state, had taken charge of the direction of the war for England. He sent out good generals to America, and supported them generously with men and supplies. Nevertheless, Montcalm achieved another brilliant success. The fort of Ticonderoga on Lake Champlain was held by

VICTORY OF TICONDEROGA

the French. Word came that the English were sending a large force up the Hudson to attack the fort. Montcalm was sent with a much smaller force to defend it. When he arrived he found that the engineers had constructed the defences badly, but he remedied the defects as far as possible. The fort stood at the head of a narrow peninsula jutting out into the lake. It could not be attacked successfully from the water, and so Montcalm set about fortifying it on the land side. He had a zigzag wall of logs set up, somewhat like a snake fence, well supplied with loopholes. In front of the wall he had a deep ditch dug, and in front of this he had fallen trees placed with their branches sharpened and pointed forward. The English were commanded by General Abercrombie, a very incompetent leader, whom Pitt had unwisely retained. Abercrombie's second in command, Howe, was a brilliant general, but unfortunately he was killed in a skirmish early in the siege. Abercrombie sent column after column of redcoats to storm the wall, but they were driven back by the withering fire of the French. At length he had to withdraw after a loss of two thousand men. Montcalm's generalship, with far inferior forces, had won another brilliant victory. Abercrombie's dismal failure brought about his immediate recall.

Montcalm's success in the defence of Ticonderoga did not blind him to the impending disaster. He knew that the end was drawing near, and that the best he could do was to delay its coming. "You must retain your foothold till the very last," was the king's command. "I shall do it, or die," was Montcalm's reply.

By the last boat that left for France in 1758, Montcalm sent a letter to his wife in which he wrote: "Thank God, it is all over till the beginning of May. We shall have desperate work in the next campaign. The enemy will have 50,000 men in the field, and we, how many? I dare not tell it. Adieu, my heart, I long for peace and you. When shall I see my Candiac again?" The foreboding that he would never return to his native land and his family grew stronger daily. His discouragement over the condition of his army increased as time went on. In his diary he wrote: "In spite of the distress and impending ruin of the colony, pleasure parties are going on all the time." While Bigot and his friends feasted at tables laden with luxuries, Montcalm and his soldiers ate horse-flesh and half rations of bread.

The year 1759 brought the closing scene in the drama of the war in Canada. In May a combined fleet and army under Admiral Saunders and General Wolfe appeared in the St. Lawrence. From that moment Quebec was isolated from the outside world, caught in the grip of British sea power. Nevertheless, the French occupied a position that was wellnigh impregnable. Montcalm had strongly fortified the north shore of the St. Lawrence from the St. Charles River to the Montmorency, a distance of six miles. Bougainville, an able commander, was in charge of the defences above Quebec, where the high banks of the river made attack difficult. Wolfe seized the south shore across from the fort when it was abandoned by Montcalm under Vaudreuil's order, but he made his main encampment on the north shore east of the Montmorency. Montcalm knew that if he could hold out till October he was safe. The British fleet would have to withdraw at the approach of winter, or be frozen in the ice.

Wolfe knew equally well that the decisive blow must be struck not later than September. On July 31st he tried to land his troops west of the Montmorency under cover of a bombardment by the fleet. Montcalm retreated from the first line of trenches to the second, higher up, from which he poured a deadly fire upon the exposed position of the English. Wolfe was compelled to withdraw with heavy loss. The day was glorious for Montcalm but disastrous for Wolfe.

Wolfe then abandoned his camp at the Montmorency and transported his troops to the south bank of the river opposite the citadel. From that moment the movements of the British were screened by the fleet, and Montcalm was completely in the dark as to their plans. He feared that they would attempt a landing on the heights above Quebec, and urged Vaudreuil to accept reinforcements to strengthen the guard there. But the governor obstinately refused Montcalm's assistance, stating that the heights were sufficiently protected from any attempt the British could make. When, on the morning of the 13th of September, word was brought to Montcalm that Wolfe's troops were in battle array on the Plains of Abraham, three miles above Quebec, he remarked, "Ah, there they are, where they have no right to be."

The rest of the story is soon told. After a hurried consultation with his officers, Montcalm decided that he would fight the invaders outside rather than inside the walls of Quebec. An open battle would be better than a siege. In a short time five battalions of French were moving against the long thin line of redcoats. A single volley from the British at forty paces, followed by a fierce bayonet charge, threw the French battalions into confusion. Montcalm rode along the wavering lines trying to restore their shattered front, but in vain. He received a mortal wound, and from that moment the rout was complete.

When told that he had only a few hours to live, Montcalm said, "So much the better, I shall not live to see the surrender of Quebec." He dictated messages of affectionate farewell to be sent to each member of his family. He sent a letter to General Townshend, the successor of Wolfe, expressing the hope that the French prisoners and the Canadian people would be kindly treated. "Be their protector as I have been their father," he said. Then, having arranged his earthly affairs, he gave himself up to prayer. And thus died a brave soldier and a chivalrous gentleman.

XVI

GENERAL JAMES WOLFE

THE BRITISH HERO OF QUEBEC

JAMES WOLFE, the conqueror of Canada, was born in the village of Westerham in Kent, England, in 1727. His father was an officer in the army, and had fought with Marlborough in the War of the Spanish Succession. As a mere lad, James developed a strong military spirit. When he was thirteen a war broke out between England and Spain, and the elder Wolfe was ordered with his regiment to Spanish America. The boy, young, slight, and delicate though he was, secured his father's permission to go along. Fortunately he became ill before the ship sailed from Portsmouth, and, much to his own disappointment, he was sent home to his mother.

Wolfe remained at school till he was fifteen, when he received a commission as ensign in a regiment that was about to embark for Flanders to fight in the War of the Austrian Succession. A year later he was joined by his younger brother Edward, and the two boys fought side by side at the battle of Dettingen in 1743. Wolfe wrote a letter to his mother giving a graphic description of the battle and expressing pride in his brother's bravery. He said, "I sometimes thought I had lost poor Ned when I saw arms, legs, and heads beaten off close by him." Edward died in Flanders shortly after this, and his death was a great grief to his brother.

At the age of eighteen Wolfe, now a lieutenant, was sent to Scotland under the Duke of Cumberland to assist in crushing the rebellion in support of Charles Edward, the Young Pretender. The army of rebels was pursued northward along the east coast of Scotland until it was

A RISING OFFICER

overtaken and scattered. Cumberland's troops were accompanied by a fleet, which sailed along the shore and kept them well provisioned. It was here that Wolfe first learned the value of close co-operation between the army and navy. He used this knowledge to good effect in his campaigns in Canada at a later time.

Wolfe was now an experienced soldier and a promising officer with prospects of speedy promotion. He was six feet three inches in height, thin and ungainly in appearance, and delicate in health. But what he lacked in strength of body was compensated by his determination of spirit. For a few years he was stationed with his regiment at Glasgow, in Scotland. When his duties permitted he studied mathematics and Latin, and read all the military works that he could secure. He realized that he had left school too early to have obtained as good an education as he needed. He was very popular with his men because he was always considerate of their welfare and took a personal interest in them. One of his captains wrote of him: "Our acting colonel is a paragon. He neither smokes, curses, nor gambles. So we make him our pattern."

Public Archives of Canada
GENERAL JAMES WOLFE

Wolfe was soon recognized as one of the most competent officers in the army. When Pitt, the secretary of state, looked about for young men to place in charge of Britain's operations in America during the Seven Years War, he selected Wolfe as one of the brigadier-generals under Amherst. To Wolfe was assigned the task of taking Louisbourg, a strong French fort on the east side of Cape Breton Island. It was built on a harbour, at the mouth of which was an island which had been strongly fortified. The French fleet was sheltered within the harbour. The fort was defended by Drucour, a gallant French general, in command of a strong and determined garrison.

Early in May, 1758, amid a stormy sea and under heavy fire from the enemy, Wolfe landed his troops on the rocky shore two miles south of the fort. Marching around the harbour, he seized a strong position on the north side. The guns from the British fleet under Admiral Boscawen silenced every gun on the fortified island. The French sank several of their vessels across the passage into the harbour to prevent the British fleet from getting in. However, the British marines rowed into the harbour in small boats and seized the remaining French vessels. Drucour now saw the futility of further defending the fort. He had succeeded in his main object of delaying the British till it was too late in the season for an attack on Quebec. So, late in July, Drucour surrendered the fort to Wolfe.

Up to this time the war in America had been going against the British. The French had won notable victories at Forts Oswego, William Henry, and Ticonderoga. The people of England were much depressed. Wolfe's capture of Louisbourg was the first signal success achieved by the British, and the drooping hopes of the nation were revived. Wolfe was everywhere in the home land acclaimed as a hero.

After the victory at Louisbourg, Wolfe sailed for England to visit his home and to make plans for the final campaign in America. His visit to his mother, now a widow, proved to be his last. The plans made for the conquest of Canada were very complete. Pitt had already stationed the British fleet off the coast of France in such a way as to cut off all communication between France and America. No further reinforcements, supplies, or equipment could reach the French forces in Canada. Admiral Saunders was to be sent out with a quarter of the whole British fleet. Three armies were to proceed against Canada: the first to attack the French forts on the Great Lakes; the second, under General

THE FINAL CAMPAIGN

Amherst, to attack Montreal by way of Lake Champlain; and the third, under Wolfe, to take Quebec. The last was by far the hardest task, and it was a tribute to Wolfe's ability that it was assigned to him.

In May, 1759, Wolfe reached Louisbourg. He had with him three brigadier-generals, Monckton, Townshend, and Murray, with 9,000 soldiers. Admiral Saunders was in command of a fleet of forty-nine men-of-war with 14,000 marines. Early in June the expedition sailed for Quebec. It took a week for the fleet to get through the narrow passage between the Isle aux Coudres and the north shore of the St. Lawrence. Captain Cook had so accurately charted the Traverse, the passage south of the Island of Orleans, that the fleet sailed through without mishap, to the great astonishment of the French, who thought the passage unnavigable without skilful pilots. On June 26th, after a twenty days' voyage, Wolfe reached the western end of the Island of Orleans, and began the twelve weeks' siege of Quebec.

The great fortress stood on the north bank of the St. Lawrence on a lofty promontory. It was defended by the Marquis de Montcalm, the alert and skilful French commander-in-chief. He had very strongly fortified with guns and trenches the shore east from Quebec as far as the Montmorency River, a distance of six miles. The Montmorency could not easily be crossed because of its high banks and swift current. Montcalm had blocked the mouth of the St. Charles at Quebec by booms of logs. West of the fortress for many miles the high steep banks of the St. Lawrence formed a natural fortification, and were guarded by a strong force under an able leader, Bougainville. Nature had done much to make the taking of Quebec a difficult problem, and Montcalm had made the difficulty greater by careful fortification.

Vaudreuil, the governor, foolishly made Montcalm withdraw from the heights across the river from the fortress. Wolfe gladly seized this position, fixed his guns, and soon had the town of Quebec in ruins, though the citadel was unharmed. He also took up a position on the east bank of the Montmorency, and made this his main encampment.

Weeks passed in futile efforts to get a foothold on the northern shore near Quebec. Both Wolfe and Montcalm knew that if nothing decisive were done before the autumn the siege would have to be given up. The approach of winter would necessitate the withdrawal of the British fleet, or it would be frozen fast in the river. Montcalm therefore directed all his energies to holding the British at bay till the autumn arrived. Wolfe was almost in despair to see the summer slipping past without his getting any nearer his goal.

On July 31st the British commander decided to make an attack near the Montmorency. For several hours the fleet bombarded the point where he proposed to land his troops. The landing was made with difficulty, and a redoubt held by the enemy was successfully stormed. The French merely retreated to another prepared position higher up the bank, from which they poured a deadly fire upon the unprotected British. A tremendous storm arose, and the skies added their thunder to the clatter of the musketry. It was useless to make any further attempt to dislodge the French. The British retired to the boats with heavy loss. Wolfe's first serious attempt to storm the enemy's position had ended in failure.

In August Wolfe became ill and was unable to leave his bed for several days. Things looked bad for the British in the absence of their leader, but the doctors "patched him up," as he put it, and, though weak, he was about again. On September 3rd, under cover of the fleet, he broke camp at the Montmorency and transferred the troops to the southern shore of the St. Lawrence. September 10th came and nothing had been accomplished. It looked as if Quebec could not be captured that year. Then an inspiration came to Wolfe. While surveying the north bank through a telescope he located a path leading up the heights about three miles above Quebec. If he could get an army up that path to the plains above without interference from the French, Quebec would be in his hands! But how might this be done in the face of the ever-watchful Montcalm?

Gradually the plan unfolded itself in Wolfe's mind. He would keep the French alarmed by the movements of the fleet below Quebec. He would have the citadel bombarded

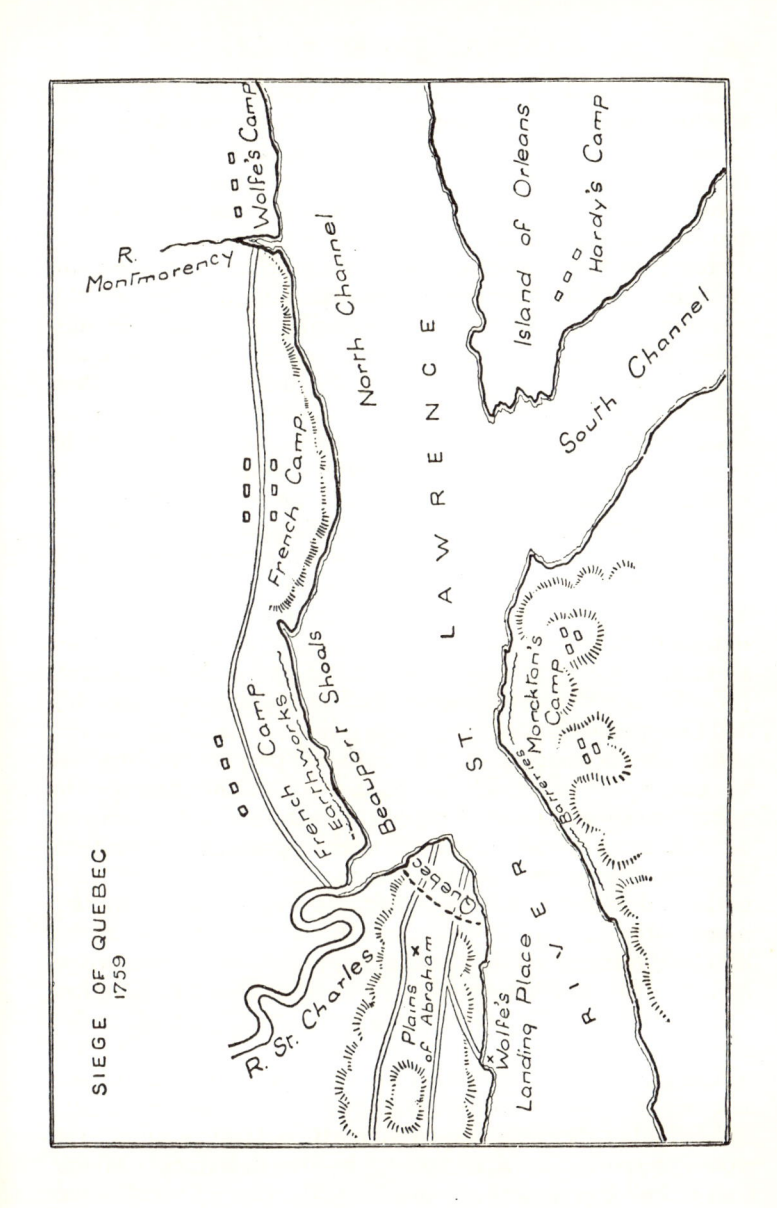

from the south shore. He would make a pretence of attempting to land above Cap Rouge, nine miles west of Quebec. Thus he would distract the attention of the French from the point at which he intended to strike. He assigned to different officers the parts of the plan they were to carry out, but kept to himself the plan as a whole.

The plan was carried out with the precision of machinery. Admiral Holmes above Quebec kept Bougainville's guards occupied in watching his movements above Cap Rouge. Admiral Saunders bombarded the shore below Quebec, and kept his marines rowing up and down the river as if preparing to land. The artillery on the south shore kept up a continuous fire upon the town. For two days these puzzling manœuvres were continued. Only one Frenchman was concerned about the point which the British seemed to ignore. Montcalm suspected that a landing might be attempted there, and sent a battalion to reinforce the guard. But Vaudreuil, the governor, derisively asked, "Have the English wings that they can fly up the heights?" So he marched Montcalm's battalion back. "I will see about increasing the guard to-morrow," he added. It was a fatal mistake. Vaudreuil's "to-morrow" gave him no chance to fulfil his promise.

On the afternoon of the 12th of September, from a warship in the river, Wolfe again surveyed by telescope the place where he intended to land his troops. He wanted to be sure that no unforeseen difficulty would interfere with his plan. The survey completed, he fell into solemn thought upon the heavy task before him on the morrow. In this mood he recited to the officers at his side several stanzas of Gray's *Elegy*, which had become famous a few years before. As he reached the line—

> The paths of glory lead but to the grave,

he paused and said, "Gentlemen, I would rather have written that poem than take Quebec to-morrow." Little did he think that he was to achieve a fame even greater than the poet's, and in the very way described in the striking line he had just quoted.

THE PLAINS OF ABRAHAM 99

That night, under cover of darkness and an autumn mist that lay upon the river, the troops were quickly transferred from the warships above Quebec to small boats. These were rowed slowly and quietly down the river in the shadow of the towering cliffs on the northern shore. Everything was done as noiselessly as possible in order not to attract the attention of the watchful guard. The officers gave orders in low tones; the soldiers sat silent in the boats; the rowers scarcely stirred the waters with their oars.

Suddenly, the challenge of an alert French sentinel rang out—"Qui vive?" "La France," replied a young Highlander with such perfect intonation that the sentinel thought the boats were manned by Frenchmen. A convoy with provisions was expected from up the river, and this made the deception easy.

The army landed on the beach at a spot that is now called Wolfe's Cove. A party of Highlanders under Captain Macdonald were the first to scramble up the heights. The leader was sharply challenged at the top, but again the reply came in such faultless French that the sentry did not recognize an enemy till it was too late. When the Highlanders swarmed over the edge of the cliff, the guard fired one volley and fled. The rest of Wolfe's army quickly climbed the heights, and at dawn were in battle array on the Plains of Abraham. Wolfe formed his men in a "thin red line" two deep across the field.

When the astonishing news that the British were in possession of the Plains of Abraham was brought to him, Montcalm with characteristic courage prepared to give instant battle. A quarter of a mile from the enemy he formed his battalions six deep, and gave the order to advance. His forces were equal in number to those of Wolfe, though he had fewer regular soldiers. But they were the victors of Ticonderoga and Montmorency, and their splendid courage was stirred once more at the prospect of another success.

Wolfe had given orders that there should be no firing from his ranks till he gave the signal. The French fired irregularly as they advanced. What supreme self-control it required on the part of the British to stand inactive under fire, to see their comrades dropping beside them, and to step silently into the vacant spaces! But they stood the strain with matchless patience. Now the French were within a hundred yards! No signal yet from Wolfe. Now they were fifty yards away! Still no signal. Would the commander never let them fire? Forty yards! At last the signal came. "Fire!" A volley like a single cannon shot flashed from the line. Under cover of the smoke the men advanced twenty paces, reloading as they ran. Another volley, followed by a fierce bayonet charge, and the enemy were put to disorderly flight. It was all over. Fifteen minutes of fighting, following seventy hours of manœuvres, terminated twelve weeks of siege and won the most important fortress in America.

Wolfe was three times wounded. As he rode along the ranks encouraging his men to hold their fire, he was struck first in the wrist and later in the thigh. But he gave no sign. Then he received a mortal wound in the breast, and would have fallen from his horse had he not been caught by two officers who sprang to his aid. "Hold me up," he said, "that the men may not see me fall." He was carried to the rear, and it was soon apparent that the end was near. Presently he heard a shout, "See, they run!" "Who run?" quickly asked the dying general. "The enemy, sir," was the reply "they are giving way everywhere." "Then I shall die content," said Wolfe. And after giving a last order to cut off the retreat of the foe, he closed his eyes in death.

Wolfe's body was conveyed to England and laid to rest in the family vault at Greenwich. On the spot where he fell is erected a monument bearing the inscription, "Here Died Wolfe Victorious." Thus Canada commemorates one of the most dramatic battles of all history, and pays tribute to one of the greatest of builders of the British Empire.

XVII

GENERAL JAMES MURRAY

THE FIRST GOVERNOR OF BRITISH CANADA

AFTER the surrender of Quebec to the British on September 18, 1759, the garrison was placed in charge of General James Murray. He was the son of a Scottish nobleman, and had given distinguished service in the army before coming to Canada. He had commanded a brigade at the siege of Louisbourg in 1758, and had been highly praised by Wolfe. He had served as a brigadier-general under Wolfe at the siege of Quebec, and at the battle of the Plains of Abraham had directed the left wing of the British army.

Murray's garrison at Quebec consisted of 3,000 men. He soon established friendly relations with the townspeople. He treated the French with kindness, and won their admiration and respect. The winter of 1759-60 was severe, and the garrison suffered intensely from cold and disease. The nuns of the convent knitted wool stockings to protect the legs of the Highlanders from the cold. The soldiers, on their part, shared their rations with the poor and hungry of the city.

De Levis, the successor of Montcalm, was in command of the French garrison at Montreal. He had not given up hope of recovering Quebec, but he knew that his best chance of success lay in an attack before the ice left the St. Lawrence in the spring. After that, any attempt would probably be hopeless, for at any moment a British fleet might sail up the river to reinforce the defenders of the fort.

In April, 1760, De Levis, with an army of 6,000 men, appeared before the walls of Quebec, expecting to take the city by siege. To his surprise Murray marched out of the citadel with his whole available force to give battle. The

British general knew that the fort was not strong enough to resist siege, and he staked his fortunes, as Montcalm had done the year before, upon an open battle. The British were outnumbered three to one, but they made a stubborn resistance. At length, however, they were overpowered by force of numbers, and retreated within the walls of the fort. The battle of St. Foy, as it is usually called, was a severe reverse for Murray.

Nevertheless, Quebec did not surrender, though De Levis did his best to batter down the walls. Day after day Murray held out in the hope that a British fleet with reinforcements would appear. Day after day De Levis maintained the siege in the hope that French ships with supplies and men would come to his aid. The eyes of the British within the fort, and the eyes of the French without, constantly swept the river for the appearance of a sail. Which would arrive first, a French or a British fleet? For many days the uncertainty continued. At length, on the 9th of May, the watchers descried a vessel sailing up the estuary. Would it fly the flag of Britain or the tricolour of France? Every telescope was anxiously trained upon it. The fate of Canada depended upon the identity of that flag. If it were the tricolour, then Canada would remain French; if it were the ensign of the British fleet, then Canada would pass to a new allegiance. For a long time no flag could be discerned at the masthead. Presently one was run up. It was the white

Public Archives of Canada
GENERAL JAMES MURRAY

CESSION OF CANADA

ensign of England, and was borne by a British man-of-war. Canada's destiny was decided—she was British! A few days later three other warships arrived. De Levis saw the futility of further attempts to capture the fortress, and withdrew to Montreal.

Later in the year three British armies converged upon Montreal: the first from the Great Lakes, the second from Lake Champlain under Amherst, and the third from Quebec under Murray. In the face of overwhelming odds De Levis surrendered the fort, and Governor Vaudreuil ceded all Canada to the British.

In the interval between the cession of Canada in 1760 and the close of the war by the Treaty of Paris in 1763, the country was placed under military rule, that is, government by the officers of the army. General Murray governed Canada from Quebec. Under him Colonel Burton had charge of the military district of Three Rivers, and General Gage the military district of Montreal.

ENGLISH MAN-OF-WAR

In 1761 a serious difficulty arose with the soldiers in the garrison at Quebec. The War Office in London had issued an order that fourpence per day should be deducted from each soldier's pay for rations that formerly had been supplied free. The soldiers were enraged at the ingratitude thus shown to those who had just won a great war. They broke out in open mutiny. Murray sympathized with the men in their resentment, but he could not allow rebellion to become rife in the garrison. He called his officers together and told them that the mutiny must be suppressed with a strong hand. Then he ordered all the troops to appear on parade. Placing two flags some distance apart, he ordered the men to march between them, on pain of instant death if they refused. He then gave the command, "Quick march!"—and every man obeyed. Murray's decisive action saved the situation. Later the difficulty about the pay was satisfactorily settled by the War Office.

Murray was asked to report to the British government the possibilities of establishing a sea-going trade with Canada. Up to this time Canada had been regarded as affording opportunities for the fur-trade and nothing more. In his report Murray dwelt upon the possibilities of developing the rich fisheries of the St. Lawrence River and Gulf. He pointed out the opportunities of using the fine timber of the forests for purposes of shipbuilding. He referred to the vast areas of fertile land suitable for agriculture. He advised an investigation into the supplies of iron near Three Rivers. Murray's report forms one of the earliest documents pointing out the advantages of Canada for immigrants.

In 1763 the Peace of Paris was signed, closing the Seven Years' War and formally transferring Canada to the British. Murray was made governor, with authority to call a General Assembly when he found the circumstances to warrant it. It was evidently the intention to establish a system of self-government in Canada. There were 65,000 people in the country, most of whom were French. Outside the militia, very few were English. The French were unused to parliamentary institutions, and did not want a General Assembly. Murray therefore did not think that circumstances warranted its establishment. Murray's great task lay in the development of a friendly relationship between the two races. In this task he succeeded so well that soon there were loud complaints from the English traders that Murray was favouring the French to the disadvantage of the English. It is certain that he stood high in the regard of the French clergy, seigneurs, and *habitants*. It is a tribute to Murray's sagacity as a statesman that he was able under very difficult circumstances to create a friendly attitude on the part of the French Canadians towards their new governors.

Murray's most serious trouble was with those of his own nationality. Now that their services were no longer necessary in the defence of the colony, the soldiers became unpopular among the civilians of Montreal. Quarrels between the two classes became frequent. A soldier was unjustly sentenced to gaol by a magistrate, and there was great indignation among his fellow-soldiers. A party of them broke into the magistrate's house, gave him a sound thrashing, and cut off his ear. Murray was called from Quebec to quell the disturbances. He tried to get over the difficulty by sending the regiment to another place. But the magistrates were loud in their complaints against Murray, and had sufficient influence with the authorities in England to secure his recall in 1766. His conduct was investigated by a committee, but he was exonerated of all blame.

General Murray deserves to be remembered in Canadian history for his bravery and skill as a general and for his tact in the treatment of the new French-speaking citizens of the Empire at a critical period after the conquest.

XVIII

PONTIAC

THE INDIAN CONSPIRATOR

For several years after the surrender of Canada, the British had serious trouble with the Indians living south and east of the Great Lakes. With the single exception of the Iroquois, all the tribes were sympathetic towards the French and hostile towards the British. The reason for this lay in the different treatment accorded the red-men by the two white races. Champlain had, it is true, made a serious mistake in provoking the enmity of the Iroquois, a mistake for which the French had to pay in a century and a half of conflict and bloodshed. But the French had in all other cases systematically cultivated the friendship of the Indians. French missionaries had been very zealous in teaching them; French traders were generous in giving them goods on credit; the French government distributed presents liberally, though at considerable cost to the treasury; and the French governors frequently received the chiefs with great pomp and ceremony.

On the other hand, the British despised the Indians, and made no attempt to conceal their scorn. The red-men were useful only as collectors of furs; they were little better than the wild beasts of the forest; the land would be well rid of them if they could be driven away. Such was the general attitude of the British towards the Indians. There were, however, a few Englishmen who thought differently. One of these was Sir William Johnson, who had a large estate on the Mohawk River near the territory of the Iroquois. Johnson was a man of broad sympathies, a brilliant military leader, and a skilful diplomatist. It was due to his influence

AN INDIAN CONSPIRACY

that the Iroquois tribes, with the exception of the Senecas, remained loyal to Britain at a time when their enmity would have had serious consequences.

After the capitulation of Montreal in 1760, the British flag was raised over the western forts. The Indians were disturbed and resentful. The hated English were taking the place of their friends, the French. There would be no more presents to the Indians. The English would settle the lands and deprive the red-men of their hunting-grounds. The French had not given up hope of recovering Canada. It would be a good thing to drive out the conquerors and restore the land to the people who had always been the friends of the red-men.

And so was formed a famous Indian conspiracy to seize the forts that had been taken over by the British. The leader in the conspiracy was Pontiac, a chief of the Ottawas. He secured an influence over the Indians by his fiery oratory, by his ingenuity in planning deeds of cruelty, and by his superior ability in treachery. They recognized in him a master-mind in plotting savagery. He united the tribes from the Mississippi to the Alleghanies and from the Great Lakes to the Ohio in a great confederacy, and induced them to take the warpath against the British. The result was that all the British forts in the west, save three, fell to the Indians; and in the year 1763 more British lives were sacrificed than during the siege of Quebec in 1759. And the pity of it was that these lives were blotted out in most cases by treachery, and not in a fair fight against recognized enemies. The story of the attacks on Forts Detroit, Michilimackinac, and Pitt will illustrate the Indian methods of attack.

Pontiac decided to strike first at Detroit because it had abundant stores of food and goods and would afford rich plunder. One morning in May, 1763, he called a council of chiefs at his camp a few miles south of Detroit, and stirred their spirits by a fiery speech denouncing the base designs of the British. The following day, under pretence of performing the peace dance for the entertainment of the garrison, Pontiac and several warriors secured entrance to the fort and made a careful survey of the defences. Major Gladwyn, the commander, received them kindly, and distributed presents when they left. Pontiac then formed a dramatic plan to seize the fort. Fifty picked warriors were to pay another "friendly" visit. Under his blanket each warrior was to conceal a gun with the barrel cut short so that it would not be noticed. Pontiac was to make a friendly speech to Major Gladwyn, at the end of which he was to present the commander with a peace belt of wampum. If Pontiac thought it wise to attack, he would present the belt with the reverse side first; but if he thought it unwise to attack, he would present it in the ordinary way. A sound of firing in the fort was to be a signal for other Indians outside the walls to rush through the gates to the assistance of the warriors inside.

Fortunately, the plot was revealed to Gladwyn by a friendly Indian, and the commander made careful preparations to meet it. Accordingly, when Pontiac and his chosen warriors were admitted to the fort on the appointed day, he was amazed to find the soldiers distributed at strategic points, and every one of them fully armed. Disguising his surprise, the chief demanded, "Why do I see so many of my father's young men standing on guard with their guns?" "I have ordered my soldiers under arms for the sake of exercise and discipline," Gladwyn replied. Seeing the futility of any attempt to execute his plan, Pontiac said, "I have come to give my father the wampum belt of peace as a token of the friendship of his red children." He then presented the belt in the ordinary way, and the baffled savages withdrew.

Foiled in his attempt to take the fort by treachery, Pontiac next tried to carry it by assault. Several hundred warriors attacked, but were held at bay. From the shelter of bushes, fences, and ridges they kept up a continuous fire upon the fort. For weeks no British soldier slept, except in his clothes with his gun across his arms. The garrison would have been starved had it not been for a friendly Frenchman named Baby, who lived on a large farm across the river from the fort. At night, when he could safely do so, he sent boatloads of meat and flour to the fort.

A SIEGE FAILS

Late in July a reinforcement of 300 men under Captain Dalyell arrived from Niagara with cannon and supplies. Dalyell decided to make a surprise attack upon Pontiac's camp by night, and, by capturing the chief, to put an end to the siege. The plan was betrayed by a spy in the fort, and when Dalyell's men in the darkness were crossing a small bridge over a stream, they were attacked by the waiting Indians. Twenty men were killed, including Dalyell, and over forty were wounded. It was a most unfortunate reverse for the British, and the Indians celebrated their victory by wild orgies of rejoicing.

In September a boat came up the river from Niagara laden with supplies. At a narrow spot in the river a fleet of canoes shot out from the overhanging bushes. A crowd of Indians swarmed over the sides of the vessel before the soldiers could turn the guns upon them. In the midst of the hand-to-hand fight that ensued on the deck, a soldier with some presence of mind and a sense of humour shouted, "Light the powder and blow up the ship." One of the Indians who knew a little English passed the dreadful threat along. In a moment the whole throng of savages leaped into the river, swam frantically to the shore, and were soon lost to view. It was a bit of comedy in the midst of tragedy. The boat with its supplies reached the fort in safety.

By October the Indians had grown tired of the siege and had begun to disperse to their homes. Pontiac's power was beginning to wane. At length, after six months' continuous siege, he gave up the attempt to capture the fort. The weary garrison at Detroit at last had rest.

The story of the fall of Fort Michilimackinac reads like the scenario of a moving-picture drama. The soldiers of the British garrison at this northern post, under Captain Etherington, were on friendly terms with the neighbouring Indians. Apparently all was peaceful. On the 4th of June the garrison was to celebrate the birthday of King George III in a programme of sports. In this celebration the Indians were invited to participate. They offered to provide part of the entertainment by arranging a game of lacrosse, an offer that was gladly accepted by the soldiers. Two teams one of Sacs and one of Chippawas, appeared on the field in front of the fort, and the game began. The ball was thrown, batted, and carried up and down the field with great energy. The players slashed, tripped, and shouldered each other in real earnest. Excited shouts arose as the tide of the game turned now in this direction and now in that. The unarmed soldiers stood along the edge of the field, watching the play with interest and encouraging their favourite team with friendly shouts. Near the gate of the fort stood two lines of stolid squaws with their blankets tightly wrapped about them. Suddenly the ball was thrown near the entrance and the excited players rushed after it. All at once lacrosse sticks were cast aside. The blankets of the squaws were thrown open. Each warrior as he passed grasped a tomahawk and a scalping-knife that had been concealed by the squaw. Every soldier was either captured or slain, and the fort and its stores fell to the savages. The capture of Fort Michilimackinac is a famous example of Indian treachery.

The defence of Fort Pitt on the Ohio River was scarcely less dramatic than that of Fort Detroit. In June, 1763, the fort was surrounded by large numbers of Indians of several different tribes. They sent messengers under a flag of truce to persuade the British commander to surrender. The Indians professed to be concerned as to the garrison's safety if he did not do so.

"Great numbers of other warriors are on their way to the attack," they said. "The fort will surely be destroyed and every soldier will be killed. Give up the fort and go home to your wives and children."

The British leader was something of a humorist and he replied in kind.

"Several thousand reinforcements are already on their way to assist us," he said. "Your friends, the Ottawas, are going to be destroyed. If you stay here you will all be killed. Your wives will be widows and your children orphans. Better get away while there is time, for we should be sorry to see you hurt. But do not tell the Ottawas, for we do not want them to escape. We are not going to give up this fort while there is a white man left in America."

IGNOMINIOUS END

Seeing that nothing could be gained by treachery, the Indians made an assault on the fort. For several weeks the siege was kept up. In the meantime Colonel Bouquet was sent from New York with a small army to the relief of the besieged fort. For days the army struggled through the difficult forest roads, a scouting party in front, the main company next, and the supplies on pack-horses in the rear. When the British were about forty miles from the fort, a large body of Indians set upon them, firing from the shelter of the trees. The disaster to Braddock's army eight years before was almost repeated. By a clever piece of strategy Bouquet led the Indians into a trap, and then sent his Highlanders upon them with the bayonet. The Indians were quickly dispersed, and their losses were so heavy that they lost heart. Bouquet had beaten them in their own style of warfare. Three days later the expedition reached Fort Pitt and the siege was raised.

Gradually Sir William Johnson and Colonel Bouquet succeeded in quieting the Indians. At length, in 1766, a council to discuss terms was called at Oswego. Here Pontiac gave a pledge of peace, and the great Indian war was over.

Three years later Pontiac was treacherously killed by another Indian who had stealthily followed him into the forest as he was leaving a drunken feast. Thus fell, by an assassin's hand, the Indian chief whose misguided plots had caused the death of many British soldiers and many warriors of his own race.

XIX

SIR GUY CARLETON

THE FATHER OF BRITISH CANADA

CANADA owes much to Sir Guy Carleton. If a less resolute man than he had been governor of Canada in 1775, this country would probably have been separated from the British Empire and made a part of the United States. The colony that had been acquired through the victory of Wolfe was kept loyal to the Empire through the strategy of Carleton when the American colonies to the south broke away. For this service alone Carleton deserves to be gratefully remembered in the history of Canada.

Guy Carleton was born in the county of Tyrone in Ireland in 1724. He entered the army at the age of eighteen. Wolfe recognized his ability and specially requested that he should be sent to Canada in 1759 as director of defences. So well did he plan the fortifications of the British during the campaign that he won the confidence of the commander-in-chief. "Grave old Carleton," as Wolfe affectionately called him, probably knew more of the plan that resulted in the capture of Quebec than any other of Wolfe's generals.

When Murray retired from the governorship in 1766 Carleton was appointed to the post, and thus began a period of service which lasted, with two brief interruptions, for thirty years.

The first great problem was to set up a form of government under which the two races in the country could work in harmony. Accordingly, in 1774, the British parliament through his influence passed the Quebec Act. This Act fixed the southern boundary of Canada at the Ohio and the western at the Mississippi. It established English law

HARMONIZING THE RACES

for the trial of criminal cases and French law for the trial of civil cases. Seigneurial tenure was confirmed as the method of holding land. The Roman Catholics were given the right to the free exercise of their religion, and the Roman Catholic clergy were allowed to collect their "accustomed dues." The government was to be directed by a governor and council containing from seventeen to twenty-three members, all of whom were to be appointed by the British parliament.

The Quebec Act was pleasing to the French seigneurs and the clergy, whose former rights were thus confirmed. But it was not satisfactory to the *habitants*, who would have preferred to be free from the exactions of the seigneurs.

Nor was the Act agreeable to the English population, who had been accustomed to government by elected representatives and not by appointed councils. But most of all, the American colonies were displeased. "Who gave the British parliament the authority," they asked, "to attach to a newly acquired French colony that great country south of the Great Lakes as far as the Ohio?" It was absurd, they said, that this valuable territory should be given to Canada.

Public Archives of Canada
SIR GUY CARLETON

Carleton soon had a more serious difficulty to meet than the dissatisfaction over the Quebec Act. To understand the nature of this difficulty, it is necessary to refer to conditions that existed in the American colonies. There were thirteen of these lying along the Atlantic coast. Britain had protected the colonies from attack by the French during the Seven Years' War. The war had cost a great deal of money, and

Britain asked the colonies to give some assistance in paying off the debt, part of which had been incurred in their protection. The colonies refused to be taxed by a parliament in which they had no representatives. "No taxation without representation," was their reply. The British parliament imposed taxes which the colonies refused to pay. At length, with so much stubbornness on the one side and so much unreasonableness on the other, the dispute developed into a bitter war which lasted several years. In the end the colonies had the better of the struggle, and Britain acknowledged their independence in 1783. Thus was established the great American republic, the United States.

In the early part of the war the rebellious Americans decided to make Canada the fourteenth colony in the revolt against Britain. In this they believed they would have small difficulty, for it was known that the French inhabitants were none too well disposed towards Britain. It was known, too, that there were in Canada many English sympathizers with the colonial cause. It was therefore determined to invade Canada, to invite the French to throw off their allegiance to Britain, to make prisoners of the loyalist governor and his army, and to consolidate Canada with the thirteen colonies. In 1775 two expeditions were fitted out for the attack: one under General Montgomery to strike at Montreal, and the other under General Arnold to proceed against Quebec. It was arranged that when Montgomery had captured Montreal he should unite his forces with Arnold's for the taking of Quebec, which was regarded as the more formidable task.

Carleton had heard of Montgomery's project of taking Montreal, but did not know of Arnold's part in the invasion. The governor therefore hurried to Montreal to prepare for Montgomery's attack. On their way the Americans took Forts Chambly and St. John's without encountering much resistance. Carleton then saw that it would be futile to attempt any defence of Montreal, and decided to retire to Quebec, from which the American attack might be more easily repelled. Accordingly, with a small flotilla, he set off down the St. Lawrence. But the winds were contrary, and

A FORTUNATE ESCAPE

for several days the boats made little progress. Reaching a narrow spot in the river at Sorel, Carleton found to his dismay that the enemy had fixed guns on both sides and that the boats could not pass. The American commander invited the governor to send a lieutenant ashore to see how impossible it was to escape. The lieutenant's report convinced Carleton that the flotilla could not get through. Carleton knew that, if he were captured, Quebec would fall and Canada would be lost. A live British governor as a prisoner would be a rich prize for the Americans! They confidently expected his surrender on the following morning.

In the night Carleton dressed himself as a French *habitant*, with grey woollen suit, red tuque and scarf, and moccasins. Leaving orders that the fleet should not surrender till the last possible moment next day, he entered a small boat with two or three of his men. In the darkness they dropped noiselessly past the American guns, paddling the boat with their hands till out of danger. Next day they reached Three Rivers, and in a larger boat the governor was conveyed to Quebec. His arrival there on November 19th was an occasion of much rejoicing in the city. In the meantime the Americans at Sorel were greatly chagrined that, though they had captured his fleet, the governor himself had slipped through their fingers.

Early in December Montgomery, having captured Montreal, joined forces with Arnold before Quebec. He sent Carleton a demand for his immediate surrender, in the course of which he said: "Should you persist in your unwarrantable defence the consequences be on your own head. Beware of destroying stores of any kind. If you do, by Heaven, there will be no mercy shown."

To this the governor's only reply was: "I will hold no communication with any rebels until they come to implore the king's pardon."

The numbers of the opposing armies were about equal, 1,800 on each side. The walls of Quebec were none too strong, but the Americans had not the artillery to batter them down. Little was done for a whole month. Then in the early morning of December 31st, 1775, during a blinding snowstorm, the Americans attacked. The fighting was severe, but the British had been expecting the assault and were prepared. Montgomery was killed, and his body was found several hours later completely buried in the snow except for one protruding hand. Arnold was severely wounded. The Americans lost 300 in killed and wounded and 400 in prisoners; while the British escaped very lightly, with a loss of only 30 in killed and wounded.

The siege did not end with this reverse. The Americans hung around Quebec for several months, hoping for reinforcements, but they made no further serious attempt at assault. Three British men-of-war appeared in the river early in May, and the Americans discreetly withdrew. Thus ended the fifth and last siege of Quebec.

In 1778 Carleton asked to be relieved of the governorship, and he retired to his estate in England. But his services were soon required by the British government for another task. To explain the nature of this task, it will be necessary again to revert to the American colonies.

Probably one-third of the three million inhabitants of the American colonies were not in sympathy with their fellow-citizens in their rebellion against the Mother Country. They wished to remain loyal to the British Crown. They refused to bear arms against Britain in the war. These Loyalists became the objects of bitter hatred on the part of their revolutionary neighbours. In some of the colonies they were deprived of the right to vote or to hold public office. In others their property was confiscated, and those who owed them money were relieved of all responsibility for payment. They were fined, imprisoned, and subjected to special taxation. Often they were compelled to suffer personal violence. They were "tarred and feathered," horsewhipped, and "rail-ridden" through the streets. In a few cases they were actually put to death as traitors. The treatment of these unfortunate people in the American colonies became so bad that Washington, the revolutionary leader, said: "I can see nothing better for them than to commit suicide."

COMING OF THE LOYALISTS

When the war was over the British government offered refuge to the Loyalists in the British dominions at the north and provided transportation for those that wished to go. Thirty-five thousand went to the Maritime provinces and settled chiefly in southern Nova Scotia and along the St. John in New Brunswick. Seven thousand settled in Quebec at Three Rivers and Sorel. Another ten thousand settled along the St. Lawrence between Lake Ontario and the Ottawa, and along the Bay of Quinte and the Niagara. In the first year or two of their residence in Canada, many of them suffered severely from lack of proper shelter, food, and clothing. They were subjected to all the hardships of pioneer life in an unbroken wilderness. The British government showed an appreciation of the sacrifices the Loyalists made in their devotion to the Empire. It gave to each a grant of land, and provided him with the necessary tools, implements, and seed grain to start farming. It also arranged for compensation for the loss of property in the colonies. Altogether Britain treated the Loyalists very generously, distributing three million acres of land and three million pounds sterling among them. Each Loyalist was given the right to append the letters "U.E." to his name, as a mark of his belief in the principle of the unity of the empire.

It was the task of Sir Guy Carleton to arrange for the transportation of the Loyalists from the United States. New York was the last post to be vacated by the British army after the treaty of peace was signed. Carleton was in command, and from there he directed the work of getting the Loyalists out of the country. This required some time, and he was pointedly asked several times by the American authorities when he would withdraw his army and give up the post. His answer invariably was: "I will withdraw only when I am sure that I have assisted to leave this country every Loyalist who wishes to go." When, at the end of 1783, the work was at length completed, Carleton again retired to his country home in England, expecting to pass the rest of his days in leisure. As a reward for his great services to the empire, he was raised to the peerage, being given the title Baron Dorchester.

I

Three years later, at the age of sixty-two, Lord Dorchester was again asked to return to Canada as governor. The coming of the Loyalists had given rise to an entirely new set of conditions which required adjustment, and Dorchester was believed to be the man to do this work. The Loyalists were dissatisfied with the government as established by the Quebec Act, and wanted a representative assembly. Dorchester proposed a federal union of Canada with the Maritime provinces, thus anticipating an event which occurred three-quarters of a century later. However, his suggestion was not approved. The Canada Act, or the Constitutional Act as it is usually called, was passed by the British parliament in 1791. It divided Canada into two provinces, Upper and Lower Canada, with the Ottawa River as the dividing line. It arranged for the election in each province of a legislative assembly by the people, and for the appointment of a legislative council by the Crown. The real government of each province was placed in the hands of an executive council, also appointed by the Crown. The Act set apart one-eighth* of the Crown lands of Upper Canada for the support of a Protestant clergy. It also arranged that lands in Upper Canada should be held by freehold tenure.

The Constitutional Act had serious defects which were apparent at a later time. It was no doubt a mistake to divide the country into two parts on racial lines. The division tended to intensify the cleavage between the two great races that constituted the citizenship of the country. It was a mistake, too, to place the administration in the hands of an appointed executive council, which might or might not accept the advice of the elected assembly. Still further, the setting apart of the "Clergy Reserves" opened the way for bitter disputes on religious grounds. The Act, however, marks a forward step in providing that the people, through their elected representatives in the assembly, should have something to say in the government of the country.

* Owing to the peculiar wording of the Act, the area set apart is frequently stated as one-seventh. The fraction one-eighth is, however, the correct amount.

FINE RECORD OF SERVICE

Lord Dorchester's work in Canada was soon completed. He left in 1796, and lived in retirement till his death in 1808. His name is associated in Canadian history with four important landmarks: the Quebec Act of 1774, the defence of Canada against the American invasion in 1775, the coming of the United Empire Loyalists in 1783, and the Constitutional Act of 1791. It is doubtful if any other man has been connected with so many outstanding events in this country. Sir Guy Carleton, Lord Dorchester, may justly be called the Father of British Canada.

XX

JOSEPH BRANT

THE MOHAWK ALLY OF BRITAIN

THE fine agricultural county of Brant and the thriving city of Brantford in the province of Ontario perpetuate the name of Joseph Brant, the famous chief of the Mohawks and the loyal ally of Britain during a troublous period of her history. In the central square of the city of Brantford stands a noble bronze statue of this notable Indian, and on the walls of a thousand schools in Ontario hangs a portrait depicting his striking figure arrayed in the bright colours dear to the heart of the red-man.

Of Brant's early life little is known. His sister, Molly Brant, was married to Sir William Johnson, the famous superintendent of the Indians, who had a large estate in the Mohawk Valley in what is now the State of New York. Under Sir William's direction the boy was sent to a school in Connecticut, where he remained for two years. In that short time he obtained a fair education, which he greatly improved by his own effort as he grew older. Two great aims seem to have been developed in his mind during these early years: first, to become a leader among his people; and second, to do everything possible to advance their religious and moral welfare. He rose rapidly in influence among the Indians, and was soon recognized as the war chief of the Six Nations.

When the American colonies revolted and declared their independence, Brant remained loyal and kept the Six Nations in allegiance to Britain. He visited England in 1775, accompanied by a British military officer from Montreal. He was introduced to many notable people, and made a fine

CRUEL WARFARE

impression. Everywhere he went the stalwart war chief, with the pleasing manners and eloquent voice, was received with enthusiasm. The visit intensified his loyalty. On his return to America he prepared his warriors for the fight against the revolting colonists.

In the years that followed, events occurred that form some of the darkest blots on the pages of American history. A terrible guerrilla warfare was waged in New York and Pennsylvania between Loyalist soldiers and the Indians on the one hand, and the revolutionists on the other. It was a bitter struggle, and there were acts of great barbarity on both sides. The cruel sufferings of some of the Loyalists at the hands of the rebels, for which there was no possible justification, have been described in the story of Sir Guy Carleton. On the other hand, it is impossible to justify the attacks upon unprotected settlements by bodies of British soldiers and their Indian allies. The marauders would descend suddenly upon a quiet village, burn the houses, and take the inhabitants prisoners or put them to death if they offered resistance. Sometimes the Indians, in spite of all restraint, massacred the prisoners. It must, however, be said in Brant's favour that he was not personally responsible for these acts of barbarism. Though he was the chief of the Indians, he was at times unable to restrain their ferocity, try as he might. Brant has been unjustly blamed by some

Public Archives of Canada
JOSEPH BRANT

writers for acts that he did not commit. The English poet Thomas Campbell, for instance, in his poem *Gertrude of Wyoming*, brands the chief as a monster of cruelty. Certain barbarous acts, in which the Indians had a part, were committed in an attack upon an American settlement in the valley of Wyoming, near the Susquehanna River. It has been proved beyond any question that Brant was not even present when the attack was made, and in no way deserved the blame that the poet placed upon him.

To these cruel attacks the Americans replied in kind. They descended in large force upon the Mohawks, consigned their villages to the flames, and put many of the inhabitants to the sword. The whole territory was laid waste, and most of the Indians who escaped went to Fort Niagara, where during the winter they suffered terribly.

By the treaty of peace that closed the Revolutionary War, only Canada, Newfoundland, and the Maritime provinces remained to Britain in America. The whole of the territory of the Six Nations passed to the United States. Joseph Brant, intensely loyal in his allegiance to Britain, declined to return to the lands of his tribe. "We will sink or swim with the British," said he. After some negotiation with the British government, he obtained a grant of land six miles wide on each side of the Grand River from its source to its mouth. This goodly area formed a part of the finest land in what is now the Province of Ontario. The title-deeds to this great heritage were given by royal authority in 1784, in recognition of the valuable services rendered by the Mohawks to the Empire in her time of need.

There was some difficulty over this land at a later time. With the large influx of United Empire Loyalists into Upper Canada, the withholding of such a large area from settlement formed a serious problem. Brant wished to sell the land, claiming that it was an absolute gift to the Indians, and that therefore they could do with it as they wished. The province claimed that the land belonged to the Indians only so long as they remained upon it. In the end the matter was settled by the government's undertaking to sell the

AN AMUSING INCIDENT

land and to invest the proceeds for the benefit of the Indians. The descendants of the Mohawks of Brant's day still live on reservations along the Grand River.

In 1785 Brant paid a second visit to England, and was again enthusiastically welcomed as the great ally of Britain during the war just closed. He was received by the king and queen and entertained by many of the nobility. An amusing episode occurred at a masquerade ball given in London. Brant appeared in the full dress of a Mohawk war chief with paint and feathers. One of the guests, believing that the war chief was one of his friends in masquerade costume, approached him and playfully pulled his nose. He was amazed to find that he had grasped a nose of flesh and blood and not part of a mask. Immediately Joseph Brant uttered a tremendous war-whoop and brandished aloft his tomahawk. He seized the astonished offender and seemed about to kill him on the spot. The other guests shrieked in terror and rushed pell-mell from the ballroom. They were induced to return only when Brant laughingly explained that he was merely having a joke at the expense of his playful friend.

Brant was ambitious to become the head of all the Indian tribes and to unite them against the encroachments of the Americans. He wished the Indians to have all that fine territory west of the Alleghanies, north of the Ohio River to the Great Lakes for their hunting and fishing grounds. When the American settlers pressed northward across the Ohio, the Indians resisted for many years. Brant was invited to Philadelphia to meet the president and to discuss with American statesmen the best means of inducing the Indians to give way to the white settlers. He was offered a large tract of land worth a hundred thousand dollars and a pension of fifteen hundred dollars a year if he would only use his influence to keep the Indians quiet. Such an offer must have been a great temptation to Brant, but believing that acceptance would make him disloyal to his race, he spurned the bribe with disdain. In the end, however, the Indians were defeated, and in a treaty of peace with the Americans they surrendered the territory north of the Ohio. Brant then realized the impossibility of an Indian confederacy to check the oncoming whites.

For the rest of his life he gave most of his attention to the establishment of a happy and prosperous nation on the banks of the Grand. Believing that the religious welfare of his people was of the first importance, he built a church about two miles from what is now the centre of the city of Brantford. For more than a century this church was called the Old Mohawk Church, but a few years ago it was given the name of His Majesty's Chapel of the Mohawks. The Bible first used there had been presented to the tribe by Queen Anne, and had been brought from the Mohawk country to the Grand. The British government presented a bell to this church after its erection, and this was the first bell to send forth its call to prayer in Upper Canada. Joseph Brant himself translated the Gospel of St. Mark and part of the Anglican Prayer Book into the Mohawk tongue, and these were used in the church services.

Brant died in 1807. To the very last his thoughts were concerned with the welfare of his people, for with his dying breath he whispered: "Have pity on the poor Indians. Do them all the good you can."

Joseph Brant played an important part in Canadian history. In holding the Six Nations loyal to the British Crown during the Revolutionary War, he did much to save Canada for Britain. Had the Six Nations fought for rather than against the Americans, had they taken the warpath northward instead of southward, it is probable that nothing could have prevented the Americans from taking Canada. Thus it is perhaps due as much to Joseph Brant as to anyone else that the Union Jack still floats over the northern half of this continent.

XXI

CAPTAIN JAMES COOK

THE EXPLORER OF THE PACIFIC

It is a matter of no small interest to Canadians that the most distinguished British navigator of all time should have been associated with important events in the history of Canada. Captain James Cook has to his credit many remarkable feats of seamanship, and at least two of them closely concerned Canada. He gave valuable assistance to Wolfe in the taking of Quebec, and he made a useful contribution to the knowledge of his time regarding the so-called "North-West Passage."

He was born in Yorkshire, England, in 1728. His father was a poor farm-labourer. The boy went to the village school for four years and picked up the elements of an education. It is a tribute to his cleverness and his industry that, with this slight equipment, he was able in later years to acquire the science of navigation and to make himself a master mariner. At the age of twelve he was apprenticed to a shopkeeper, but the work was so hard and dull, and his treatment was so harsh, that he decided to go to sea. He was employed on a small sailing-vessel carrying coal from Newcastle to the Baltic Sea.

For thirteen years he remained at this trade, employing his leisure time in studying and in adding to his knowledge of seamanship. Then came his first great opportunity. War broke out between the English and French in America, and men were needed for the British navy. Cook was appointed to an important post on a warship.

In 1759 he was at Quebec with Wolfe. The British general wanted a dependable man to make soundings of the St.

CAPTAIN JAMES COOK

Lawrence between the Island of Orleans and the northern shore of the river. He wished to use the fleet in his attempt to take the fortress, but it would not be safe to do so unless his seamen knew the spots dangerous to navigation. To James Cook fell the task of sounding the river and making charts. Most of this work he did at night under cover of darkness. On one occasion while thus engaged he narrowly escaped capture by some Indians. They pursued him in their canoes, and had just caught up with him when he touched shore and escaped over the bow of his boat. When at length the work was finished he presented a complete chart of the soundings of the river in the neighbourhood of Quebec. The French were amazed that the British fleet was able to navigate the dangerous northern channel so successfully. They believed that one of their own pilots had given the enemy the necessary information. Later Captain Cook made a survey of the St. Lawrence below Quebec and of the coast of Newfoundland. He prepared charts which are still used by navigators.

Public Archives of Canada
CAPTAIN COOK

In 1768 Captain Cook, who was by this time recognized as the foremost mariner of England, was given charge of an expedition to Tahiti, in the Southern Pacific, to make certain astronomical observations. Having completed this task, he went on a voyage of exploration in these little known seas.

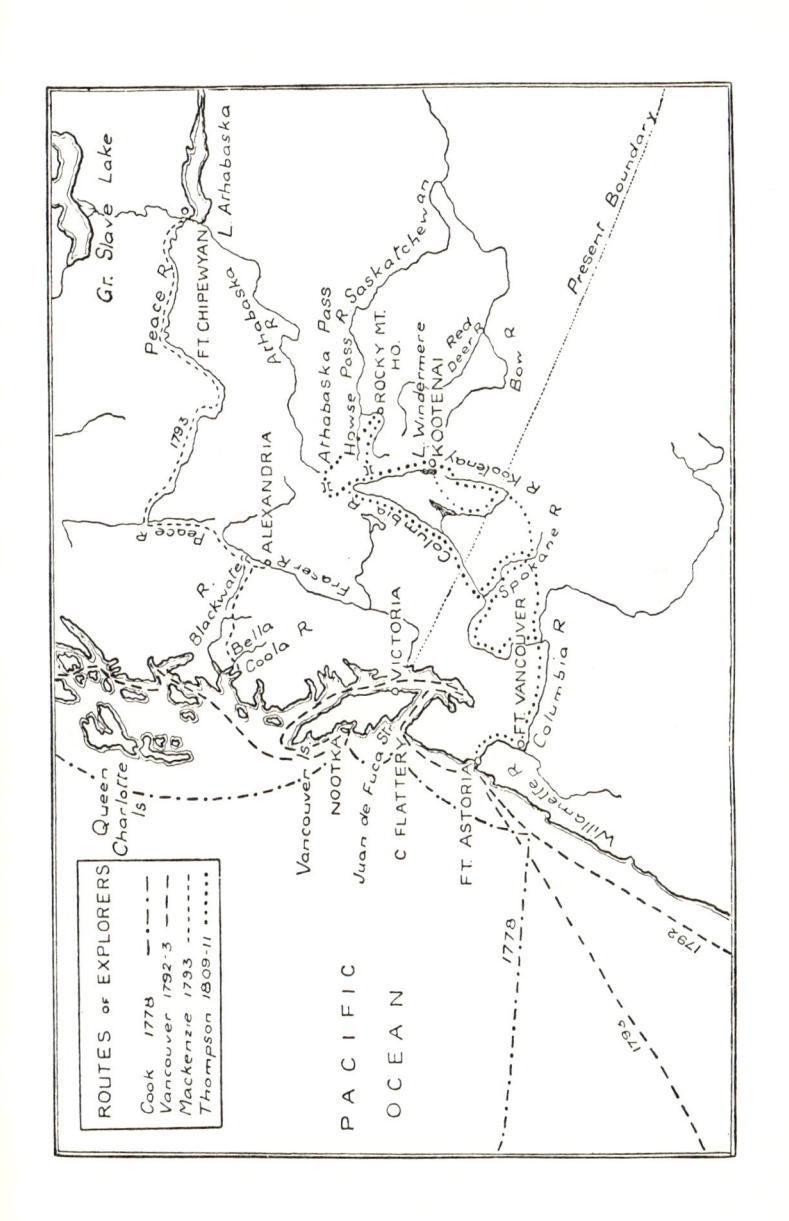

He reached New Zealand, which had been discovered by Tasman many years before, but which was believed to be a part of a great southern continent. He spent six months in circumnavigating and exploring the islands. In particular he explored the strait which separates the North from the South island, and which now bears his name. The natives were hostile, and on this account Cook was unable to explore the interior.

Leaving New Zealand, he sailed westward to Australia. He surveyed the east coast, and called it New South Wales, because he thought it resembled the Welsh coast at home. He took possession of the country for England. The natives were again hostile, and no serious attempt to explore the interior was made. He later wrote an interesting account of the people, animals, and products of the coast.

Captain Cook headed a second exploring expedition to the southern seas in 1772. The purpose of this was to get authentic information about a southern continent that was supposed to exist there. He sailed by way of the Cape of Good Hope and then south-eastward. He penetrated about four degrees beyond the Antarctic Circle, the farthest south that any navigator had ever gone up to that time. The great masses of floating ice in that region convinced him that there was no southern continent, or that if one did exist, it must be perpetually covered with ice and snow and must be of no use for human habitation. He touched at many islands in the Southern Pacific—the Friendly Islands, the New Hebrides, New Caledonia, and others. He came home around the southern end of South America, having completely circumnavigated the southern hemisphere of the earth. On this voyage, which took three years, he had sailed over 50,000 miles, more than twice the distance around the earth. He lost only one man out of more than a hundred in the crews. He managed to give the men the proper kind of food to ward off scurvy.

From the standpoint of Canada, the most important voyage made by Captain Cook was his third and last, begun in 1776. The British government had offered a reward of £20,000 to anyone who would discover the North-West Passage, in

A MISSION UNFULFILLED

quest of which so many sailors had striven in vain. All previous efforts had been made from the Atlantic westward. It was now proposed to reverse the route, and to attempt it from the Pacific eastward. For this purpose Captain Cook was given charge of two vessels, the *Resolution* and the *Discovery*. He sailed around the Cape of Good Hope, touched Tasmania, New Zealand, the Society Islands, and the Sandwich Islands, and sighted the American coast north of California. He saw Cape Flattery, but missed Juan de Fuca Strait. He landed at Nootka Sound on the west coast of Vancouver Island, which, of course, he thought part of the mainland.

Nootka was a pleasant spot, and the sailors were glad to land after many months at sea. The Indians were friendly, and swarmed about the ships in brightly painted canoes. They exchanged beaver and otter skins for nails, knives, and kettles. The sailors prolonged their stay for a month, and then suddenly the kindly attitude of the Indians changed to unfriendliness. Captain Cook deemed it wise not to delay his departure longer.

The expedition continued its northerly course along the coast, threading bays and inlets in the constant hope of finding an easterly passage. At one point the Indians had swords, guns, and powder, and the hopes of the sailors rose. They believed that the natives must have secured these things from the Hudson's Bay Company, and that therefore the Company's posts could not be far away. If that were true, the long-sought passage to the Atlantic might be close at hand. The sailors forgot that the Indians had been for years in contact with Russian traders from the West, a fact that accounted for their possession of these unexpected weapons. Week after week the northward voyage continued. Captain Cook's hopes began to fade when he found that the coast constantly bore away to the westward. However, he directed his course through Behring Sea, past Cape Prince of Wales, the most westerly point of America, into the Arctic Ocean. For some distance along the northern shore of Alaska he proceeded, until he came upon a great wall of ice twelve feet high which barred further progress.

The tremendous masses of ice convinced him that there was no feasible passage through the Arctic. Icy Cape, north of Alaska, marks the most easterly point reached by Captain Cook.

The homeward voyage took him to the Sandwich Islands, about which he was anxious to get more information. The natives regarded the sailors as supernatural beings and paid them great honour. Unfortunately, in securing timber to repair the ships, the sailors desecrated the graves of the dead. The natives resented this and showed great displeasure. However, they permitted the ships to sail without disturbance. But a gale arose and broke off the mast of the *Resolution*. The ship had to be put back to the islands for repair. The natives were sullen and refused to assist. Then they stole a rowboat from the *Discovery*. Captain Cook landed to recover it. An altercation arose. A native struck him with a stone. The sailors, fearing that their leader's life was in danger, fired a volley among the islanders. Several were killed and wounded. In the confusion that followed, Captain Cook was stabbed to death by a native with a dagger. His men recovered his body with difficulty. They consigned it to the ocean in a sailor's funeral. Under such unfortunate circumstances ended the career of the foremost navigator of his time.

Captain Cook performed several valuable services in the interest of science and geography. He explored the western coast of North America for over three thousand miles. He secured a great deal of definite information regarding the islands of the Pacific. He brought the mystery of the North-West Passage one stage nearer final solution. His greatest service to the Empire consisted, however, in planting the British flag upon what have proved to be two of the most valuable of the Empire's overseas dominions, Australia and New Zealand.

XXII

SAMUEL HEARNE

THE TRAVELLER OF THE BARREN LANDS

On a map of Canada find Fort Churchill, on the west side of Hudson Bay. Trace a straight line from Fort Churchill to the mouth of the Mackenzie River. This line roughly marks the boundary between the great Canadian forest to the south and the barren lands to the north. In the barren lands there is little but a waste of rocks broken by many wide lakes and rapid rivers. A few spruce-trees and stunted shrubs grow among the rocks, and patches of grass and moss here and there afford food for the herds of caribou that wander over the region during the summer. It is the most desolate region in all Canada, and has been seldom crossed by white men. Locate the Coppermine River, flowing into the Arctic east of Great Bear Lake, and calculate the distance from the mouth of this river to Fort Churchill. You will find it to be nearly a thousand miles.

A knowledge of these facts of geography is necessary to an understanding of the explorations of Samuel Hearne, a clerk of the Hudson's Bay Company at Fort Churchill. The Indians brought to this trading-post stories of a wonderful river of the north, on the banks of which there were great mountains of pure copper. In proof of their tales they showed weapons and tools roughly fashioned out of copper which had been obtained, they said, at this northern river. This stream of fabulous wealth, according to the Indians, was called by the English the Coppermine River, and it became the object of much curiosity and speculation. Moses Norton, the governor of the post at Churchill, secured the consent of the Company to send an expedition to find out the truth of the stories. He selected for the purpose Samuel Hearne, a young man of twenty-four, who had already gained considerable knowledge of the west coast of the Bay, and was skilled in the use of the scientific instruments of that day.

In November, 1769, Hearne set out north-westward with two white companions and several Indian guides. The latter were secretly determined that the white men should not reach their goal, so they purposely led Hearne through the barren lands. There was no shelter from the Arctic winds which swept over the region. The guides provided little game, and food was therefore scarce. They daily poured into the ears of the Englishmen horrible tales of the hunger and cold to be endured if they persisted in their plan. Hearne, however, pressed doggedly on until the Indians deserted him. Without guides it would have been folly to go farther. Hearne therefore turned back, after having gone two hundred miles. He reached the post in safety after an absence of five weeks.

Public Archives of Canada
SAMUEL HEARNE

In February of the next year Hearne set out on his second attempt to reach the Coppermine, taking with him as companions only six Indians. The hardships that they suffered on this journey were terrible. They had only one small tent to shelter them from the bitter cold of the northern winter. When the snow melted, they had to discard their sledges and carry their provisions and equipment on their backs. Their food had to be eaten raw, for they had no means of making a fire. As winter passed into spring, food became scarcer. For four days they were entirely without any. For seven days at another time they had only a few berries, some leather, and burnt bones to eat.

At length they met a large party of Indian hunters, and Hearne's guides wished to join the chase. It was useless to protest. Hearne was compelled to go along. Soon the party came upon some herds of caribou. These the hunters recklessly slaughtered, and, with the improvidence characteristic of the Indian, ate only the tender parts, throwing away the rest. Hearne wasted much time going from place to place with the Indians in their hunt, without getting any nearer to the object of his quest.

One day his quadrant, the instrument by which he determined the latitude of his location, was blown over by the wind and broken. This was perhaps a fortunate accident, for it compelled Hearne to turn homeward. Had he gone forward with his poor equipment and his treacherous guides, he would probably have been lost for ever.

On his way back he fell in with another party of Indians, who coolly plundered him of nearly all he had. He would doubtless have perished had he not, by a fortunate chance, met an Indian chief who was a friend of the English. The chief provided him with warm clothing and food, and accompanied him back to Fort Churchill, which he reached late in November, 1770. Hearne's journey on this occasion had occupied nine months.

Within two weeks of his return Hearne, accompanied by the friendly chief, started on his third attempt to reach Coppermine. This time he proceeded westward through the wooded territory towards Lake Athabaska. Again he suffered greatly from cold and hunger. He spent a foodless Christmas, and wrote in his journal that he would gladly have eaten, if he could have had the chance, the refuse from his friends' tables in England on that festive day.

Late in December he was joined by a large party of the tribesmen of his guide. Soon game became plentiful, and several days were passed by the Indians in feasting. Then, proceeding northward, they met another wandering tribe, the Copper Indians, who were on the warpath against the Eskimos. These Indians had never before seen a white man,

ROUTES OF HEARNE
MACKENZIE & FRANKLIN

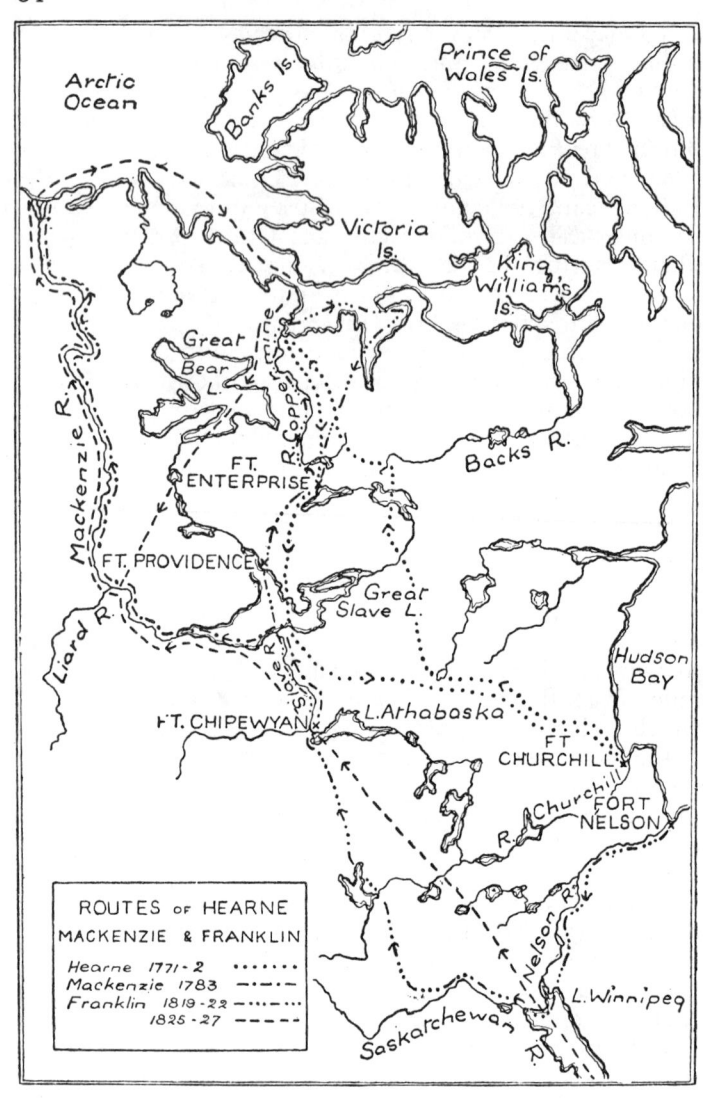

Hearne 1771-2 ....
Mackenzie 1783 –·–·–
Franklin 1819-22 ––··––··
        1825-27 – – – –

A DISAPPOINTING DISCOVERY 135

and spoke in derisive terms of Hearne's colour. "His skin is like birch bark and his hair is like a buffalo's tail," they said.

On July 13th Hearne reached the Coppermine River. But before he could make any exploration of it, he was compelled to witness an inhuman act of warfare. The Indians learned that a party of Eskimos were encamped a few miles down the river. They moved forward rapidly and silently during the night, though not in darkness. In this latitude at this season of the year the sun shines brightly on the horizon at midnight. The Indians fell upon the sleeping Eskimos, massacred every man, woman, and child, and plundered the camp. Hearne protested in vain against the inhumanity of the act; he was merely ridiculed by the Indians for what they considered his weakness. They regarded what they had done as an act of justifiable warfare.

Having completed their warlike task, the Indians accompanied Hearne to the mouth of the Coppermine at the Arctic Ocean. He erected a great heap of stones to signify that he had taken possession of the region for the Hudson's Bay Company. On the way back the Indians led Hearne to what they called the copper mountains, about thirty miles from the mouth of the river. In the rocks, among which a tumultuous river ran, Hearne found some traces of the metal. But certainly there was no mountain of copper such as the Indians claimed existed there. Hearne picked up a piece of the metal, about four pounds in weight, and carried it back with him to the fort. This memento of Hearne's expedition a century and a half ago is still in the possession of the Hudson's Bay Company. Once more a white man had learned to his sorrow that the Indian tales of the wonders of unknown lands must be heavily discounted.

Hearne's journey of more than a thousand miles back to Fort Churchill was made under great difficulties. On the way he discovered Great Slave Lake, which he crossed on the ice in mid-winter. He reached the post in June, 1772, having been absent about a year and a half. Though his journeys, undertaken and carried through at great hazard, had little practical result, they proved at least one thing—that there is no north-west passage to the Pacific through Hudson Bay. Hearne was rewarded for his service to the Company by being made governor of Fort Churchill.

XXIII

SIR ALEXANDER MACKENZIE

THE CONQUEROR OF THE ROCKIES

Two important achievements in the exploration of Canada stand to the credit of Alexander Mackenzie. He was the discoverer of that great river which bears his name, and which, through numberless tributaries, carries the melted snows of the Rockies and of the great northern plains in a mighty flood to the Arctic. He was also the first to reach the Pacific by an overland route over the rugged mountain ranges of the West, thus solving the great problem which had been the despair of Cartier, Champlain, La Salle, and La Vérendrye. Mackenzie's two great exploits make a stirring tale of endurance, daring, and perseverance, in the face of difficulties which have had few parallels in the history of Canada.

Alexander Mackenzie was a Scotsman, who had come to Canada as a young man to engage in the fur-trade. In a few years he had become a partner in the North-West Company, a newly established rival of the Hudson's Bay Company for the fur-trade. He saw the commanding position of Lake Athabaska, situated at the end of a chain of lakes from the east and at the junction of the two great rivers from the west and south, the Peace and the Athabaska. Under his direction a trading-post of the North-West Company was established on the lake and named Chipewyan. Then Mackenzie turned his attention to the possibilities of the country to the north. He knew that somewhere there must be a river carrying a mighty volume of water northward to the Arctic. He determined to search for this great waterway, believing that if it were discovered it would be useful in the development of the fur-trade in the Far North.

Accordingly, at the beginning of June, 1789, accompanied by several French Canadians and a few Indian guides, Mackenzie set out with canoes northward down the Slave River. In about a week the party reached Great Slave Lake, which was still covered with ice even at that season of the year. Drawing their canoes and supplies on sledges or carrying them on their backs, they searched for three weeks, in weather growing gradually warmer, before they found the outlet of the lake. On July 1st they discovered the great northern river, issuing from the extreme western end of the lake. They at once embarked upon its turbulent waters.

Five days later the party reached the point where the waters of Great Bear Lake are poured in a blue flood into the Mackenzie. Near here they met a number of Indians, who did their best to frighten the explorers into giving up their enterprise. The savages told terrifying tales of tremendous waterfalls and horrible monsters to be met on the lower stretches of the river. Mackenzie was not to be daunted, however. He seized one of the Indians as a guide and continued the journey. This guide deserted, but another was secured, also by force.

Soon the boatmen began to murmur against going forward. The long days and short nights of summer in this high latitude, the desolate and uninhabited shores, the numberless

Public Archives of Canada
SIR ALEXANDER MACKENZIE

TRACING A GREAT RIVER 139

swirling rapids, the long and difficult portages, all combined to fill them with unrest and fear. Mackenzie bargained with the men for seven days more, and agreed that, if the mouth of the river were not reached within that time, he would allow them to turn back. One is reminded of the difficulties of Columbus with his sailors under somewhat similar circumstances three centuries earlier.

Before the end of the stipulated time Mackenzie had reached his goal. On July 12th, from an elevation on an island on which he had landed, he could see the Arctic. He had arrived at a delta in the river where it emptied into the ocean. There could be no doubt that it was the ocean, for whales could be seen sporting in the water some distance away. Some of the men had the hardihood to set out in their frail canoes in pursuit of the whales. Fortunately a fog descended and put a stop to this dangerous sport. Because of this incident the delta was named Whale Island.

Mackenzie spent three days at the mouth of the river making observations. He set up a wooden post bearing his own name, the number of persons in the party, the date, and the latitude. On July 15th he started on the homeward journey, which was much more difficult because it was against the current. Fortunately food was plentiful. The men were able to add to their supplies by gathering berries and shooting game along the shores. Mackenzie noted evidences of the presence of coal and petroleum in the territory through which they passed. At one point he found a great seam of coal burning in the bank of the river. It had evidently been started from the camp-fire of some Indian hunting-party. At times the men had to haul the canoes over long rapids, at other times they were able to hoist sail and to speed along for miles over smooth waters.

At length, on September 12th, after an absence of 102 days, Mackenzie reached Fort Chipewyan. He had penetrated almost fifteen hundred miles northward. He was the first white man to traverse a part of Canada in which there are to-day many trading-posts of the Hudson's Bay Company and many mission stations for the education of the Indians.

He was also the first to point out the possibilities of this region in the production of coal and petroleum.

Mackenzie's overland journey to the Pacific was attended with even more trials and dangers than his journey to the Arctic. In the autumn of 1792, accompanied by a fellow-Scotsman and a few French Canadians and Indian guides, he left Chipewyan and ascended the Peace River to a point about four hundred miles from its mouth. Here the party erected a fort and spent the winter making preparations for continuing the journey early the following spring. They built a large birch-bark canoe, twenty-five feet in length, very light and strong. In this, early in May, 1793, they proceeded up the river.

There are few streams more tumultuous than the Peace in its course through the passes of the Rockies. Its foaming cataracts, precipitous banks, and dangerous rocks make it wellnigh impossible to navigate. Mackenzie and his men toiled for weeks up this difficult river, now paddling where the current permitted, now pulling the heavily laden canoe over rapids with tow-lines, now carrying it on their backs up the steep banks and through unbroken forest. So difficult was the route that some days they were unable to advance more than three miles. They entered the Parsnip River, the southern branch of the Peace, and followed it to its source. Thence they made a short portage across the height of land to a little stream, now called the Bad River, a tributary of the Fraser.

They were now going with the current, but the journey was even more difficult than before, for dangerous rocks could not so easily be seen and avoided. Soon the canoe was hurled against a boulder and overturned. The men clung to the sides of the boat, and, by a fortunate chance, were swept ashore in safety. The canoe was broken, the supplies were drenched, and half the powder and all of the bullets were lost. Mackenzie and his men patched up the canoe and continued their course. They entered the swift-flowing Fraser and swept down its turbulent course for many miles.

At one point hostile Indians sent showers of stones and arrows from the high banks upon the explorers. Mackenzie

OVERLAND TO THE PACIFIC

landed on the opposite shore, and, laying some trinkets upon the ground, made friendly gestures towards the savages. They cautiously approached, and when they were convinced that he intended friendship, they consented to accept the peace-offerings. By means of signs Mackenzie learned that the shortest way to the ocean was to retrace his route for a considerable distance and to ascend a tributary of the Fraser towards the west.

Acting upon this information, Mackenzie went back for fifty miles up the Fraser. He found a western tributary, now called the Blackwater, which he ascended to its source. Here the canoe was abandoned, and the men, each carrying a load of ninety pounds on his back, made a long portage over another height of land to the Bella Coola River. By this time the whole party were barefooted and their clothing was reduced to shreds and tatters. They secured some dug-outs from Indians and paddled down the river into Burke Channel, an arm of the Pacific. The long and perilous journey, more than twelve hundred miles in length, was over. On a rock facing an inlet of the great western ocean, Mackenzie painted in large red letters this inscription: "Alexander Mackenzie, from Canada by land, 22nd July, 1793. Latitude 52° 20′ 48″ N."

As the Indians were unfriendly, Mackenzie found it advisable to leave the coast two days after his arrival. The return journey was safely made in exactly a month. A few years later Mackenzie retired to Scotland and wrote a detailed account of his two memorable journeys. He was knighted by the king in recognition of his distinguished services in the exploration of Canada.

XXIV

CAPTAIN GEORGE VANCOUVER

THE GEOGRAPHER OF THE PACIFIC COAST

A LARGE, rich, and fertile island situated off the western coast of Canada, and a great city with a magnificent harbour on the mainland opposite the island, bear the name of Vancouver. They owe this name to the famous English navigator of the latter half of the eighteenth century, Captain George Vancouver.

Vancouver became a sailor at the age of thirteen, and he crowded into his short life of forty years a great deal of adventure and romance and some important achievements. He was a companion of Captain Cook in his famous second and third voyages, and shared with him all the thrilling experiences of those memorable expeditions.

It will be remembered that during his third voyage Captain Cook had landed at Nootka Sound, on the west coast of Vancouver Island. Later, a pioneer trader, Captain James Meares, had established a trade in furs with the Indians at that point. The Spaniards, who occupied most of the western coast of America at this time, maintained their right to this territory by virtue of prior discovery, claiming that they had landed there three years before Captain Cook's arrival. So it came about that Spanish officers seized three ships belonging to Captain Meares which they found at Nootka. Meares appealed to the British government for redress, and war between England and Spain over the incident was narrowly averted. However, after some negotiation, Spain agreed to surrender the disputed territory. Captain George Vancouver was sent by the British government to take over the surrendered territory for Britain. He was instructed also to

CHARTING THE WEST COAST 143

survey the western coast of America from California to Cook's Inlet to discover, if possible, some passage from the Pacific to the Great Lakes.

The expedition set sail in 1791 in two vessels, the *Discovery* and the *Chatham*. It followed the route taken by Captain Cook fifteen years before, sailing by way of the Cape of Good Hope, touching New Zealand, Australia, and the Sandwich Islands, and reaching the American coast at California in 1792.

Vancouver carefully surveyed the coast northward. By an unlucky chance he missed the mouth of the Columbia River. Two weeks later an American, Captain Robert Gray, entered the Columbia and laid the foundation of the claim of the United States to the territory about this point. Had Vancouver not missed the discovery of this great river at this time, it is possible that the territory now included in the States of Oregon and Washington might have been a part of Canada.

Public Archives of Canada
CAPTAIN GEORGE VANCOUVER

Vancouver entered the Strait of Juan de Fuca, which Cook missed, and explored the Gulf of Georgia. A fog hid the mouth of the Fraser River, and he passed it by as he had passed the Columbia. He sailed around the island, thus proving that it was not part of the mainland, as Cook had supposed. Thus quite rightly the island bears Vancouver's name. He reached Nootka, and arranged for the surrender of the territory by the Spaniards.

Vancouver has left an interesting account of the Indians of the island. He described them as lighter in colour than the Indians of other parts of America. They stained their bodies and their faces with red, black, or white paint mixed with oil, over which they sprinkled pieces of mica to make it glitter. They were fond of wearing wooden masks carved in the most fantastic forms to represent birds, animals, and sea monsters. They were great thieves, and stole from the boats everything they could carry away. Vancouver suspected that they were cannibals too, for they brought human skulls which they offered in trade.

In 1794 Vancouver carried out a careful survey of the west coast of the mainland as far north as Cook Inlet. He explored Portland Channel, Lynn Canal, Prince William Sound, and Cook Inlet. Captain Cook had suspected that the latter might be a river communicating with the interior, but Vancouver proved that it was merely a deep bay. Vancouver carefully charted the coast as he went along, and was thus the first to supply accurate information of the western side of North America.

Vancouver took possession of the Columbia River and the territory through which it ran. He ignored the fact that Gray had previously planted the American flag there. This was the basis of the rival claims of the British and Americans to this large and valuable territory. The dispute continued for many years, and was not settled till the Oregon Treaty was negotiated in 1846.

On a second visit that he paid to the Sandwich Islands during this voyage, Vancouver received the submission of the natives to Britain. For some reason this addition to the Empire was never ratified, and these islands were never brought under the British flag.

Vancouver returned to England in 1794 by way of Cape Horn, thus circumnavigating the globe during the course of his memorable voyage. He set to work upon the story of his explorations, but died before he had completed it.

Vancouver shares with Captain Cook the honour of making the most important discoveries along the western coast of North America.

XXV

DAVID THOMPSON

THE SURVEYOR OF THE GREAT WEST

A WELSH lad, brought up in a charity school in old London, came to Hudson Bay near the close of the eighteenth century, and spent nearly thirty years in exploring and charting what is now the Canadian and American West. He underwent hardships such as seldom fall to the lot of man, and overcame difficulties almost insuperable in penetrating regions never before trodden by the feet of white men. He made voluminous notes of his journeys, which contain geographical information of the most valuable kind. He made maps and charts which were the basis of all subsequent maps of the West, and some of which remain unchanged to this day. This man died at the age of eighty-seven, blind, friendless, and in dire poverty. He lay in a forgotten grave for seventy years. Only recently has his name been rescued from oblivion and his valuable services to Canada given belated recognition. This man was David Thompson, fur-trader, explorer, land-surveyor, and geographer.

At the Grey Coat School in London, to which the lad was sent at the age of seven on the death of his father, he was trained in mathematics and navigation. When he was fourteen years of age a request came to the school authorities from the Hudson's Bay Company for boys to enter its service as apprentices. Only two boys were available, of whom David was one. In terror of the hardships of life in the far north, the other boy ran away from school and was never heard of again. Young Thompson, however, was delighted at the prospect of a life of adventure, and gladly embarked on the voyage to the Bay.

After spending two unprofitable years at Fort Churchill, Thompson was transferred to York Factory, the headquarters of the Company, 150 miles down the coast at the mouth of the Hayes River. He was sent with a company of traders to open up new posts in the Saskatchewan valley, so that the Company might compete more successfully with its rival, the North-West Company, for the trade with the Indians. He was fortunate in spending a winter at Cumberland House, a post on the lower Saskatchewan, in company with Philip Turnor, a competent surveyor and astronomer. Sitting at the feet of this man during the long winter evenings, he acquired an interest in land-surveying which determined his future career. Then and there he resolved that he would not always be a mere fur-trader; he would be a surveyor and geographer; he would survey and chart the Great West for posterity.

For eleven years Thompson was engaged in opening up new fields of trade and in cultivating friendly relations with the Indians. Everywhere he went he carried his sextant, telescope, compass, and charts. The Indians looked upon him as a sort of supernatural being, and gave him the name "The man who looks at the stars." His most notable achievement during that period was the exploration and charting of a new route to Lake Athabaska by way of the Churchill River.

One incident during this expedition is illustrative of the hardship and danger that Thompson had to undergo not once but many times. With two Indian guides, he had reached his destination over a route never before followed by a white man. He was returning up the tumultuous Black River which connects Lake Athabaska with Lake Wollaston. The guides were towing the canoe up a roaring rapid. Thompson was in the canoe steering with a paddle. The guides got the tow-rope entangled with a tree on the bank. The canoe swung out into the middle of the stream, and Thompson saw that the only possibility of safety was to cut the tow-line and head the canoe downstream. He slashed the rope with his knife, and the canoe shot down the cataract. It struck a protruding boulder and overturned.

UNDER A NEW MASTER 147

Thompson was dashed against the jagged rocks, but, almost by miracle, he reached the bank, bruised and bleeding, his foot gashed by the sharp rocks, and his clothing torn to shreds. Fortunately the canoe was recovered, together with the tent, axe, gun, and surveying instruments, but the food supply was lost. By tearing up the tent, Thompson clothed himself and bandaged his wounded foot, while the guides repaired the damaged canoe. They were three hundred miles from the fort, without food in a region destitute of game. They were so reduced by hunger that they actually ate the flesh of two young eagles, and this unusual food made them violently ill. When after many days Thompson staggered into the fort, he was a mere skeleton, almost unrecognizable by his friends.

For some years Thompson had felt that his efforts in exploration were not appreciated by the officials of the Hudson's Bay Company. In 1797, after thirteen years of faithful service, he determined to leave what he regarded as an ungrateful organization, and to join the ranks of the newer North-West Company, where he might have wider scope for his talents. Accordingly, he made his way to Grand Portage, the headquarters of the North-Westers on Lake Superior. He was cordially received by the officials there, and given the important post of astronomer and surveyor.

During the year that followed, Thompson completed the most extensive, most rapid, and most brilliant piece of survey work of his career. He covered that vast territory from Winnipeg River and Lake Winnipegosis on the north, the source of the Assiniboine on the west, the upper waters of the Missouri on the south, and Sault Ste. Marie on the east. The work was carried out in the face of the most difficult conditions—hostile Indians on every hand, temperatures as low as 40° below zero during the winter, breaking ice, melting snow, and floods during the spring. When the survey was finished and the charts and notes were presented to the officials of the Company, Thompson was complimented upon having completed in ten months a task that ordinarily would have required two years.

DAVID THOMPSON

An important feature of this survey was the discovery of the upper waters of the Mississippi. Among the many small lakes and ponds through which the river flows near its beginning, Thompson decided that Turtle Lake was best entitled to be considered its source. Several years later American surveyors determined that the neighbouring Lake Itaska was the real beginning. This, however, scarcely deprives Thompson of the distinction of being the virtual discoverer of the source of the mighty river of the south.

During the next eight years Thompson was engaged in the fur-trade in the Far West on the upper waters of the Saskatchewan, Athabaska, and Peace. But always he found time to survey and chart the country and to make extensive notes of the physical features, the wild life, the Indian tribes and their habits and customs. He had in view an overland journey to the Pacific across the Rocky Mountains, a feat that had been accomplished by Sir Alexander Mackenzie in 1793 by way of the Peace River. Unfortunately for Canada, the demands of the fur-trade kept Thompson too much occupied to permit him to undertake this task as early as he desired. In 1806 two Americans, Lewis and Clark, made an overland journey to the Pacific, during which they descended the lower waters of the Columbia. It was disappointing to Thompson that the Americans had anticipated him in his project. However, he determined to find this great river of the West—the Columbia—and to trace it throughout its whole course. The chief obstacle to his purpose was the hostile attitude of the Piegan Indians, the horsemen of the far western plains, who were determined to prevent traders from crossing the mountains.

In 1807 Thompson was stationed at Rocky Mountain House, on the upper waters of the Saskatchewan. The Piegans had gone south on an errand of war, and the pass through which the Saskatchewan emerges was momentarily unguarded. Thompson made hasty preparations for a dash across the mountains. After incredible difficulties he got through the pass and found himself on the bank of a little river, now known as the Blaeberry. "May God in His mercy give me to see where its waters flow into the ocean!" he

A DIFFICULT TASK

exclaimed. Six days later he reached the Columbia, built canoes, and traced the river upwards to an expansion now known as Lake Windermere. Here he erected a building on the steep bank of the river, and fortified it strongly with stockades on the three exposed sides to make it proof against Indian attack.

As Thompson expected, the Piegans were soon on the scene, but they hesitated to attack so strong a fort. They hung about for several days, expecting him to surrender for lack of food and water. But he was well provided with food, and he secured a plentiful supply of water by lowering his kettles at night down the steep bank to the river below. He admitted two Indian scouts to the fort, showed them his six men and ten guns, and impressed them with the strength of his position. He sent the scouts away with a large quantity of tobacco for the warriors and a splendid pipe for the chief. As the Indians' store of tobacco was low at the time, the gifts were gratefully accepted, and after that tribal honour forbade further attack upon the fort. "Thus by the mercy of Providence I averted the danger," wrote Thompson in his diary. Later in the year he explored the Columbia to its source and also its tributary, the Kootenay; but strangely enough he made no attempt to follow the great river to its mouth.

In 1810 the North-West Company learned that John Jacob Astor, a New York merchant, had formed a fur-trading company and had fitted out two expeditions for the mouth of the Columbia. One was to go by ship around Cape Horn and the other overland, following the trail of Lewis and Clark. The North-Westers at Fort William determined to beat the Americans to the Pacific and plant a trading-post there before they could arrive.

The task was assigned to Thompson. He found the pass at the Saskatchewan guarded by the Piegans, making it impossible for him to get through the mountains at that point. Thereupon he decided to go northward and try the Athabaska Pass. After weeks of infinite hardship, battling against avalanche and glacier, enduring intense cold and short rations, he got across the Great Divide. By the end

L

of January, 1811, he had reached the Columbia once more.

Then he made a mistake which cost him much valuable time in his race to the Pacific. Instead of going northward down the river, rounding the bend, and sweeping southward towards the mouth, he chose to go back to the source and strike overland to the Spokane River, through which he eventually arrived at the Columbia again. On its bank he hoisted the British flag and claimed the territory for Great Britain and the North-West Company, thus ignoring the prior claim of the Americans through the discovery of Lewis and Clark five years before. In July, 1811, Thompson, with little further difficulty, reached the mouth of the Columbia, only to find that the sea-going party of Astorians had already arrived. He had lost the race by a scant two months! Realizing the futility of planting a post for his company in the face of such competition, he retraced his route up the Columbia. Though too late in reaching its mouth to be regarded as its discoverer, he had at least won the honour of being the first white man to traverse its upper waters.

Thompson's work as an explorer was now completed. He returned to the Company's headquarters at Fort William, made his report, and then proceeded to Montreal. He spent the next year finishing his great map of the West, embodying his life-work. This map hung for many years in the great hall of Fort William, and is now preserved in the Ontario Archives. He was later employed for several years in surveying and charting the international boundary between Canada and the United States after the war of 1812.

Thompson settled in the village of Williamstown in Glengarry County, expecting to pass the rest of his days in peace and in the enjoyment of the moderate wealth he had accumulated during his years of trade. But misfortune fell upon him. He lent money to a struggling church to erect a building. When the church was unable to repay the money, he promptly cancelled the debt. His sons failed in business and lost the money he provided. Soon the savings of a lifetime were gone. He retired to Longueuil, near Montreal. His eyesight failed, and he became utterly destitute. He pawned his beloved instruments, and even his clothing, for food. Near the end of his life he made this pathetic entry in his diary: "This day borrowed 2s. 6d. from a friend. Thank God for this relief." He died in 1857, and his grave lay forgotten and unmarked for many years. Thus came to a pitiable end the strenuous and fruitful life of "the greatest land geographer of all time."

Fortunately for the good name of Canada, David Thompson has been given his meed of fame, though at a late hour. Some years ago the Hudson's Bay Company set up in his honour a typical trading-post at Lake Windermere in British Columbia, near the site of his own Fort Kootenai. In 1926 a memorial was placed at his grave in Mount Royal Cemetery in Montreal by the Canadian Historical Association. Recent historical writers have endeavoured to cultivate in the Canadian people some appreciation of the great services that he rendered this country.

XXVI

COLONEL JOHN GRAVES SIMCOE

THE FOUNDER OF UPPER CANADA

JOHN GRAVES SIMCOE has been called the Father of Upper Canada, because he did more than anyone else in the early days of the province to fill it with sturdy settlers and to establish its government upon a firm foundation.

Simcoe was born in northern England, the son of an officer who fought with Wolfe at Quebec. Quite naturally he became a soldier, and was one of the British officers in America during the Revolutionary War. Later he was elected a member of the British parliament, and in 1791 was appointed the first governor of Upper Canada under the Constitutional Act.

The Upper Canada to which Simcoe came in 1792 was quite different from the Province of Ontario of to-day. Where there are now fertile, well-cultivated farms and busy towns and cities, there was then unbroken forest. Where there is now a network of roads and railways penetrating in all directions a well-settled country, there were then only a few Indian trails through the wilderness. Where there are now thousands of comfortable homes of a prosperous people, there were then only a few scattered log cabins of settlers struggling against untold difficulties to secure the bare necessities of life for their families. The wonderful changes that have come over the Province of Ontario in the last century and a half can best be appreciated by understanding something of the conditions under which the pioneers lived and worked.

The principal settlements of the United Empire Loyalists who came to Canada in 1784 were along the St. Lawrence,

LIFE OF THE PIONEERS 153

the Bay of Quinte, and the Niagara. The Loyalists came very poorly equipped to start life in the woods. In many cases they had little more than the clothing on their backs and a few household utensils, saved from the wreck of their former homes. The government came to their assistance during the first year and provided them with flour and pork, hoes and axes, and seed grain.

Each Loyalist set to work to clear his bush farm. Trees were chopped down, and a rude log hut was quickly set up

MIGRATION OF UNITED EMPIRE LOYALISTS

to shelter the family. The chinks between the logs were stopped with moss and clay. The roof was made of "troughs," or hollowed-out pieces of logs, overlapping each other in such a way as to keep out the rain. A chimney and a huge fireplace were constructed of stones. A few pieces of furniture were put together from sticks of timber, roughly hewn out of logs. There was no scarcity of fuel for the fireplace, and the Loyalist family were quite comfortable in their little cabin even in the coldest days of winter.

Around the cabin an open space was cleared by felling the trees and burning the logs. Among the stumps the ground was turned up with hoes and the seed was sown. Fortunately the land was fertile and yielded an abundant harvest. The ripened grain was cut with a sickle and threshed with a flail.

In the absence of mills to grind the wheat, the settlers invented a method of doing this for themselves. The wheat was placed on the top of a stump that had been hollowed out, and then it was crushed by pounding it with a heavy stone. The process was laborious, but it produced a flour out of which a wholesome bread was made. For other food the early settlers had considerable variety. The forests abounded with deer, wild fowl, berries, and nuts, and the lakes and rivers teemed with fish.

The Indians were usually friendly, and from them the pioneers learned much that was useful in the primitive conditions amid which they had to live. The Indians taught them how to tan deerskin and to make it into clothing, how to snare game in the forest, how to weave baskets from willow and basswood, and how to make sugar from the maple-tree. Every home was a manufacturing centre. The father fashioned the shoes of the family from animal hides, tanned by himself into leather. The mother spun the wool of the sheep into yarn and knitted the stockings, mittens, and scarfs. Someone in the neighbourhood would have a loom upon which would be woven the material for the clothing of the little community.

In a few years mills for the grinding of grain and the sawing of lumber began to be built at points where water-power was available. Often the settler would trudge long distances over forest trails with a sack of wheat on his back, and return with a sack of flour that was lighter only by the amount of the miller's toll. As roads were hewn out of the woods the ox-cart was used to convey the "grist" to the flour-mill, and the sleigh in winter to carry the logs to the saw-mill. The early roads were very bad. Streams were crossed by log bridges, and swampy places by corduroy roads, made by laying logs across the path and covering these lightly with earth. It is a far cry from the corduroy roads and the ox-cart of pioneer days to the paved roads and the automobile of the present.

SOCIAL ACTIVITIES

The religious and educational welfare of the early settlers at first received little attention. Soon, however, the itinerant preacher made his way from place to place, bringing to each little community at long intervals the services of the church. Soon, too, each settlement set up its little log school for the education of the children. The early teachers were often retired soldiers or immigrants from the United States, who had little fitness for the work of teaching. They had to eke out their slender salaries by "boarding around" with the families of their pupils, an arrangement that could not have been very satisfactory to either party.

The lives of the pioneers, though filled with hardship and discomfort, were not unhappy. They had their share of homely joys and simple pleasures. Social events often took the form of "bees," in which co-operative work and pleasure were combined. There were "logging bees," when the men with their ox-teams met at the farm of a neighbour to help him clear away and burn the logs and stumps from part of his land. There were "raisings," when the men chose sides, and, in friendly but earnest competition, quickly set up the timbers of a barn. There were "quilting bees," at which the women assisted a neighbour to add to her family store of bedding. A "bee" usually wound up with an evening of mirth and jollity, music and dancing, in which the whole community participated with whole-hearted pleasure.

It was to such a province and to such a people that John Graves Simcoe came as governor in 1792. His ideas of

Public Archives of Canada
COLONEL JOHN GRAVES SIMCOE

government were unsuited to a pioneer province like Upper Canada. He hoped to establish an aristocracy of military officers and landed proprietors, who would constitute the government. But he speedily learned that the people who elected the members of the assembly chose men like themselves for the office. This was a disappointment to Simcoe, but nevertheless he threw himself with energy into the duties of his position, and in the few years that he was governor he did much for the welfare of the province.

In 1792 the first parliament of Upper Canada met at Newark, a little town on the Niagara River which had been chosen as the capital. Parliament was opened by Simcoe with all the pomp and ceremony that attends the opening of the British parliament at Westminster. Cannon boomed from the fort, and the governor arrived accompanied by a military escort. He read a speech from the throne, modelled closely upon that delivered by the sovereign at the beginning of the parliamentary session at London. Seven members of the council and sixteen members of the assembly met at the first session, which lasted a month. Acts were passed establishing trial by jury and setting up British law as the law of the province. In the session of 1793 provision was made for the payment of bounties for the destruction of bears and wolves, and an Act was passed for the abolition of slavery in the province. It would seem that some of the Loyalists had adopted the practice of holding negroes as slaves, as was done at this time in the United States. Our early legislators had humanitarian principles that were put into practice here more than seventy years before similar principles were adopted in the neighbouring republic. The first parliament also provided for free grants of land to settlers from the United States, but required that each settler should take an oath of allegiance to the British Crown.

Simcoe became convinced that war was imminent between Great Britain and the United States, and he deemed it unsafe to have the provincial capital so close to the guns of an American fort as Newark was. In a journey westward that

A NEW CAPITAL 157

he made in 1793, he came upon what he believed would be an excellent site for the capital at the forks of the Thames River, where the city of London now stands. To Simcoe's mind this point had several important advantages. It was away from the international boundary, on a navigable river, and surrounded by a fertile and well-wooded country. He accordingly recommended that the provincial capital be established at this point, but Lord Dorchester at Quebec disapproved of the plan. Thus London narrowly missed being made the capital of the province. Simcoe had a road put through from the head of Burlington Bay to the forks of the Thames, a road which he named Dundas Street, in honour of a British minister of the time.

Later Simcoe chose a site for the capital across the lake from Niagara at a point between the Don and the Humber Rivers. This appeared to the governor a suitable place because of the fine harbour, which would make a good naval station in time of war. Here a town was laid out and called York, after the Duke of York, the son of George III. Simcoe spent the winter of 1793-94 at York in a canvas house. Before he left the province he arranged for the erection of temporary government buildings at the new capital. At a later time the name York was changed to the beautiful Indian name Toronto, which means "the meeting-place."

In the fall of 1793 Simcoe made another important journey, this time northward from York. He walked to the Holland River, and proceeded by canoe down this stream to Lake Simcoe, and thence down the Severn River to Georgian Bay. He believed this might be made the trade route between the Upper Lakes and the St. Lawrence, in preference to the route by way of the French River, Lake Nipissing, and the Ottawa River, which had been used for more than a century. Accordingly he had a road surveyed from York northward, which he called Yonge Street, after another British minister of the time.

Simcoe did not get along well with Lord Dorchester, the governor of Lower Canada. The latter was the commander-in-chief of the Canadian militia, and resented Simcoe's interference in military matters. In 1796 Simcoe asked to be recalled. He was appointed governor of San Domingo, but his health failed in the tropical climate of this island, and he returned to England. Later he was appointed commander-in-chief for India, but, before he could take over the duties of this position, he died, in 1806.

The name of the first governor of Upper Canada is borne in Ontario by a lake, a county, a town, and many streets and public buildings. A statue has been erected to his memory in Queen's Park, Toronto. The bronze figure, garbed in military uniform, with long coat, knee-breeches, and sword, may be seen on the lawn south-east of the provincial parliament buildings.

XXVII

SIR ISAAC BROCK

THE MILITARY HERO OF 1812

As we sail up the Niagara River towards Queenston or approach this village by the highway from St. Catharines, we see, many miles before we reach it, a beautiful shaft towering nearly two hundred feet above the lofty bank of the river. It is Brock's monument on Queenston Heights, erected to the memory of the man who laid down his life in defence of Canada against an invasion by the Americans more than a hundred years ago. The monument is a striking mark of the gratitude of the Canadian people to Sir Isaac Brock, whose leadership saved Canada at a critical moment during the war with the United States. In the honour roll of military heroes of our country, the name of Brock stands beside the names of Wolfe and Montcalm.

Brock was born in Guernsey, one of the Channel Islands south of England, in 1769, the year in which two other famous soldiers, Wellington and Napoleon, were born. He came of fighting stock. On both his father's and his mother's side there had been soldiers for many generations back. As a boy he delighted to read of military exploits and to listen to tales of the deeds of his soldier ancestors. Small wonder that he too decided to be a soldier.

Young Isaac was strong-limbed, athletic, and venturesome. He could scale the highest cliff near his island home, sail a boat in the stormiest water, break the wildest pony to the saddle, or swim a mile in a turbulent sea. At fifteen he was sent to a school at Rotterdam, in Holland, in order to learn French. He was the champion boxer and swimmer in the school, if not the best scholar. At sixteen he was an ensign in the army, and at twenty-seven he was colonel of the 49th Battalion. During all the years that he was climbing in rank, he studied hard to fit himself for a place still higher up.

For some time he was stationed with his regiment in Barbados and Jamaica, and the climate of these tropical islands nearly ruined his health. His first active service was in Holland under Sir John Moore during the war against Napoleon. In an engagement there he narrowly escaped being killed. He was struck by a bullet in the neck, but happened to be wearing a thick scarf which prevented a serious wound. Later he was with Nelson at the bombardment of Copenhagen, and stood beside him on the flagship *Elephant* when the great admiral put the telescope to his blind eye and said that he could not see the signal of the commander to retire. The lesson was not lost upon Brock, as we shall see later.

Public Archives of Canada
SIR ISAAC BROCK

In 1802, much to his own displeasure, Brock was ordered with his regiment to Canada. He was disappointed, because there was peace in Canada while there was war in Europe. He feared that his chance of active service was gone for good. Little did he think that his opportunity for most valuable service to the Empire would come to him in that far-off colony.

Soon after his arrival in Canada Brock was stationed at

WAR CLOUDS

Fort York, near the struggling village that Simcoe had laid out on the north shore of Lake Ontario. A pillar on the exhibition grounds at Toronto now marks the site of the former fort. There were many disloyal people in Upper Canada at that time, most of whom were recent immigrants from the United States. The monotony of garrison life and the disloyal atmosphere of the place began to tell upon the soldiers. Desertions to the United States began to be frequent. One day six soldiers deserted and set off in a boat across the lake to Niagara. When the news was brought to Brock he took several men in another boat and rowed all night across the lake in pursuit, the commander himself taking his turn at the oars. In the morning the deserters were surprised on the American shore and were brought back. Brock's firmness in discipline, coupled with his fairness and kindness, won the confidence of the soldiers. His manly bearing and his devotion to duty inspired them with loyalty, and soon desertions ceased. Brock was to the last a hero in the eyes of his men.

To a man of Brock's restless energy the first few years that he spent in Canada were disappointing in the extreme. While his brother officers were winning fame on the battlefields of Europe, he was compelled to remain inactive in a peaceful country. Then things began to happen which reconciled him to staying in Canada. War clouds began to gather on the Canadian horizon. For thirty years the United States had looked with longing eyes upon Canada, and believed that it would be an easy task to wrest her from the Mother Country. A good excuse for an attack was found in the conditions that grew out of Britain's war with Napoleon. The Americans were eager to make as much as possible out of trade with Europe. In an attempt to strike at Britain through her trade Napoleon issued a decree that no nation should trade with Britain, and threatened to seize all vessels found so doing. Britain replied that any vessel entering a French port without first calling at a British port would be liable to seizure. American shipping began to suffer from these vexatious orders, particularly at the hands of the British. A further cause of irritation lay in the British claim of the right to search American vessels for deserters.

SIR ISAAC BROCK

Annoyance grew into hostility, and hostility into war, which was declared by the Americans in 1812.

In the meantime Brock had been promoted to the rank of brigadier-general, and was acting governor of Upper Canada in the absence of Sir Francis Gore, who had, on account of ill-health, gone home to England on leave. The commander-in-chief of the Canadian forces was Sir George Prevost, who thought that war might yet be averted, and ordered Brock not to make any offensive move against the Americans. But Brock, remembering the example of Nelson at Copenhagen, took matters largely into his own hands. He believed that the salvation of Canada lay in vigorous attack on the enemy, and not in weak inactivity till they attacked. So he sent word to the commander of the garrison at St. Joseph Island to take the American fort at Michilimackinac, at the head of Lake Michigan. This fort was easily captured, and the British thus won the confidence of the Indians of the west.

Brock then resolved upon an attack upon Fort Detroit. General Hull, the American commander at this point, had crossed the river at Sandwich, and had issued a high-sounding proclamation to the Canadians, inviting them to throw off the yoke of Britain and threatening severe penalties if there were any sign of resistance. The Americans then plundered and laid waste the farms in the neighbourhood, but did not attempt to take Fort Malden, near Amherstburg. Brock proceeded to Fort Malden by way of Lake Erie with seven hundred men, more than half of whom were volunteers. The voyage was very stormy and took five days. Arriving at Fort Malden, he found that Hull had withdrawn to his own side of the river.

On the night of his arrival Brock was visited by Tecumseh, a famous chief of the Shawnees, who was a bitter enemy of the Americans. Tecumseh was in command of six hundred Indian braves, eager to attack the hated foe. The meeting between the two great leaders was memorable. Both were striking figures: the British general, fair-haired, erect, dressed in brilliant uniform; the Indian chief, swarthy, keen-eyed, sinewy, arrayed in deerskin and feathers. One glance was

AN AMAZING SURRENDER 163

sufficient for each to read the other. Turning to his companions, Tecumseh exclaimed, "This is a man!" This opinion was received by a chorus of assent from his dusky followers. The British commander and the Indian chief clasped hands, and thus sealed a compact of friendship and mutual support.

On a piece of birch bark, with his scalping-knife, Tecumseh traced for Brock a plan of Detroit. The fort was surrounded by a high, strongly-built palisade. Outside was a deep and wide ditch filled with water. The fort was armed with thirty guns, and defended by 2,500 well-equipped soldiers. It was apparent that to take the fort with scarcely more than half this number of men would be a formidable task. Together Brock and Tecumseh formed a plan of attack. Under cover of darkness the Indians would cross the river to protect the British landing the following morning. Brock would take his men across from Sandwich and advance upon the fort from the west.

In the meantime Brock sent to Hull a demand for the surrender of his garrison. Whether the American commander was panic-stricken by the possibility of an Indian massacre, or was misled as to the number of the British assailants, or was simply afraid to fight, has never been very clear. At any rate, when Brock advanced upon the fort the white flag was speedily run up. Hull laid down his arms, gave up the fort with its munitions and supplies, and surrendered the whole State of Michigan to the British. More than two thousand American soldiers were sent as prisoners to Quebec. Brock had not lost a single man. It was an amazing victory, and the news aroused great enthusiasm both in Canada and in England.

Brock at once went to Fort George, at the mouth of the Niagara, intending to sweep the Americans from that frontier. To his astonishment he learned that Sir George Prevost had agreed with General Dearborn, the American commander, to an armistice, that is, a cessation of hostilities, for several weeks. This was a most unwise proceeding, for it gave the Americans a chance to bring up additional men, guns, and supplies to strengthen their position. Had he been allowed to begin a campaign at once, Brock might easily have captured or destroyed the American forts and removed all possibility of danger at the Niagara frontier. When the armistice ended and warfare was resumed, the Americans were greatly superior to the British in numbers, and Brock's chance of victory had almost disappeared.

On the morning of October 13, 1812, the Americans began crossing the river in boats from Lewiston to Queenston. They were met by a heavy fire from the Canadian shore. The boats were thrown into confusion and many turned back. A large number of Americans, however, succeeded in landing, though their leader, Van Rensselaer, was severely wounded and had to be taken back to the American shore.

The sound of the cannonade aroused Brock at Fort George, seven miles distant, and he at once hurried to Queenston. On the way he met Lieutenant Jarvis, who was galloping to the fort to inform him of the attack. Without reining his horse, Brock waved the messenger to turn back. Riding by the general's side, the lieutenant delivered his message. Brock then ordered him to ride on to the fort and to tell General Sheaffe to bring with all haste every available man to Queenston. Then galloping forward he reached the village.

After giving directions for repelling the invaders, he proceeded to the Heights in order that he might get a better view of the whole action. There he found a company on guard and a single gun that was bombarding the opposite shore. Thinking that there was no danger from the Americans on the Heights, he sent the company to reinforce the soldiers in the village below. Brock remained with eight artillerymen in charge of the gun. In the meantime a company of sixty Americans under Captain Wool had secretly climbed the Heights by a path that had been left unguarded. They swarmed over the edge of the cliff upon the astonished artillerymen, who had just time to spike the gun and beat a hasty retreat.

The loss of a gun is always a severe blow to the pride of a British soldier, and Brock immediately called for volunteers to regain the gun that had been captured. Taking a hundred

A TRAGIC VICTORY

men, he began to scale the Heights, under a continuous fire from the Americans, who by this time numbered more than three hundred. The British pressed doggedly forward up the perilous ascent. They reached the top with Brock at their head, waving his sword and shouting encouragement. They rushed for the gun, but the next moment their leader was struck down by a bullet in the breast. The tall figure in the brilliant uniform had been all too good a mark for an American rifle. Thus fell, with victory almost within his grasp, one of the bravest of British military leaders, one who well deserves the name "The Hero of Upper Canada."

The death of Brock was a serious blow to the British, but the cry "Avenge the General!" inspired them to greater effort against the enemy. General Sheaffe, in response to Brock's order in the early morning, marched with a thousand men from Fort George, climbed the Heights by a road two miles from the river, and attacked from the rear the sixteen hundred Americans then assembled on the Heights. The charge was completely successful. The Americans broke and fled. Some scrambled down the Heights, and were either killed by falling over the rocks or drowned in attempting to swim the river. The Americans lost 300 killed and wounded and 1,000 prisoners, while the British loss was only 110. But the joy in the brilliant victory was dimmed by the death of the gallant leader.

Brock was buried at Fort George by his sorrowing comrades-in-arms. A monument to his memory was erected on Queenston Heights some years later, but this was blown up by a rebel. The present monument was erected in 1853. Brock's body, together with that of Colonel Macdonell, a gallant soldier who died of wounds the same day as Brock, rests in a vault beneath the monument.

XXVIII

TECUMSEH

THE WAR CHIEF OF THE SHAWNEES

A STRANGE and romantic figure crosses the stage of Canadian history for a fleeting moment and is gone. The figure is Tecumseh, the Shawnee chief, bravest of all the red-men, and typical of all that is best in Indian character. Three outstanding Indian chiefs have set their mark upon the pages of our history—Pontiac, Brant, and Tecumseh—but the greatest of these is Tecumseh.

He was born about the same time as that other great soldier with whose name his own is inseparably associated—General Brock. His boyhood was passed in the valley of the Ohio amid troublous times. White settlers from the American colonies were pushing their way westward from the Alleghanies and northward from the Ohio into the hunting and fishing grounds of the Indians. The red-men were fighting to hold them back, but it was a losing battle. As a young man Tecumseh had several encounters with the "Long-knives," as the Indians called the whites. He saw his father and oldest brother killed in these battles. Gradually there grew in his mind the ambition of uniting all the Indian tribes together in a great confederacy to stem the tide of white settlement, and to retain for his race some of the territory which was all its own before the European set foot in America. We have seen that Pontiac and Brant had dreamed the same dream, but in vain. And we shall now see that Tecumseh's vision of Indian supremacy was also destined to remain unfulfilled. The resistless flood of white immigration continued, and the red-men were pushed farther and farther back, until most of them were confined in a few

A DEFENSIVE LEAGUE 167

reservations here and there, which the whites in their generosity assigned to them. But that was many years after Tecumseh's time.

In 1794, when Tecumseh was about twenty-five years of age, the Indians suffered a severe defeat at the hands of the Americans at a great battle on the Maumee River, south of Lake Erie. By a treaty of peace the Indians surrendered a large territory north of the Ohio. Tecumseh and his tribe retired to a region along the Tippecanoe River, in what is now the State of Indiana. For several years he busied himself among the various tribes, trying to bind them together in a defensive league against white aggression. For this purpose he made use of his younger brother, who professed to have supernatural powers, and who, because of this, was called the Prophet. Tecumseh probably did not believe the claims of his brother, but he saw an opportunity to use the superstitious nature of his race to secure his ends. With great eloquence and power the Prophet preached that, if the Indians would only give up the customs and habits that they had learned from the whites, they might recover their former greatness. They must discard linen and wool, and wear deerskin for clothing; they must give up eating the flesh of sheep and cattle, and return to the flesh of the deer and buffalo; they must throw away their guns and resume the bow and arrow; they must abstain entirely from drinking fire-water. The Prophet gained great influence among the tribes, and for several years Tecumseh's league seemed likely

Public Archives of Canada
TECUMSEH

to succeed. Unfortunately, however, the opportunity for success was destroyed through the folly of the Prophet himself. In 1811, while Tecumseh was absent, the Prophet attempted to gain some glory for himself by advising a surprise attack upon an American army under General Harrison. His plans miscarried, and the battle of Tippecanoe was a crushing defeat for the Indians. The spell of the Prophet's power was broken, and Tecumseh saw the futility of his league.

The next year the war between Great Britain and the United States broke out. Tecumseh's experience with the Americans had taught him that he could expect nothing from an alliance with them. Whatever hope there was for his race lay in an alliance with the British. Accordingly, with six hundred warriors, he appeared at Fort Malden, near Amherstburg, and pledged his allegiance to Britain.

The meeting of Tecumseh and General Brock at Fort Malden is one of the dramatic incidents of Canadian history. It was the evening of Brock's arrival. Word was brought to the general that the Indian chief wished to see him. Brock ordered that he should be brought in at once. They met in the dimly lighted tent, Brock surrounded by a few of his officers, Tecumseh accompanied by several of his warriors. It was a striking picture—the dark, straight, keen-eyed chief in deerskin suit and moccasins, facing the fair-haired, tall, dignified British leader in the brilliant uniform.

"I am glad to meet the great chief of the Shawnees," said Brock. "I have heard much of the bravery of his Indian warriors. I have brought my soldiers so that they may take lessons in warfare from them. The great father across the sea is proud that his children of the forest wish to fight under his flag."

"The Indians are glad that the great father has sent his soldiers to assist them," replied Tecumseh. "His red children are ready to shed their last drop of blood in his service."

The leaders looked each other in the eye for a moment, and then each spontaneously stepped forward. Their hands met in a warm clasp, and thus was sealed a compact of permanent friendship.

Turning to the warriors who accompanied him, Tecumseh exclaimed, "This is a man!" His sentiment was echoed by loud exclamations of assent from the red-men.

"The task of taking Detroit will be difficult," said the general. "The fort is strongly defended with both men and guns."

"It will not be hard," returned the chief. "Let the Indian show his white brother how to do it."

And taking his scalping-knife, he drew upon a sheet of birch bark a complete and detailed plan of the fort, and suggested a way of attack.

"If the general will follow this plan," Tecumseh concluded, "the Long-knives will give up the fort to-morrow."

"If prisoners are taken, I hope that there will be no bloodshed," said Brock with some concern. "You will not let your warriors attack those who surrender?"

"Have no fear," answered the chief. "The red-men despise the Long-knives too much for that."

Before he retired that night Brock wrote to one of his officers concerning his newly found ally: "A more sagacious or gallant warrior does not exist." To Hull, the American leader, Brock wrote a despatch commanding him to surrender the fort, and adding significantly: "You must be aware that the numerous bodies of Indians who have attached themselves to my troops will be beyond my control the moment the contest commences."

The plan agreed upon by Brock and Tecumseh was carried out to the letter. In the darkness of the night of August 15, 1812, the Indian chief crossed the river at Sandwich with his warriors; in the early dawn of the morning, the British leader followed with several hundred soldiers, their crossing being protected by the Indians. To the amazement of both leaders, Hull surrendered the fort without a shot. Two thousand five hundred Americans, sheltered by a strong, well-armed fort, gave themselves up to half that number of adversaries.

Tecumseh was full of admiration for Brock's leadership.

"We saw you standing erect in the boat while crossing the river," said he, "and we saw that you were the first to land. Your boldness frightened the enemy."

Brock took off his silken sash and placed it over the shoulders of his Indian ally.

"Keep this as a memento of our victory," he said.

Next morning he observed that Tecumseh was not wearing the sash.

"I gave it to Roundhead, the Wyandot chief," he explained. "He is an older and abler warrior than I am, and deserves it more."

Brock hurried to the Niagara frontier, and left Tecumseh and his Indians to co-operate with the British along the western frontier. The news of the gallant general's death at Queenston Heights shortly afterwards was a sad blow to the Indian chief. From that moment he began to fear for the success of the British arms in the struggle. General Procter was the leader in the west, and Tecumseh had little confidence in his generalship.

In 1813 the American forces in the west greatly outnumbered the British. Procter was forced to abandon Detroit and to retreat eastward, closely followed by General Harrison, the American leader, with five thousand men. Tecumseh repeatedly urged Procter to make a stand against the enemy. At last, on reaching Moraviantown, six miles beyond the present city of Chatham, the retreat was halted. Here a favourable position was chosen. The Thames River was on one side and a cedar swamp was on the other. Midway between the two, Procter placed the only cannon he had, and awaited the American attack without preparing any other defences. Tecumseh posted his Indians in the swamp to fire upon the enemy from cover.

"Father, have a big heart," said the chief to the British leader in saying farewell to him before the battle.

"Brother warriors," he said to his own men, "we enter an engagement to-day from which I shall not return."

Harrison, with greatly superior strength, charged the British position, captured the gun, and put Procter and his army to flight.

AN UNKNOWN GRAVE

In the meantime, Colonel Johnston with a body of Americans was trying to dislodge the Indians from the swamp. It was a veritable "valley of death" for the Americans. They were nearly all killed. To make the victory complete Tecumseh himself rushed upon Johnston with tomahawk upraised to strike him down. Before the blow could fall, the American fired upon the chief with his pistol. Tecumseh fell dead.

His sorrowing followers carried his body from the field. Where they buried him nobody knows. No stately monument has been set up in his memory. But his name will live in the pages of Canadian history as the last great Indian ally of the British, and as the friend and colleague of the best loved of her generals in Canada, the hero of Queenston Heights.

XXIX

LAURA SECORD

THE HEROINE OF BEAVER DAMS

AMONG the heroines of Canadian history Laura Secord occupies a foremost place. She is to Upper Canada what Madeleine de Verchères is to Lower Canada. The great deed with which her name is connected occurred during the war with the United States, a period that brought forth many heroic acts on the part of both men and women.

Laura Secord's maiden name was Ingersoll. Her family lived in Massachusetts at the time of the Revolutionary War. Her father was a merchant, and after the war was over his business declined so much that he decided to seek a new home amid the fertile lands of Canada. The family migrated to Oxford county and began farming. The town of Ingersoll is named after them. Later they went to Queenston, where Laura Ingersoll was married to James Secord, whose family were ardent United Empire Loyalists.

James Secord was one of the followers of General Brock at Queenston Heights, and was severely wounded during the engagement. As he lay helpless on the side of the cliff, word of his plight was brought to his wife. Without thinking of danger, she at once went out to search for him. She had just

LAURA SECORD'S COTTAGE

found him when three American soldiers came up and were about to club him to death. Mrs. Secord threw herself between them and her husband, begging them to kill her and spare him. Fortunately, just at that moment Captain Wool, the American leader, appeared. Taking in the situation at a glance, he severely reprimanded the soldiers and ordered that the wounded man should be carried to a place of safety. It is pleasant to record such an act of humanity on the part of an enemy during this period of bitter warfare. This incident marked the beginning of a friendship between the British soldier and the American officer, which continued long after the war was over. Mrs. Secord nursed her husband back to health, but it was many months before he completely recovered.

The particular exploit that has made Laura Secord famous took place in June of the following year, 1813. At this time Queenston was in possession of the Americans. They had sent scouting parties out in every direction, and had captured and sent as prisoners to the United States all the men of military age that they could find in the neighbourhood. As James Secord had not yet recovered from his wounds, he was not molested.

The British commander, General Vincent, had abandoned Fort George and had retreated to Burlington Heights, near the present city of Hamilton. However, he maintained two strong outposts, and from these scouts were sent out, who harassed the Americans and hindered their progress. Lieutenant Fitzgibbon, a young and clever officer, who had been a favourite of Brock, obtained permission to raise a volunteer corps for scouting purposes. He selected fifty men and dressed them in reversible coats, red on one side and grey on the other. They wore the grey side out when scouting the woods so as not to be seen easily by the enemy. Fitzgibbon's headquarters were at Beaver Dams, about thirteen miles from Queenston. From here he attacked the Americans, now here, now there, striking a blow quickly and then disappearing. In this method of harassing the Americans he was ably assisted by a company of Indians under Captain Ducharme. The Americans decided that if they could capture Fitzgibbon Upper Canada would soon be theirs.

A number of American officers were billeted at the Secord home in Queenston. At dinner one day Mrs. Secord overheard them discussing with Colonel Boerstler, the commander, a plan for the capture of Fitzgibbon. She decided that Fitzgibbon must be warned of the danger and put on his guard. But how was it to be done? Her husband was still too weak to go, and there was nobody else to send. She made up her mind to go herself. The danger would be great, but her patriotic spirit was equal to the attempt. Accordingly, in the early hours of the following morning before daylight she set out. The severe illness of her brother at St. David's was the excuse that she gave the sentinel for her early start, and she was allowed to pass. She reached St. David's just at sunrise. Her niece accompanied her to Shipman's Corners, now St. Catharines, but could go no farther because her feet had become sore from the long walk.

Public Archives of Canada
LAURA SECORD

From this point Mrs. Secord continued her perilous journey alone. She could not go by the travelled road, for she would have been stopped by the enemy. She had to walk through the pathless woods, ever on the alert for American scouts. That she passed through the enemy lines without being discovered is almost a miracle. The season had been rainy. The swamps were flooded and the creeks swollen with water. She had to cross streams and pools again and again over fallen logs on her hands and knees.

A MERITED MEMORIAL

To make the conditions even more trying, the day was very hot.

As she approached Fitzgibbon's position she came unexpectedly upon some Indian scouts. She was much frightened, for the Indians at that time showed scant respect to women. Though they could not speak English, she made them understand that she had a message for Fitzgibbon, and at length she was conducted to him. Fitzgibbon was very grateful to the woman who, in order to bring him warning, had walked twenty miles under the most difficult conditions and through the greatest dangers. He afterwards said that he did not understand how a woman with so frail a body could have accomplished such a journey. It is believed that the commander had already been informed by Indian scouts of the American plan; but, though this may be true, the glory of Laura Secord's heroic act is in no way dimmed. The qualities of the woman which command admiration are the patriotism which inspired the achievement and the determination which carried it through.

Fitzgibbon, knowing now the enemy's purposes, formed his plans accordingly. When the American commander, sure of an easy victory, approached Beaver Dams, he was ambushed by the Indians; and, fearing a massacre, he surrendered with over five hundred men to Fitzgibbon. The latter generously gave the credit of the victory to the Indians, who had done all the fighting.

Laura Secord lived for fifty-five years after this event, and died at the great age of ninety-three. A monument to her memory was erected in 1912 on Queenston Heights, near the more imposing one of General Brock. It bears this inscription: "This monument has been erected by the Government of Canada to Laura Ingersoll Secord, who saved her husband's life in the battle on these Heights, October 13, 1812, and who risked her own in carrying to Captain Fitzgibbon the information which enabled him to win the victory of Beaver Dams."

XXX

THE EARL OF SELKIRK

THE COLONIZER OF THE WEST

THOMAS DOUGLAS, Earl of Selkirk, was one of the great colonizers of Canada and the founder of the first permanent settlement in the Canadian West. He was born in Scotland in 1771, the scion of a noble house that had for centuries been famous in Scottish history. As he was the youngest of seven brothers, he had no expectation of succeeding to his father's estates and title. On this account he prepared himself to make his own way in the world. He went to the University of Edinburgh, and had quite a creditable career there. During his course he was one of nineteen young men who formed "The Club," an organization that had for its purpose the study and discussion of social and political questions. Sir Walter Scott, who afterwards became a famous author, was also a member, and between him and Douglas there was formed a lifelong friendship.

The six elder brothers of Douglas died one by one, and, when his father died also, he found himself in possession of an earldom, large estates, and great wealth. The Earl of Selkirk, as he now was, began at once to look about him to see in what way he might be of some service to his fellow-men. He had read Sir Alexander Mackenzie's book of explorations in Western Canada, and was impressed with the possibilities of that great land as a place for settlement.

At this time the condition of many of the Scottish Highlanders was pitiable. Their lands had been bought up by wool-growers, who had turned the farms into sheep pastures. Many of the Highlanders, thus deprived of their means of livelihood, were on the verge of starvation. Their plight

EARLY COLONIZING VENTURES 177

excited the sympathy of Selkirk. He formed the plan of transporting them to Canada, where they might begin life anew in a land of plenty. Accordingly, he persuaded eight hundred of the inhabitants of the Island of Skye to emigrate. In three vessels they sailed in the summer of 1803, and were landed on Prince Edward Island, where Selkirk had secured a large grant of land. The colony was a success from the beginning. Many of the present inhabitants of the island province are descendants of the settlers who came out with Selkirk more than a hundred years ago.

Selkirk next bought a large tract of land south of Lake St. Clair in Upper Canada, and settled more than a hundred Highlanders there in 1804. This was known as the "Baldoon" settlement. It was not so successful as the Prince Edward Island venture. The land was flat, poorly drained, and at that time unsuitable for farming. During the first year more than a third of the colonists died of fever. At a later time, during the war of 1812, the settlers' farms were devastated by invading Americans. Many descendants of the Baldoon colonists still live in the counties of Essex and Kent.

Public Archives of Canada
LORD SELKIRK

The most important of Selkirk's colonizing efforts was the planting of the Red River Colony, the story of which deserves to be told in some detail.

Ever since it obtained its charter in 1670, the Hudson's Bay Company had maintained its claim upon those lands which drain into Hudson Bay. A glance at the map of Canada will show how immense that territory is. It comprises not only the lands immediately surrounding the Bay, but also those drained by the Saskatchewan, the Assiniboine, and the Red Rivers, whose waters are eventually poured into the Bay. A large part of what is now the three prairie provinces of Canada, as well as a part of the States of Minnesota and Dakota, was included in the territory claimed by the Hudson's Bay Company. At first the Company established trading-posts only on the Bay, and required the Indians to make long journeys from the interior to bring their furs to the posts. Towards the end of the eighteenth century a rival fur-trading organization, called the North-West Company, was established among the Scotch merchants of Montreal. This Company pushed its trade very vigorously in the region west of the Great Lakes to the foot of the Rocky Mountains. It established posts at convenient points, and the western Indians found it much easier to sell their furs to the new Company than to make the long and arduous journey to the posts of the older Company on the Bay. Thus the Hudson's Bay Company was also compelled to establish posts in the interior, and it frequently happened that the posts of the two Companies were only a few miles apart. Rivalry grew into hostility, and encounters which sometimes ended in bloodshed became frequent between the traders of the rival companies. The trade of the Hudson's Bay Company was so seriously impaired that its shares began to fall in value.

It was at this point that Lord Selkirk saw a great opporportunity. He had formed the project of planting a colony in the fertile lands surrounding the Red River, and decided that the best way to secure this territory was to buy up the shares of the Hudson's Bay Company. When he had secured a controlling interest in the Company, he induced the other shareholders to give him a grant of over 100,000 square miles of the Red River lands in order that he might colonize this territory. He then distributed pamphlets throughout Scotland setting forth his plans and inviting people to join the proposed colony.

RED RIVER COLONY

The North-West Company at once set up an active opposition to Lord Selkirk's scheme upon the plea that the colonization of this country would destroy the fur-trade. The agents of the Company did their best to discourage emigrants from going. They slandered Selkirk, saying that his scheme was designed only for making money for himself. They said that nothing would ever grow on the lands in the Red River territory, and that settlers would be sure to starve or freeze to death.

Notwithstanding all this, in the summer of 1811 a party of 105 persons under Captain Miles Macdonell, who had been appointed governor of the new colony, set sail from Scotland in three old vessels of the Hudson's Bay Company. After a stormy passage of two months, during which many died of "ship fever," they landed at York Factory, on the west side of Hudson Bay, where the Nelson and Hayes Rivers discharge their waters. They built themselves rude huts, and spent a winter of much suffering from cold and disease. Scurvy broke out, the result of a diet of salt meat; but the victims were cured by taking the sap of the white spruce. In the spring of 1812 the colonists ascended the Hayes River, made a portage to Lake Winnipeg, and went up the Red River to a point where the city of Winnipeg now stands. Here they built a fort and named it Fort Douglas, from the family name of Lord Selkirk. The colonists suffered greatly from cold during the following winter, but they did not lack for food, as they were able to secure a supply of buffalo meat.

In the spring of 1813 the colony was strengthened by the arrival of nearly one hundred more immigrants, who had come to Fort Churchill the autumn before and had wintered at that far northern point. The new-comers were good farmers. They sowed wheat, which yielded an abundant harvest. Consequently the food supply was better the following winter. But trouble started with the North-West traders at Fort Gibraltar, a mile or so from Fort Douglas, at the junction of the Red and the Assiniboine. As a measure of protection from starvation, Governor Macdonell ordered that no food supplies should be sent out of the territory.

The North-Westers were used to sending supplies from the Red River country to their western posts, and paid no attention to the governor's command. Then Macdonell had the Company's supplies at Fort Souris seized. A violent quarrel resulted. In the end the North-West traders drove out the colonists, burned their dwellings, and sent the governor as a prisoner to Montreal. The discouraged settlers started for Hudson Bay on their way home to Scotland.

In the meantime Colin Robertson, a servant of the Hudson's Bay Company and a friend of Selkirk, arrived at the Red River by way of the Great Lakes with a company of *voyageurs*. Upon learning the fate of the colony, he started northward after the fleeing settlers. He overtook them at Lake Winnipeg, brought them back, and re-established them on their farms.

The following year, 1815, a fourth contingent of colonists arrived under the leadership of Robert Semple, who had been appointed governor of the Hudson's Bay Company. Semple took Fort Gibraltar and drove out the North-West traders. These, however, incited the Métis half-breeds to attack the colony. Under Cuthbert Grant, a clerk of the North-West Company, the Métis made a sudden descent upon the settlers. When the news of their coming was brought to Semple, he rode out with twenty men to parley with them. The party was quickly surrounded by the assailants and practically all were slain. This tragedy is known as the massacre of Seven Oaks. Again the colonists were expelled and their homes were given to the flames. It looked as if the Red River Colony was for ever destroyed.

A monument on Main Street, Winnipeg, commemorates this unfortunate episode, and bears this inscription: "Seven Oaks. Erected in 1891 by the Manitoba Historical Society, Through the Generosity of the Countess of Selkirk, on the site of Seven Oaks, Where Fell Governor Robert Semple and Twenty of his Officers and Men, June 19, 1816."

Before news of the occurrence at Seven Oaks reached Lord Selkirk, he had started west by way of the Great Lakes with a company of a hundred discharged soldiers, whom he had persuaded to go out to the colony. When he reached the North-West Company's post at Fort William, he heard of

PIONEER STAGE COACH, 1834.

By courtesy of the Ross Robertson Collection, Toronto Public Library.

THE SILVER CHIEF

the expulsion of his colonists. In his capacity of justice of the peace he tried the officials of the Company, and sent nine of them as prisoners to York for further trial for their actions against the colony. Then Selkirk proceeded west, and in July, 1817, he set foot for the first time upon the site of his colony.

He first arranged a treaty with the Indians. He treated them with great respect and kindness, and, because of his liberality in making gifts, they called him the "Silver Chief." They readily agreed to give up their rights to a strip of land along the Red and Assiniboine Rivers in return for an annual payment of two hundred pounds of tobacco. The decision as to the width of the land to be surrendered gave some difficulty. The Indians were unused to the white man's methods of measurement. At length the Earl proposed that the land should extend on each side of the rivers as far as a horse could be seen on the open prairie. This was a measurement that the Indians could understand, and the suggestion was accepted.

Then the Earl visited the low-roofed homes of the colonists by the river. He paused at the churchyard to look sadly at the rude headstones and newly made mounds of earth. The people crowded about him to grasp his hand. Presently he said: "It is my wish that the parish be called Kildonan, after your old parish at home in Scotland. Here you shall build your church, and over there across that little stream you shall build a school for your children."

When Selkirk returned to Upper Canada, suits were brought against him in the courts by the North-West Company for his actions at Fort William. He was heavily fined for what the courts decided were illegal acts. He returned to Scotland a disappointed man. His health was broken, and he died in 1820, his death doubtless hastened by worry over his ventures in colonization. A year later the rival trading companies buried the hatchet and united their forces.

Though Lord Selkirk's Red River Colony had a struggle for a few years against difficult conditions, it gradually grew prosperous. On the site of the original settlement there now stands the proud city of Winnipeg. The great Province of Manitoba has, in the space of a hundred years, grown from the little colony planted amid so much stress and hardship. The pity of it is that the beginnings of settlement in the Canadian West should have been associated with so much bitter quarrel and cruel bloodshed, and that the greed of traders should have done so much to hinder a great colonization scheme. Selkirk's great dream was at length realized, but he died before the fruits of his work were apparent. Well does he deserve the tribute of his friend, Sir Walter Scott, who wrote of him: "I never knew in my life a man of more generous and disinterested disposition, or one whose talents and perseverance were better qualified to bring great and national schemes to conclusion."

XXXI

SIR JOHN FRANKLIN

THE DISCOVERER OF THE NORTH-WEST PASSAGE

Of all the expeditions into the Arctic regions north of Canada, those of Sir John Franklin are the most memorable. The stories of these expeditions form a record of endurance, determination, and heroism that stirs our blood and fires our imagination. Franklin made three expeditions into the north. In the first two he made important discoveries, and in the last he met a tragic death before he had quite attained his great ambition.

As a small boy Franklin was filled with a love of the sea. One school holiday, with a companion, he walked twelve miles to look at the sea for the first time, and then and there he made up his mind to be a sailor. His father did not approve of his choice of a career, and, in order to cure him of what he thought was merely a passing fancy, he sent him on a long voyage. The boy returned with a stronger determination than ever to be a sailor. At the age of fourteen he entered the navy, and before he was twenty he had been in action in the famous battles of Copenhagen and Trafalgar. He had also been on an exploring expedition to Australia, and had been wrecked on a sandbar hundreds of miles from land, from which perilous position he was fortunately rescued. His coolness in danger, his resourcefulness in difficulty, his cheerfulness in discouraging situations, and his ability to manage men were soon recognized, and he made rapid advance in the navy.

When the war with Napoleon was over and many officers and seamen were thrown out of employment, the attention of Britain was once more directed to Polar exploration.

In 1819 Franklin was given command of an expedition which was to proceed overland from Hudson Bay to the Arctic Ocean. The purpose was to trace the coast from the Mackenzie to the Coppermine, and thus connect up the discoveries of Mackenzie and Hearne. Franklin's three principal companions were Dr. Richardson, Lieutenant Hood, and Lieutenant Back. The expedition landed at York Factory, and proceeded up the Hayes River, through Lake Winnipeg, and up the Saskatchewan. During the winter they reached Fort Chipewyan on Lake Athabaska, and in the following summer made their way to Fort Providence, on the north shore of Great Slave Lake. Thence they started, with insufficient supplies and poor equipment, for the Coppermine River.

The brief Arctic summer was now closing, and they found it impossible to reach the ocean that season. Near the headwaters of the Coppermine they built a rude shelter, which they named Fort Enterprise. Here they spent the winter of 1820–21. Their hardships were great. The cold was intense. The temperature inside the fort was many degrees below zero a few feet from the fire, and often went as low as forty below zero at night. The trees froze so solidly that the men's axes splintered in the attempt to cut fuel. Their food consisted of a little fish and deer meat, and on Sunday a cup of chocolate extra. Sunday was always a day of rest, and Franklin read to his men the service of the Church of England.

Public Archives of Canada
SIR JOHN FRANKLIN

ARCTIC HARDSHIPS

In the summer of 1821 the explorers descended the Coppermine to its mouth, and in two canoes they followed the Arctic coast nearly five hundred miles eastward. When they turned again westward the Arctic winter had already set in, and, on account of the ice, it was impossible to return the way they came. So they set off overland for Fort Enterprise. The hardships of that journey were almost beyond belief. It was bitterly cold. Their food failed. For weeks they toiled forward over the wastes of snow and ice. They had nothing to eat but weeds scraped from the rocks and a few fragments of deer flesh left by the wolves. They struggled on till they were within forty miles of Fort Enterprise. Here Lieutenant Hood became so weak and ill that he could not go forward.

It was arranged that Dr. Richardson and two or three of the men should stay with Hood while the others went on to Fort Enterprise. The sick man was sheltered in a tent. A few days later, when Richardson returned from a search for food, he found Hood dead. An Indian in the party had become insane and had murdered him. The madman was evidently bent upon killing the others in the same way. Richardson did the only possible thing under the circumstances. Rather than have the whole party killed in cold blood he put a bullet through the madman's head. The untimely death of Lieutenant Hood cut short the career of a promising young officer.

In the meantime Franklin's party had reached the rude shelter of Fort Enterprise. It was impossible to secure enough food, and they were reduced to digging for scraps among the refuse heaps of the year before. They tore up the floor of the fort to get fuel to keep them warm. They resolved on a desperate attempt to reach Fort Providence, but Franklin broke a snowshoe when he had gone only a few miles, and he had to turn back, taking a few companions with him. Lieutenant Back continued the journey, and fortunately reached his destination in safety.

Franklin and his companions lay helpless and starving at Fort Enterprise for many days. It was thus that Richardson and his party, almost equally weak from lack of food, found them when they staggered in. Each party was shocked at the wasted appearance of the others. Day by day the men grew weaker from cold and slow starvation. One day a herd of deer passed close by their door, but not one in the party had strength enough to raise a gun to shoot. Several of the men died. At last, before it was too late, relief came. Lieutenant Back had reached Fort Providence and had sent back a supply of food. Gradually the men recovered their health and strength, and were soon able to set out on the return journey to York Factory. This took seven weeks. Altogether, in three years, the explorers had covered a distance of over five thousand miles.

Franklin's second expedition to the Arctic was made in 1825. Dr. Richardson and Back were again his companions. They went by way of the St. Lawrence to York (now Toronto), thence to Georgian Bay and Lake Superior and then overland to the Mackenzie River. They spent the winter on the shore of Great Bear Lake, and in the following spring pushed on down the Mackenzie to its mouth. Here the party divided into two groups. Franklin went westward and traced the northern coast of Alaska for several hundred miles. Richardson went eastward as far as the mouth of the Coppermine.

The North-West Passage, the goal of Arctic explorers for centuries, was now all but won. A northern waterway westward through Baffin Bay, Lancaster Sound, and Barrow Strait to Melville Sound was already known. A more southerly waterway eastward from Bering Strait to beyond the Coppermine was also known. The two waterways overlapped. It remained only to discover the connecting passage between the two and the great riddle of the North-West Passage would be solved.

Sir John Franklin was chosen for the task of finding the missing link in the great mystery. In 1845, when he was nearly sixty years of age, he started on his third expedition to the Arctic. He commanded two large vessels, the *Erebus* and the *Terror*, manned by 134 sailors and stocked with provisions to last for three years. These ships were very large and powerful for that time. In addition to sails, each

A MYSTERIOUS FATE

had a twenty-horse-power engine, and it was thought that the vessels would easily be propelled through the Polar seas. We know now how mistaken the people then were. We know that much larger ships with engines of many thousand horse-power are helpless against the great icepacks of the Arctic. The *Erebus* and *Terror* reached the west coast of Greenland in July. They were sighted by a whaling-ship in Lancaster Sound late in that month. For fourteen years no

ABANDONING THE "EREBUS" AND "TERROR"

further direct news of either the vessels or the crews reached England.

For three years there was little public anxiety for their safety. When the ships did not then return, people began to grow alarmed. Expedition after expedition was fitted out to search for the Franklin party, and the British government offered a reward of £10,000 for their rescue or for reliable news of their fate. No trace of them was secured till 1851, when their first winter quarters on Beechey Island were discovered. It was evident that their food supply must have run low sooner than was expected. Thousands of cans of spoiled meat that had been discarded as unfit for food were found here. In 1854 Dr. Rae, an employee of the

Hudson's Bay Company, obtained further news of the ill-fated party from Eskimos. These people told him that, several years before, they had seen a large party of white men hauling a boat and sledges over the snow. One of them seemed the chief. Later the Eskimos found many dead bodies under an overturned boat. Dr. Rae secured many articles which the Eskimos had collected. Among these were guns, telescopes, compasses, spoons, knives, and forks, together with a small silver plate engraved with Franklin's name. It was plain that Rae had obtained authentic news of the fate of the party, and he was paid the reward offered by the government.

But it was not till 1859 that final proof of the sad disaster was secured. In that year McClintock, an explorer who had been sent by Lady Franklin in a last effort to find her husband, returned with a document which set all doubts at rest. In a heap of stones on King William's Island he had discovered a paper written by some of the officers of the Franklin expedition in 1847. This stated that the *Erebus* and *Terror* had been caught in the icepack during the second winter and had to be abandoned. The note added that Sir John Franklin had died on June 11, 1847.

Further traces of the ill-fated expedition have been recently brought to light. In the year 1926 some Arctic travellers picked up on King William's Island several articles that undoubtedly formed part of the equipment of the Franklin party. Among these were wooden bowls and fragments of navy cloth similar to those used in the Royal Navy of Franklin's day, pieces of shoe leather, scraps of iron and brass, and parts of oak sled-runners.

Though Amundsen, the Norwegian, was the first man actually to sail a vessel from the Atlantic to the Pacific through the Arctic Ocean, a feat which he accomplished in 1904, Sir John Franklin will always be regarded as the real discoverer of the North-West Passage. It was Franklin who found the missing link north and south between the known passages from the Atlantic and from the Pacific. He and his gallant companions endured untold hardship and suffering, and laid down their lives in the interest of science and geography.

XXXII

WILLIAM LYON MACKENZIE

THE ENEMY OF THE FAMILY COMPACT

WHATEVER else may be said of William Lyon Mackenzie, it is certain that he played no small part in bringing about certain much-needed reforms in Upper Canada. He will be remembered in Canadian history as the doughty champion of the right of the people to govern themselves. However we may disapprove of the means that he took to gain his ends, we cannot but approve of the ends themselves.

The seeds of the troubles against which Mackenzie struggled were sown in the Constitutional Act of 1791; the harvest was reaped in the rebellion which he headed in 1837. It will be recalled that the Constitutional Act provided for a legislative assembly to be elected by the people, and for a legislative council and an executive council to be appointed by the crown. The real government of the province was in the hands of the executive council, which paid little heed to the wishes of the people's representatives in the assembly. The executive council was able to fill most of the public offices with its friends, and to spend the public money to suit itself. The council and its officials were called by their enemies the Family Compact, probably because the members stuck so closely together to keep control of the government.

Another source of dissatisfaction was the method of dealing with the settlement of the land. In every township a portion of the land had been set apart as crown reserves. The friends of the government secured large blocks of these crown lands, and held them in the hope of getting high prices. This hindered the settlement by real farmers. At that time vacant land was not taxed. The settlers had therefore to pay all the taxes, while the owners of unoccupied lands escaped taxation altogether.

The clergy reserves caused another difficulty. The Constitutional Act had set apart one-eighth of the land of each township "for the support of a Protestant clergy." The Family Compact maintained that "a Protestant clergy" meant the clergy of the Church of England. Naturally, other Protestant denominations disagreed with this view and claimed a share in these lands. A long and bitter dispute, extending over many years, arose out of this situation.

It was while Upper Canada was in the midst of these political difficulties that Mackenzie, a young man of twenty-five, arrived from Scotland. He went into business first at York, then at Dundas, but was not very successful. Then he became editor of a newspaper, *The Colonial Advocate*, at Queenston. He soon began to make serious attacks upon the government. His principal demand was that the executive council should be made responsible to the assembly. He maintained that the members of the council should be removable from office if the members of the assembly, who were the representatives of the people, considered it advisable. In other words, he advocated what we to-day know as responsible government.

Public Archives of Canada
WILLIAM LYON MACKENZIE

Within a year Mackenzie moved his newspaper to York, this being a more promising field for the exercise of his influence. After he had made a particularly abusive onslaught in his paper against the Family Compact, several young men one night broke into his office, destroyed his presses, and threw his type into the lake. Mackenzie took the matter to the courts, and secured heavy damages from the perpetrators of the outrage. Before this time he had been nearly bankrupt, but now he was able to secure a new and better newspaper equipment. Besides, he had enlisted the sympathy of a great many people who thought that he was being persecuted for maintaining their rights.

Soon after this he was elected member of the assembly for York. He continued his attacks upon the government on the floor of the House. His language was often violent and extravagant, and aroused strong resentment on the part of his opponents. He was presently charged with publishing the proceedings of the assembly without authority and with libelling the members. He was expelled from the House, but was promptly re-elected by a large majority by his constituents. Again he was expelled and declared incapable of being elected, but again the voters of York sent him back as their member. Five times he was elected and expelled, and the whole proceeding became ridiculous. On one occasion he attempted to take his seat in the assembly, encouraged by sympathizers in the galleries. He was seized by the sergeant-at-arms and forcibly ejected, amid general confusion on the floor of the House.

In an interval between elections Mackenzie went to England, hoping to get the help of the authorities there in righting conditions in the province. He made speeches, wrote letters to the newspapers, published pamphlets, and talked to members of the British government. He succeeded in convincing the colonial secretary that something was wrong. Orders were given to the governor to remove some of the abuses, but nothing came of it.

In 1834 the town of York became incorporated as the city of Toronto, and Mackenzie's popularity was attested by his election as the first mayor. During the year cholera swept through the city, and side by side with his personal and political enemy, Dr. Strachan, he fought the scourge with tireless energy. But he was often indiscreet in both word and action. His popularity waned, and in the following year he was defeated in the election for mayor.

However, shortly afterwards Mackenzie was again elected member of the assembly for York. This time he was allowed to take his seat, as his party, the Reformers, were in the majority. He strongly attacked the executive council for appointing their friends to office. In the election of 1836 the governor, Sir Francis Bond Head, quite improperly took an active part. He succeeded in persuading many people that the Reformers were disloyal, and therefore should not be elected. As a result Mackenzie and many other prominent Reformers were defeated.

This reverse seems to have embittered Mackenzie and to have convinced him that reform was impossible without resort to open rebellion. He became editor of another newspaper, *The Constitution*, in which he made more and more reckless attacks upon the government. He began to hold secret meetings of his friends at various places, and at these meetings he urged an armed rising. Troops were secretly drilled at several points in anticipation of an early clash at arms. Mackenzie proposed that his followers should march upon Toronto, take the governor prisoner, seize the parliament buildings, and set up a provisional government. Everything seemed to favour the scheme. The government appeared to be unaware that trouble was brewing, for no steps were taken to prevent a rising. The governor moved the militia to Kingston, and the arms stored at the city hall were left unprotected.

Mackenzie planned that the attack upon Toronto should be made on December 7th, 1837. The rebels were to assemble at Montgomery's Tavern on Yonge Street, three miles north of Toronto, and were to march upon the capital to an easy victory. Then the date was changed to the 4th, and misunderstanding arose. Everything went wrong among the rebels. They lacked experienced military leaders. They were not properly armed. They began to lose confidence in Mackenzie. Many in disgust left for their homes. The projected attack was not made on the 4th of December, and the delay was fatal to the chances of the rebels.

A REBELLION CRUSHED

In the meantime the government learned of the proposed attack, and hastily assembled some loyalist volunteers under Colonel McNab and Colonel Fitzgibbon, the latter a hero of 1812. The loyalist forces, numbering about 1,100, marched upon the 700 poorly armed and ill-prepared rebels. A few shots were exchanged. In twenty minutes the fight was over. The rebels broke and fled. Only one was killed as a result of the brief encounter. The loyalists did not lose a man. It was almost a bloodless rebellion.

After the ignominious rout of his misguided followers, Mackenzie lost no time in fleeing from the scene. He made his way westward from Toronto around the head of the lake to the Niagara frontier. A reward of one thousand pounds was offered by the government for his capture. But he had many devoted friends, who assisted him in hiding from his pursuers. After a series of hairbreadth escapes, he crossed the Niagara in safety. Had he been captured, he would doubtless have been tried, convicted of treason, and hanged. Two of his followers, Samuel Lount and Peter Matthews, suffered this fate later, in spite of strong efforts to secure their pardon. Both were worthy men apart from their unfortunate association with the ill-starred rebellion.

Notwithstanding the utter failure of his resort to arms, Mackenzie continued his activities against the government from the shelter of the American boundary. At Buffalo he gathered a number of sympathizers, mainly low adventurers from American cities, and took possession of Navy Island in the Niagara River. He intended to fortify it and use it as a base from which to attack Canada. But a body of loyalists seized the rebel supply ship, the *Caroline*, and shelled the motley army from its position. Mackenzie gave up the idea of an attack by an armed force, but he did his best by newspaper writings to stir up trouble between the United States and Canada. He was soon arrested by American law officers, and was sentenced to gaol at Rochester for eighteen months for breach of the Neutrality Act. He served eleven months of his sentence and was then released. For several years after this he made a precarious livelihood in journalism.

WILLIAM LYON MACKENZIE

In 1849, through the Amnesty Act passed by the Baldwin-La Fontaine administration, Mackenzie secured pardon for the part he had taken in the rebellion. He returned from the United States, and once more entered political life. He was elected member for Haldimand, and spent seven more years in the legislature. But he was no longer the fiery agitator of former years. It was a different province to which he had come back. The old political evils against which he had fought had largely disappeared. How they had changed belongs to another story. He resigned his seat in 1858, and died three years later. And so ended a turbulent and misguided career, which was not, however, without good effect in improving the form of government in Upper Canada.

The Historic Sites and Monuments Board of Canada has recently placed a tablet on Postal Station K on Yonge Street, Toronto, the inscription of which reads as follows: "Site of Montgomery's Tavern. Original headquarters of William Lyon Mackenzie, leader in the Upper Canada Rebellion. Scene of brief skirmish on 7th December, 1837, resulting in defeat of insurgents by loyal militia commanded by Lieut.-Col. James Fitzgibbon. This uprising, an outcome of serious grievances against the dominant 'Family Compact,' was an important factor in bringing about the legislative union of Upper and Lower Canada in 1841, and the permanent establishment in Canada of responsible government, a principle then first extended to a British colony. Erected 1928."

XXXIII

LOUIS JOSEPH PAPINEAU

THE TRIBUNE OF LOWER CANADA

WHAT William Lyon Mackenzie was to Upper Canada, Louis Joseph Papineau was to Lower Canada. These two men, living in different parts of Canada during the same period, were much alike in many ways. They had the same enthusiasm for the cause they believed right, the same determination in pressing for the removal of wrongs, the same love of freedom, the same eloquence of speech, and the same lack of self-restraint in language and action. Both adopted the same unfortunate method to meet similar political conditions in the two provinces: they stirred up their followers to armed rebellion against the government. Both suffered years of exile from their country in consequence of their misguided policy; both were eventually pardoned and returned to political life in the provinces from which they had fled; both were in no small measure influential in bringing about the most important political reform that was ever needed in this country.

The Constitutional Act had produced practically the same conditions in Lower Canada as it had in Upper Canada. The legislative assembly, which represented the people, had no control over the executive and legislative councils, which were appointed by the crown. The measures passed by the assembly were continually thrown out by the council. Public offices were filled by favourites of the government. In addition to these grievances, which were the same in both provinces, there was in Lower Canada the further difficulty of nationality. The majority of the people were French, and hence the assembly was largely of that nationality. On the other hand, the councils were largely English, since the members were appointed by the British government. The bitterness of feeling between the assembly and the councils was thus intensified by racial differences.

Papineau, as a young man of twenty-six, was elected a member of the assembly. He soon became recognized as the leader in the fight against the injustice and corruption of the councils. He was chosen as Speaker, and continued in that office for many years. In 1822 a bill was introduced in the British parliament to unite Upper and Lower Canada in one province. Papineau feared that such a union would undermine the influence of the French people and make them subservient to the English. He went as a delegate to London to oppose the bill, and succeeded in stirring up enough opposition against it to secure its withdrawal before it was brought to a vote in the House.

Public Archives of Canada
LOUIS JOSEPH PAPINEAU

On his return to Canada he attacked the governor, Lord Dalhousie, who was disposed to be friendly towards the French. At length Dalhousie, stung by these attacks, refused to recognize Papineau as Speaker of the assembly. A petition was sent to London for the removal of the governor, and the request was granted. But it was not a change of governor so much as a change of government that was needed. Papineau made unceasing demand that the legislative council should be elective, that the French should have their fair share of public offices, and that the

Canadian National Railways.

QUEBEC: THE FORTRESS CLIFF.

assembly should have absolute control of the revenues of the province. The British government would not agree to an elective council, but offered the assembly complete control of the revenues if it would make permanent provision for the salaries of judges and other public officials. This concession Papineau refused to accept.

Papineau seems gradually to have lost faith in the willingness of the British government to redress the grievances of Lower Canada. He became more and more a passionate agitator against British institutions, and openly expressed his preference for the American form of government. He appears to have desired either the annexation of the province to the United States or the establishment of a republican form of government in the province. At any rate, the violence of his attacks upon the governor and the councils increased. He had a large and devoted following among the younger members of the assembly. Some who afterwards played conspicuous and honourable parts in the history of Canada were among his supporters, notably Georges E. Cartier, Louis H. Lafontaine, and Étienne P. Taché. But many of Papineau's former friends were disturbed by his disloyal speeches and turned against him. He also lost the support of the bishops and clergy of the Roman Catholic Church, who would not countenance any disloyalty to Britain.

The followers of Papineau called themselves "Patriots." In the summer of 1837 they began to hold meetings at various places in the province, particularly after the church services on Sunday, when large numbers of people were gathered together. At these meetings passionate speeches denouncing the government were made by the leaders. Riots took place in Montreal. The government ordered the arrest of Papineau, and he fled to the United States. A considerable body of "Patriots" assembled at St. Denis near the Richelieu, and fortified themselves so securely that they were able to repel an attack by loyalist troops. This success encouraged the "Patriots," and gave an impetus to the rebellion. An unfortunate incident at this time was the brutal murder of Lieutenant Weir, a loyalist officer, by some of the "Patriots." This action stirred the indignation of the loyalist volunteers, and their rallying cry in subsequent engagements was "Remember Jack Weir."

A few days later an attack was made upon the rebels at St. Charles, a few miles south of St. Denis. The rebels were badly led and poorly armed, and they were dispersed after forty of their number had been killed. This engagement really ended the rebellion in the region of the Richelieu. The "Patriots" disbanded, and most of their leaders fled to the United States, though one of the foremost, Dr. Wolfred Nelson, was captured and imprisoned in Montreal.

A more serious engagement occurred a few weeks later at St. Eustache, at the mouth of the Ottawa west of Montreal. Here a large number of rebels had assembled, and though urged by the parish priest to go quietly to their homes, they refused to disperse. About the middle of December Sir John Colborne led some volunteers against the rebels, who had taken possession of the church and fortified it against the loyalists. Severe fighting occurred, and at length the church was burned. Many of the rebels were shot down, and the homes of the people were pillaged and given over to the flames. This incident is another dark stain in the history of the rebellion. Colborne did not—perhaps could not—restrain his volunteers in their determination to avenge the murder of Lieutenant Weir.

The Lower Canadian rebellion of 1837 was now over, and had resulted in as complete a fiasco as its counterpart in Upper Canada. The rebels were neither adequately armed nor directed by experienced leaders. But the main causes of its failure were the ban of the Roman Catholic Church and the opposition of the majority of the French people.

The rebellions in Upper and Lower Canada awakened the British government to the necessity of doing something decisive with regard to political abuses in Canada. It resolved to appoint a commissioner to inquire into the causes of the disturbance and to suggest remedies for the difficulties. The man chosen for this task was John George Lambton, the Earl of Durham. He was a keen student of political affairs, with strong opinions and good judgment.

He had already held the responsible position of British ambassa_or at St. Petersburg. He arrived in Canada in 1838, and at once proclaimed a general amnesty, that is, a pardon of those who had taken part in the rebellions. He made, however, exceptions in the cases of twenty-four men. Eight of these were in prison in Canada, and sixteen were exiles in the United States. The latter were forbidden to return to Canada on pain of death. The eight prisoners were sent to Bermuda. This was a most generous method of dealing with the rebels. But Lord Durham's enemies in England and the opponents of the government there at once protested that his sentences were unjust and illegal. After a lengthy debate in the British parliament the sentences were annulled. Lord Durham believed that he had been given authority for what he had done, and strongly resented the action of the government. He at once resigned his commissionership and returned to England, after having been only five months in Canada.

In that brief period Lord Durham had gained a clearer insight than any Englishman before his time into the real political situation in Canada and the difficulties of the government. In his "Report on the Affairs of British North America," which he presented to the government of England in 1839, he ascribed the rebellion to two causes: first, the unfriendliness between the two great races in Canada; and second, the irresponsibility of the councils to the representatives of the people. The two main remedies that he proposed for these difficulties were: first, the union of Upper and Lower Canada as a means of bringing together the two races; and second, the establishment of responsible government by making the executive council answerable for its actions to the legislative assembly. It took several years to put Durham's wise recommendations into full effect, but when this was completely done the political difficulties that resulted in the rebellions disappeared.

Lord Durham had hardly left the shores of Canada when a second rebellion occurred. Some of the banished leaders returned and stirred up the *habitants* in the neighbourhood of the Richelieu with the hope of assistance from American sympathizers. When they found that no American aid was forthcoming, most of them returned to their homes. However, about 2,500, armed with pitchforks and pikes, gathered at Napierville. Sir John Colborne soon put the rabble to flight. The rebellion was over in a week. Twelve of the leaders were captured, tried, and executed.

Of Papineau there is little more to tell. After the rebellion he spent several years of exile in the United States and France, was pardoned, and returned to his native province. He was a member of the united parliament from 1847 till 1854, but wielded little influence even among his compatriots. He spent the last years of his life in retirement, and died in 1871.

XXXIV

LORD SYDENHAM

THE DIPLOMATIST OF THE UNION

LORD DURHAM was the statesman who diagnosed the disease which brought about the outbreaks in Upper and Lower Canada in 1837. It was he who also prescribed the remedy for the ills. However, it remained for other statesmen to see that the remedy was applied. The first of these was Charles Poulett Thomson, later Lord Sydenham, who came to Canada as governor-general in 1839. He soon found that the two Canadas were much like foolish children who do not want to take the doctor's medicine. They objected and grew stubborn; but at last, under the persuasive influence of the new governor, they consented to take the remedy which Lord Durham had prescribed. Before the governor's untimely death in 1841 both provinces were well on the way to recovery.

Charles Poulett Thomson was an English business man who had travelled extensively in Europe. Through his association with the people of many countries, he had learned to speak several languages, and had acquired polished and pleasing manners. His geniality, courtesy, and tact made friends for him wherever he went. He had made a special study of the trade conditions between European nations, and was soon regarded as an authority in that field. He was elected member of parliament first for Dover and later for Manchester, then as now one of the chief trade centres of England. His marked abilities soon won for him a place in the ministry of Lord Grey.

In 1839 he was offered the post of governor-general of Canada, and, believing that he would have an opportunity to render a great service to the Empire, he accepted the appointment. He was a friend of Lord Durham; he had studied his Report on the affairs of Canada, and he was convinced that the scheme set forth therein was the only cure for the situation. He came to Canada with the definite intention of bringing about the union of the two provinces

Public Archives of Canada
LORD SYDENHAM

as Lord Durham had advised. This was a task not easily accomplished, as events proved.

On his arrival at Quebec Thomson found that there was no government in operation in Lower Canada. Lord Durham had suspended the constitution the previous year. There was, however, a legislative council that had been appointed by Sir John Colborne. The governor called these men together, and readily obtained their consent to the principle of union. He then hurried to Toronto. There he found a

UNION ACCOMPLISHED

legislature indeed, but a legislature split into groups, each clamouring for something different. There seemed little prospect that a majority could be secured for any particular scheme. But the governor set himself to work. He met the members individually and privately. He argued, persuaded, cajoled. Gradually his personal charm and diplomacy won the day. A majority of the members were pledged to support the union.

Before the end of the year 1839 the governor had drafted the bill for the union of the provinces and had forwarded it to the British government. Fortunately he secured what Durham had failed to receive, the support of the authorities in England. The British parliament passed the Act of Union in 1840 along the lines that Thomson had advised. This Act provided that the two provinces, Upper and Lower Canada, should be united under one government, in which each province should have equal representation. The government was to consist of a legislative assembly of eighty-four members elected by the people, and a legislative council of forty members appointed by the crown. No definite provision was made as to responsible government, but the governor arranged that the assembly should have control of the public revenues on condition that it would provide for a permanent civil list, that is, for the payment of salaries to judges and other officials of the government.

In recognition of his services in bringing about the union, the British government made Thomson a peer, with the title "Baron Sydenham of Sydenham in Kent and Toronto in Canada."

In the autumn of 1840 there was an election campaign for the new legislative assembly. Sydenham was anxious that a majority of members should be elected who would be favourable to the union. He took an active part in the campaign. In Lower Canada he found the French strongly opposed to the union, as they feared that their nationality would be submerged. Nevertheless, the charming manners and tactful speeches of the governor were not without their effect upon the responsive French-Canadians, and he was everywhere received with cordiality. In Upper Canada his tour was a triumphal procession. He was accompanied from place to place by an escort of two or three hundred farmers with music, flags, and guns. He was especially delighted with the enthusiasm of the people for his candidates in the election. But he was impressed above all with the beauty and richness of the country. He paid justifiable tribute to Ontario when he wrote in a letter to a friend: "You can conceive of nothing finer. A climate certainly the best in North America—the most magnificent soil in the world—four feet of vegetable mould—the greater part of it admirably watered. In a word, there is land enough and capabilities enough for some millions of people and for one of the finest provinces in the world."

It is difficult for us in this day to understand how a governor-general of Canada could justifiably take an active part in a political campaign. We have become accustomed to the idea of his standing impartially aside, taking always the advice of his responsible ministers, and doing nothing of a political nature on his own authority. We must remember, however, that in Sydenham's time the principle of responsible government had not yet become established. Sydenham was working towards that goal, but he apparently felt that the country was not quite ready for it. It is perhaps fortunate that Canada had in those troublous times a benevolent despot to set things right. Had Sydenham not actively intervened in the situation, it is quite probable that the union would have broken up, and the two provinces would have been plunged into political chaos worse than before.

The elections of 1841 resulted in the return of a majority in favour of the union. Kingston was chosen as the capital of the united provinces. A hospital was made into a parliament building, and a warehouse was used for government offices. An old stone mansion facing Lake Ontario was fitted up for the governor's residence. Sydenham directed the legislation of the first session of the legislature and succeeded in having some useful laws passed.

Two other achievements besides the union stand to the credit of Sydenham. The first of these was the partial, though not complete, settlement of the Clergy Reserves question.

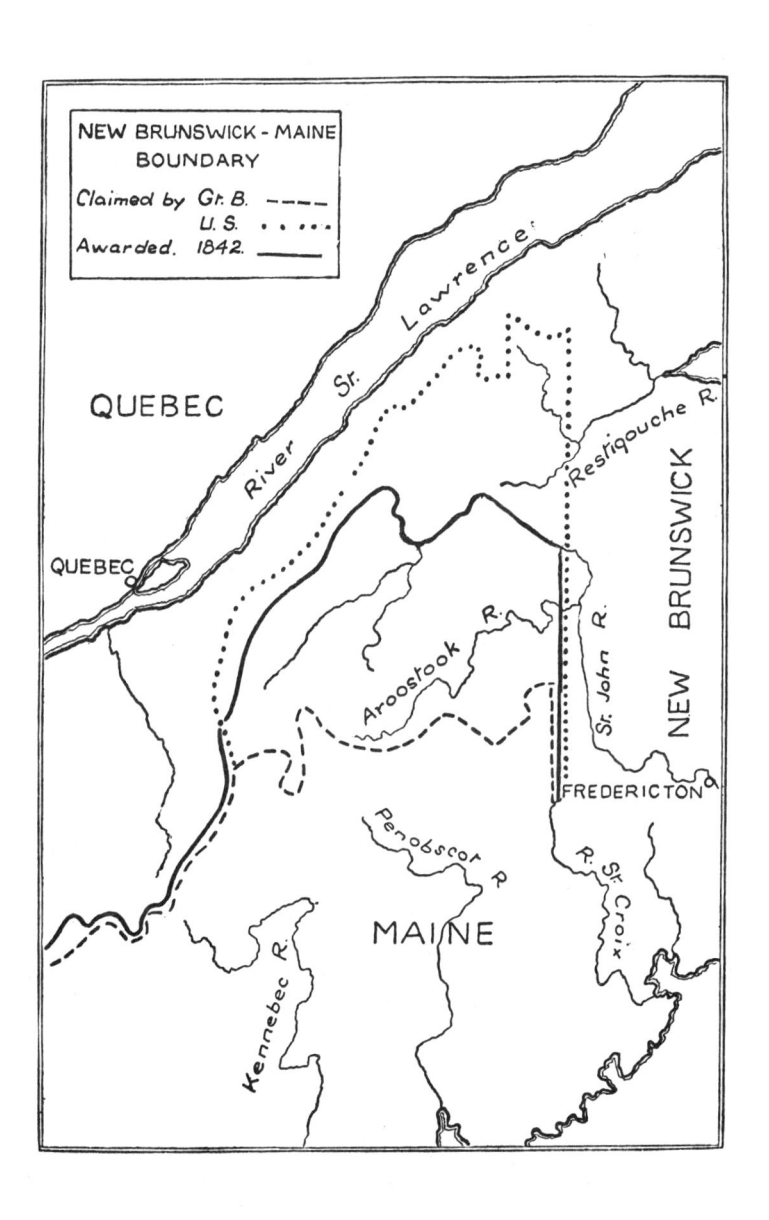

NEW BRUNSWICK - MAINE
BOUNDARY
Claimed by Gt. B. ----
U. S. . . . . .
Awarded. 1842. ———

It will be recalled that one of the clauses of the Constitutional Act of 1791 provided for setting aside one-eighth of the crown lands of Upper Canada for the support of a Protestant clergy. These lands were unoccupied and untaxed. They therefore hindered the settlement of the country and increased the settlers' taxes. All these lands were at first claimed by the Church of England. But other Protestant denominations claimed a share. The existence of the Clergy Reserves was therefore a cause of much bitterness in the province. Sydenham's plan of settlement was to sell the lands and to divide the income from the proceeds annually among the various Protestant denominations in proportion to the number of adherents. The plan was not wholly satisfactory to any of the interested parties, but the persuasive influence of the governor again carried the day. A bill embodying Sydenham's proposals was passed by the British parliament. The old sore was relieved, if not cured.

The second achievement of Sydenham was the foundation of municipal government. He had the country divided into small units, each of which was given power to manage its own local affairs through a council elected by the people. The people of each district were thus able to provide roads, drains, and bridges, by taxing themselves for these purposes. By this plan Sydenham conferred upon the country one of the most important means of self-government.

In addition to his many duties as governor of Canada at a critical period, Lord Sydenham was able to give some attention to the affairs of the other British colonies in America. His advice was sought upon the vexed question of the boundary between New Brunswick and Maine. He did not live to see the final settlement of this dispute, but during the negotiations his tact and diplomacy did much to avert serious consequences.

The dispute over the Maine boundary dated from 1783, when the American colonies were granted their independence. The clause of the treaty which defined the boundary between the new republic and the British colonies was very vague. It stated that the boundary was to be: (1) the St. Croix River; (2) a line north from the source of the St. Croix

THE MAINE BOUNDARY

to the highlands separating the rivers which flow into the St. Lawrence from those that flow into the Atlantic; (3) a line traced along this watershed to the 45th parallel of latitude; (4) the 45th parallel to the St. Lawrence; (5) the Great Lakes and rivers westward to the Lake of the Woods; (6) a line to the source of the Mississippi.

By an arrangement made in 1818 between Great Britain and the United States, the boundary from the Lake of the Woods to the Rocky Mountains was fixed at the 49th parallel of latitude. The boundary beyond the Rockies was not determined till 1846, when it was agreed to continue the 49th parallel as the dividing line to the Pacific.

The principal cause of difficulty lay in the vagueness of the definition of the boundary between Maine and New Brunswick. What river was meant by the St. Croix? At the time of the treaty of 1783 there was no such river. It was at length decided that the Schoodic River was meant. But the Schoodic had two branches. After some discussion, Britain agreed to accept the east branch as the boundary. Then there was doubt as to the location of the highlands specified in the treaty. It was found that the watershed separating the flow of the rivers into the Atlantic and into the St. Lawrence was a marshy plateau and not a range of hills. This, said Britain, could not be the highlands meant. A range of low hills farther south was claimed as the boundary by Britain. The matter was at one time referred to the King of the Netherlands as arbitrator. He made an award which was rejected by the United States.

The dispute very nearly ended in war at one stage. Lumbermen of Maine got into a quarrel with lumbermen of New Brunswick over their respective rights. Troops were sent to the scene by both sides, and only the good sense of the leaders averted a clash.

At last the question was referred to a commission consisting of Lord Ashburton, representing Britain, and Daniel Webster, representing the United States. As a result of the deliberations of the two commissioners, the Ashburton treaty was framed in 1842. This awarded seven thousand square miles of the disputed territory to Maine and five thousand to

New Brunswick, and fixed the present boundary line. It seemed at the time as if New Brunswick had been unfairly treated, and Lord Ashburton was roundly abused for sacrificing British interests. But, as a matter of fact, New Brunswick got nine hundred square miles more than had been assigned to her by the King of the Netherlands several years before. Maine was very much dissatisfied with the award, and was only appeased by a large grant of money from the federal government at Washington. It is now generally agreed by historians that the decision reached was a fair interpretation of the treaty of 1783, and that therefore neither party suffered unduly as a result of the award.

Besides determining the international boundary, the Ashburton treaty contained a section, drafted by Lord Sydenham the year before, providing for sending back for trial in their own country fugitives charged with certain crimes. This procedure is called *extradition*.

Having established the union of the two provinces upon a firm basis, Lord Sydenham felt that his mission in Canada was accomplished. His health had suffered under the heavy strain of his two years' work, and he asked to be recalled. But he was never to return to his home land. One morning while riding he was thrown from his horse and one of his legs was broken. He contracted lockjaw, and after two weeks of intense suffering he died. On his death-bed he composed the speech with which he hoped to close the session of the legislature. The last words of this speech formed a prayer for the welfare of the country for which he had done so much: "May Almighty God bless your labours, and pour down upon this province all those blessings which in my heart I am desirous it should enjoy."

XXXV

ROBERT BALDWIN

THE GREAT REFORMER

To Robert Baldwin, more perhaps than to any other man, is due the credit for the establishment of responsible government in Canada. To attain this was the purpose that dominated his political career. So strongly and constantly did he strive to establish the principle of ministerial responsibility that he has been called "a man with but one idea." Since Baldwin's day the government has always been answerable to the people for its acts, that is, the government may at any time be removed from office by the vote of the representatives of the people in the legislature. Since his day no governor has presumed to take any political action except upon the advice of his responsible ministers.

Robert Baldwin was born in the town of York, now Toronto, in 1804. He attended Dr. Strachan's grammar school, and was head boy in his class. He was not a brilliant student, but what he lacked in cleverness he made up in industry and perseverance. He took up the study of law and was called to the bar. At the age of twenty-five he was elected member of the legislature of Upper Canada for the constituency of York. At that time William Lyon Mackenzie was in the midst of his fight against the Family Compact. Baldwin sympathized with Mackenzie in his aims, but would never countenance the violent measures that he took to gain his ends. Baldwin was soon recognized as one of the leaders of the moderate Reformers, who would take no part in the rebellion of 1837, and who tried to dissuade the extremists from their rash and ill-fated enterprise. He stood sorrowfully aside while hot-headed friends made wreck of a just cause by a foolish resort to arms.

When the rebellion was over and the union of the provinces accomplished, Lord Sydenham, the governor, invited Baldwin to be a member of his executive council. Baldwin accepted, but later, when he found that Sydenham did not intend to give a full measure of responsible government, he resigned. He had the satisfaction soon afterwards of seeing his great scheme adopted. He was invited in 1842 by Sir Charles Bagot, the governor who followed Lord Sydenham, to form a government. He joined with Louis H. LaFontaine, one of the French leaders, and selected his colleagues from the members of the assembly, thus forming the first responsible ministry in Canada. Sir Charles Bagot died the next year, and was succeeded by Sir Charles Metcalfe. The latter was an honest and well-meaning man, but because of his experience and training as an administrator in India and Jamaica, he was unsuited for the position as governor of a self-governing colony. He was strongly opposed to the system of responsible government, and was immediately in conflict with the ministry, which soon resigned. In the election that followed, the governor threw himself with great vigour into the campaign, and succeeded in persuading the people to elect a majority of members opposed to the Reformers. For the moment the cause for which Baldwin had fought seemed lost. However, it proved to be only a temporary reverse. This was the last election in Canada in which a governor took an active part. The

Public Archives of Canada
ROBERT BALDWIN

THE GREAT MINISTRY

feeling of the people was aroused so strongly against Metcalfe that he was recalled.

A year later Britain sent out the Earl of Elgin, a Scottish nobleman, who proved to be one of the best governors that Canada ever had, though for a time he was most unpopular. He had high ideals of government, and determined to conduct himself as a constitutional governor, that is, to act upon the advice of his responsible ministers.

In 1847, after the defeat of the existing government, Lord Elgin asked Robert Baldwin to form a ministry. In conjunction with his French-Canadian colleague, LaFontaine, Baldwin formed what is known in Canadian history as "The Great Administration," because of the high character of its members and the important measures that it brought about. It lasted till 1851. One of the most valuable things that it did was to pass the Municipal Corporations Act in 1849, giving to the counties and the townships, villages, towns, and cities of Upper Canada a system of municipal government which permitted them to manage their own local affairs. Baldwin took the Municipal Act of Lord Sydenham's time and changed and extended it so as to suit existing conditions. The best tribute that can be paid to this Act is that the municipal institutions which Baldwin set up remain to-day in practically the same form.

The rebellion of 1837–38 had caused the loss of considerable property to many people in Lower Canada. Buildings and crops had been damaged or destroyed, and cattle and food supplies had been seized during the progress of the struggle. Naturally, those who had suffered in this way through no fault of their own looked to the government to make good their losses. Accordingly, in 1849, the Baldwin-LaFontaine government introduced the Rebellion Losses Bill to provide for the compensation of these people.

Great excitement and resentment was aroused throughout the country. The cry went forth that rebels were to be paid as well as loyalists. Strong protests and demonstrations against the bill were made in many places. Nevertheless, in the face of a public opinion strongly opposed to it, the bill was passed by the assembly. Then many people looked to the governor to disallow the bill, or at least to refer it to the home government. But Lord Elgin held that, as a constitutional governor, he was bound to accept the advice of his ministers, and he accordingly gave his assent. An excited mob broke into the parliament buildings at Montreal, drove out the members, smashed the windows and furniture, and set fire to the place. The buildings, including a valuable library, were completely destroyed. Lord Elgin was publicly insulted, his carriage was pelted with stones and he narrowly escaped serious bodily injury in the streets. Such was the price he paid for being a constitutional governor.

The excitement died down as quickly as it had arisen. The burning of the legislative buildings and the atrocious treatment given to the queen's representative had a sobering effect upon the people. And later, when it was seen how fairly the distribution of the money voted by the government for the compensation of losses was carried out, the people realized how inexcusable had been the disturbances.

This event marks the complete establishment of responsible government in this country. Lord Elgin, first among the governors of Canada, set the seal of his approval upon the principle of ministerial responsibility. Robert Baldwin, first among Canadian statesmen, succeeded in having the principle given practical effect. The long struggle, carrying in its train the two rebellions of 1837-38 and the riots of 1849, was at an end. Henceforth the right of the Canadian people to govern themselves through their elected representatives was never to be questioned.

But the disturbances in Montreal cost that city the honour of being the capital of Canada. For several years after the burning of the parliament buildings the legislature met alternately at Toronto and Quebec, spending four years at each place. In 1858 Queen Victoria chose as capital Ottawa, a small lumber city on the river of the same name. It had the advantage of central location at a distance from the American border. It had, moreover, a very picturesque situation on a commanding bluff of the river, thus lending itself to the beautification that a national capital demands.

The little lumber hamlet of seventy years ago has been transformed into a stately city, a capital of which all Canadians should be justly proud. Parliament met in Ottawa for the first time in 1865.

His great purpose of establishing responsible government having been achieved, Baldwin soon grew weary of political life. His party became divided, and he felt that the leadership was passing from him. He resigned from the government in 1851, and spent the remainder of his days in retirement in Toronto. The great Reformer died in 1858, at the early age of fifty-four.

XXXVI

SIR LOUIS LAFONTAINE

FRENCH-CANADIAN STATESMAN AND JURIST

No story of the political life of Robert Baldwin would be complete without reference to his friend and colleague, Louis H. LaFontaine. What Baldwin was to Upper Canada, LaFontaine was to Lower Canada. Mackenzie and Papineau in their respective provinces had fought against the abuses of the government and had unwisely resorted to force of arms; Baldwin and LaFontaine also struggled to secure reforms, but wisely brought them to effect by force of argument and persuasion. Next to Sir Georges Cartier and Sir Wilfrid Laurier, Sir Louis LaFontaine exercised the greatest influence of all French-Canadians upon the political life of Canada.

LaFontaine was born in 1807, the son of a farmer. As a student at college he was remarkable for his mental alertness and for his independence of thought. Like Baldwin, he studied law, and at an early age was elected to the legislature of his province. He was one of the younger members that gathered around Papineau and became imbued with his political ideals. But LaFontaine was rather a supporter than a follower, for he was too clear-headed to be carried away by the extravagant proposals of the fiery agitator. Nevertheless, his constitutional soberness of mind did not prevent him from making violent speeches, which he lived to regret later. However, he strongly opposed Papineau's counsels to resort to arms, and did his best to dissuade his compatriots from open rebellion. When he saw that his effort in this direction was futile, he thought it wise to leave the country for a time, and he spent two years in England and France.

AN INFLUENTIAL LEADER 215

In 1838 LaFontaine returned to Canada, and was placed under arrest for being implicated in the violent disturbances of the previous year. There was no excuse for this action, for he had not taken any part in the disorders. He was presently released without trial. From that moment the French-Canadians turned from Papineau and looked to LaFontaine to lead them out of the political wilderness in which they had wandered for more than forty years.

LaFontaine was opposed to the union of the two Canadas. In his public addresses he protested against the proposal to give Lower Canada the same number of representatives in the assembly as Upper Canada, though its population was considerably larger. He also objected strongly to making English the only official language of the legislature, claiming that French should be placed on a plane of equality with English. Lord Sydenham, the governor, who was anxious to conciliate those who were opposed to the union, offered him a position in his cabinet as solicitor-general for Lower Canada, but the offer was declined. However, once the union was accomplished, LaFontaine with fine patriotism set to work to make it a success. But for his strong influence among the French the union might have been wrecked.

Public Archives of Canada
SIR LOUIS LAFONTAINE

In the new parliament elected after the union he was without a seat, having been defeated in his own constituency of Terrebonne. However, through the intervention of

Baldwin he was soon afterwards elected for one of the Yorks, and thus took his seat as a French-Canadian member for an exclusively English-speaking constituency in Upper Canada. He soon became recognized as a leader of the moderate French-speaking Reformers. He supported Baldwin in his demand for responsible government. He was invited in 1842 to a seat in the cabinet of Sir Charles Bagot, but he declined to accept it, realizing that this cabinet was in no sense a responsible ministry.

Later in the same year, at the governor's request, he joined with Baldwin in the formation of the first ministry chosen from the members of the assembly, the first responsible government in Canada. In the election that followed, the Reformers were successful, though Baldwin was defeated in York. LaFontaine promptly found him a seat in Rimouski, thus returning a service that Baldwin had done him a short time before.

From 1842 to 1851 LaFontaine was closely associated with Baldwin in all the political activities of the united provinces. As a member of the great administration of 1847, he shared with his colleague the honours of its achievements. He constantly strove to secure recognition of the rights of his race in language, laws, and parliamentary representation. Largely through his influence the French language was placed on an equality with English in the parliament of Canada. At the same time he united with Baldwin in the constant effort to bring about a better understanding and more friendly relationship between the two great races of Canada.

Weary of political life, LaFontaine resigned from the ministry in 1851 at the same time as Baldwin. Shortly afterwards he was appointed chief justice of Lower Canada, and filled the position for many years with distinguished ability. In recognition of his outstanding political services, he was created a baronet by Queen Victoria in 1854, thus attaining a distinction rarely conferred on Canadians in those days. He died in 1864, and his name is held in honour as a great Reformer not only by his compatriots, but also by all English-speaking Canadians.

TWOFOLD ACCOMPLISHMENT

Sir Louis LaFontaine was a man of striking personality and commanding presence. In appearance he resembled Napoleon Bonaparte, and the likeness was frequently commented upon by the French people when he visited France.

On Parliament Hill in Ottawa, on the brow of the bluff overlooking the river, stands a striking memorial to the two great statesmen, Baldwin and LaFontaine, whose united efforts did much to establish responsible government on a firm basis and to harmonize and bring into closer sympathy the English-speaking and the French-speaking citizens of Canada.

XXXVII

BISHOP STRACHAN

EDUCATOR, CHURCHMAN, AND STATESMAN

FEW men in Canada have had so great an influence in so many fields as the Rev. Dr. John Strachan, the first Anglican bishop of Toronto. He was first a great schoolmaster who had much to do in promoting higher education in Upper Canada; he was later a clergyman and bishop who was responsible in no small degree for laying the foundation of the influence of the Anglican church in the religious life of the province; and he was a statesman who exerted considerable power in the troubled political conditions of his time.

John Strachan was born in humble circumstances in Aberdeen in Scotland in 1778. When the boy was sixteen years of age, his father, who worked in the quarries, was killed in an explosion. The burden of supporting the family then fell largely upon John as the oldest member. He secured work as a private tutor and studied hard in his spare moments. In this way he was able to assist his family and at the same time to obtain a degree from King's College, Aberdeen. The hard experiences of his early life made him a strong man, but not a gentle one; they made him intolerant of the failures and weaknesses of humanity, a characteristic that remained until age had laid its mellowing influence upon him.

It was about this time that Governor Simcoe was planning to bring about better educational conditions in Upper Canada. He had in mind the establishment of grammar schools for the education of gentlemen's sons, and as soon as possible the founding of a provincial university. He had inquiries made to secure a young man from the Old Land

A FAMOUS SCHOOLMASTER

who would be capable of undertaking the work. John Strachan was selected for the task. He was now twenty-one years of age, and he set out from Scotland with high hopes of accomplishing a great educational work in the new colony.

After a long and stormy voyage he reached Canada, only to find that Governor Simcoe had resigned his post and had returned to England without making any arrangements for the great work that Strachan was expected to do. The young man was very much depressed. "If I had had twenty pounds in my pocket," he afterwards told a friend, "I should have returned to Scotland immediately. But in truth I had not so much as twenty shillings. So I had to stay."

He found employment in the home of Mr. Cartwright in Kingston, teaching his boys and those of several neighbouring families. Here he spent three years in congenial work amid pleasant companionship. He devoted his spare time to the study of theology, and was ordained as a priest in the Anglican church. He was appointed to the parish at Cornwall, where, in addition to his church duties, he carried on a grammar school which soon became famous. Many men who were leaders in the political life of the province at a later time were educated at this school. Strachan was an excellent teacher, and exerted a profound influence upon the boys in his charge.

Public Archives of Canada
BISHOP STRACHAN

In the course of a few years Dr. Strachan was asked to take charge of the parish of York and of a grammar school there. Though loath to leave the congenial atmosphere of Cornwall, he was prevailed upon to accept the invitation.

These were the days of the war with the United States. On the voyage from Cornwall to York the captain of the boat upon which he had taken passage with his family sighted what he took to be an American war vessel. The captain was so overcome with fear that Dr. Strachan himself took command of the situation, and ordered the single gun with which the boat was equipped to be made ready for defence. Fortunately, the strange vessel proved to be Canadian and no engagement was necessary, but the incident illustrates the fearless character of the man.

At York, during the troublous years of the war, Dr. Strachan was of great assistance to the British. He was the friend and adviser of Brock and was active in providing for the comfort and relief of the sick and wounded. After the fort was captured by the Americans in 1813, General Dearborn was angered because some of his men had been killed in an explosion for which he blamed the Canadians. "The town shall smoke for this," he said. When Dr. Strachan heard of this decision he went boldly to Dearborn, and, pointing out that the explosion had been an accident, he forcibly forbade the general to burn the town. Whether the American was cowed by the wrath of the fiery Scot or was convinced by his argument of the injustice of such an act will never be known, but at any rate the town was not given over to the flames.

In 1834 Canada was visited by a dreadful scourge, the cholera. The disease was brought by immigrants from Europe, and swept through the towns and villages, carrying off hundreds of people. In York whole families were wiped out. The people were in a panic. Dr. Strachan went in and out among them, comforting and relieving the stricken and steadying the survivors by his courage. He took charge of the situation, and with military sternness dictated the measures of relief that should be taken. No task was too menial for him to perform, no danger too great for him to face. When at last the plague was stayed, the people realized that but for the heroism and endurance of Dr. Strachan the toll of death would have been greater.

During the long struggle between the Family Compact

A FOUNDER OF UNIVERSITIES

and the Reformers, Dr. Strachan sided with the former, and his attacks upon his opponents were frequent and forcible. In particular, he was strongly opposed to their proposals to do away with the Clergy Reserves, and maintained the exclusive right of the Anglican church to these lands. He was offered a seat in the executive council by the governor, and accepted it, thinking that in this way he would be better able to maintain what he believed to be the rights of his church. The most useful thing that he did during this period was to secure money for the establishment of grammar schools at various points in the province. In this way he did a great deal to advance the cause of education in those pioneer days.

In 1827 Dr. Strachan was able to realize partially his long dream of establishing a provincial university. He went to England and secured from the British parliament a charter for King's College. Among the provisions of the charter was one to the effect that the professors were to be members of the Anglican church and accept all its doctrines. There was much opposition in the legislature to this proposal. It was not till 1843, after the provisions of the charter had been greatly modified, that the college was opened. Six years later, largely at the instance of Robert Baldwin, it was removed entirely from the influence of the Anglican church, and its name was changed to the University of Toronto. Baldwin had been one of Strachan's pupils and greatly admired his old master, but he felt that the provincial university should be secularized.

Dr. Strachan was so indignant at this action, which he regarded as little short of the robbery of his church, that he at once set about the establishment of another college where its doctrines would be observed and taught. Although now an old man, he proceeded to England and secured a charter for another university. With tireless energy he made a canvass for subscriptions among his friends, and on his return to Canada successfully established in 1852 Trinity University, an institution that flourished for many years, and to-day forms a unit in the federation known as the University of Toronto.

In the meantime, in 1839, he had been appointed the first Anglican bishop of Toronto. He laboured hard for many years, setting up new churches, holding confirmation services, and preaching in all the settled parts of the province. He continued this work with undiminished vigour till he was well over eighty years of age. The death of his beloved wife, with whom he had lived happily for nearly sixty years, was a great blow to him. Soon afterwards it was evident that his physical powers were failing. He died in 1865 at the age of eighty-seven, and was buried beneath the chancel of St. James' Cathedral, the church he had built in Toronto. He was mourned by all classes of people, who felt that a great man had gone.

The year 1927 was a red-letter year in university affairs in Ontario. It marked the centenary of the University of Toronto and the seventy-fifth anniversary of the founding of Trinity University. In the celebrations that marked these events, the name of Bishop Strachan, the founder of both of these great institutions of learning, was duly honoured.

John Strachan is a shining example of a poor boy who rose to a high and influential position by dint of perseverance and determination. In three fields, education, religion, and politics, he has left his mark upon the history of Canada. Though many people disagreed with his views on religious and political questions, it was universally recognized that his industry, his energy, his courage, his moral strength, and his religious zeal were worthy of all admiration.

XXXVIII

DR. EGERTON RYERSON

THE FOUNDER OF A GREAT SCHOOL SYSTEM

BESIDE the name of Bishop Strachan in the roll of Upper Canadian educators and statesmen should be placed that of Dr. Egerton Ryerson. The two men were alike in many respects. Both began life as schoolmasters; both later entered the Christian ministry, the one the Anglican, the other the Methodist; both played important parts in determining the educational policy of the province; both founded colleges that are still in active operation; both had much to do at one time or other in moulding political opinion. The two men lived at the same time and were active forces in Upper Canada for many years. Though their views were opposite on many questions, and though they were for many years engaged in bitter controversy, they agreed in their desire to promote the educational and religious welfare of the people of their province.

Egerton Ryerson was born in Norfolk County in 1803. He came of United Empire Loyalist stock, a fact of which he was always very proud. His father emigrated from New Jersey, first to New Brunswick and later to Upper Canada. In the war of 1812 the elder Ryerson was a colonel in command of a body of militia, and saw active service on the Niagara frontier. Young Egerton was sent to the common school, but received most of his early education from his mother. Later he was sent to a grammar school, and made such rapid progress that at the age of sixteen he acted for some time as a teacher in the school.

At an early age he became an ardent member of the Methodist church. His father, who was an Anglican, was so

DR. EGERTON RYERSON

much displeased that he gave the boy the choice of either giving up the Methodist church or leaving home. He chose the latter alternative, and, much to his mother's sorrow, he went to the London District grammar school, where he secured a position as teacher. Here he spent two years filled with hard work. One day his father appeared at the school and asked him to go home to help carry on the work of the farm. It was characteristic of the young man that he did not hesitate in carrying out what he felt to be his duty. He left the classroom and returned to the home from which he had been turned in anger two years before.

For some years young Ryerson carried on the laborious work of the farm and studied as well. He had determined to enter the ministry of the Methodist church. So he ploughed and sowed and reaped in the fields all day, and read Latin and Greek far into the night. His unremitting toil early and late brought on an attack of brain fever, which nearly ended his days. He recovered, however, and at the age of twenty-two he was admitted to the ministry of his church.

Public Archives of Canada

DR. EGERTON RYERSON

His first circuit was in the Niagara peninsula. He rode from place to place on horseback, preaching several times a week, and often preparing his sermons on the road. He was later transferred to a circuit at York. In a few years he became one of the recognized leaders of the Methodist church. When it was proposed to establish a church paper, Ryerson was chosen as editor. Thus the *Christian Guardian*, the organ of that great religious body, was founded. Through

EDUCATIONAL LEADERSHIP 225

its columns Ryerson assailed with great vigour the claims of Bishop Strachan and his supporters that the Anglican church had the exclusive right to the Clergy Reserves.

In 1835 it was felt that the Methodist church should have a college of its own. Ryerson went to England to secure a charter and to obtain subscriptions for its establishment. He succeeded in both missions, and thus the Methodist body was able to set up Victoria University, which was first located at Cobourg. Many years later it was transferred to Toronto, where it is still a flourishing institution and an important unit in the federation of the University of Toronto.

While Ryerson was in England he wrote several letters to *The Times*, combating the views that William Lyon Mackenzie was spreading throughout the country on the political issues in Upper Canada. He was thus able to give the English people a more accurate idea of the real situation in the province. He pointed out that Mackenzie's views tended to republicanism, and meant the separation of Canada from the Mother Country. Ryerson wrote constantly in the columns of his own paper against the opinions and tactics of Mackenzie, and doubtless influenced on the side of loyalty many people who otherwise might have joined the malcontents in the ill-starred rebellion of 1837.

Ryerson assisted Lord Durham by making several valuable suggestions for his famous Report. He was friendly with Lord Sydenham and Sir Charles Bagot, and he supported Sir Charles Metcalfe in his campaign against responsible government, thus making what many people believe to have been the greatest mistake of his life. In 1844 he was appointed by Metcalfe as Chief Superintendent of Education for Upper Canada. It was in that capacity that Ryerson accomplished the great work for which he most deserves to be remembered.

At this time, it should be noted, the people of Upper Canada had poor opportunities to secure an education for their children. The common schools were not well distributed, and there were few grammar schools. They were given little assistance by the government, and were supported largely by the people who sent their children to them, that is, they were fee schools. The teachers were untrained and often ill-educated. There were no textbooks. The task that Dr. Ryerson had to undertake was to mould this inadequate provision for the training of the children into a systematic scheme of education for the province.

In preparation for this task he made a tour of the United States, Great Britain and Ireland, and continental Europe, visiting schools and studying the various systems of education in operation in these countries. He selected from what he saw the details that he thought suited to a country in the pioneer stage, and added other features of his own. In 1846 he presented his report, which was adopted by the legislature. His scheme, though it has been extended and modified in many respects, is practically the system of education that Ontario has to-day. It provided for the division of the townships into small units, called school sections, each of which was to provide its own school and engage its own teacher. Provision was also made for a supply of textbooks and for the training of teachers in a normal school to be established in Toronto. Higher education was provided through the extension of the grammar-school system. The scheme was well suited to the conditions of the time and secured general approval.

Ryerson was unable to realize his ideal completely in the beginning. He had a vision of education for all provided at public expense. He was unable for many years to persuade either the legislature or the people that the state owed an education to every child, and that this should be financed from public funds. Most people clung to the belief that the education of the children was the responsibility of their parents, and that those who had no children should not be required to help to pay for the education of other people's children. Ryerson did not direct his campaign wholly from his office in Toronto. He went up and down the country addressing public meetings and preaching with great earnestness the doctrine of free and compulsory education. Gradually the people began to accept the idea, and before his work was finished Ryerson had succeeded in putting all the elementary schools on a free basis. The principle has been extended since his time, and to-day a free elementary and secondary education in public, separate, high, technical, and normal schools is available to every child in Ontario.

Dr. Ryerson remained in the service of the government as Superintendent of Education for thirty-two years. He retired in 1876, and devoted his time for several years to finishing a voluminous history of the United Empire Loyalists, on which he had devoted his spare moments for some time before his retirement. He died in 1882. He will always be remembered in Ontario as an earnest preacher of Methodism and a vigorous controversialist, but above all as the founder of the educational system of the province.

XXXIX

SIR JAMES DOUGLAS

THE FOUNDER OF BRITISH COLUMBIA

AMONG the builders of Canada, Sir James Douglas deservedly occupies a high position. It was largely due to his work and influence west of the Rocky Mountains in the middle of the last century that the great territory that now forms the province of British Columbia remained under the British flag and did not pass into the possession of the United States. He maintained law and order there at a difficult period, established a settled government, and held the country loyal to the British crown.

As his name might suggest, James Douglas was of Scottish origin. He came to the Canadian West at an early age and entered the service of the North-West Company, a Scottish fur-trading organization, and the bitter rival of the Hudson's Bay Company. When the two companies at length joined forces in 1821, he continued in the service of the united organization.

Douglas was a tall, swarthy man of great bodily strength and endurance. "The Black Douglas" his friends called him, because of his resemblance in many respects to his great Scottish namesake. He was cool in the presence of danger, resourceful in difficulty, and masterful in the management of men. His devotion to duty, his grasp of detail, and his ability in organization won the favour of the officials of the Company, and he rose rapidly in the service. His career reminds one of that of Lord Strathcona in the same service at a later time.

Douglas was soon chief agent west of the Rockies in charge of an important post, Fort St. James, near the head of

INFLUENCE AMONG INDIANS

the Fraser River. Here he had opportunity to exercise his ability in managing the fickle Indians of the Pacific coast. Weakness, unfairness, or lack of tact in his dealings with them would have been fatal. But his unwavering courage and his strict integrity won the confidence and obedience of these savage tribes. As a result there were no Indian atrocities west of the Rockies such as were committed in the white settlements of the western States during the same period. The reason was that Douglas inspired in the savages a wholesome fear of punishment and a firm belief in his honesty and fairness. His methods recall those of Frontenac in dealing with the Iroquois at an earlier period. Two incidents of widely different character will illustrate these methods.

Two Indians had murdered two employees of the Hudson's Bay Company. One of the murderers was immediately caught, tried and hanged.

Public Archives of Canada
SIR JAMES DOUGLAS

The other escaped and could not be found. Some months later he ventured back to the fort. Word of his presence in the neighbourhood was brought to Douglas, who set out forthwith to arrest the man. He found the Indian hiding beneath a pile of camp equipment. He seized the skulking victim by the hair of the head, dragged him forth, and despatched him on the spot with his own hands. Such "wild justice," swift and relentless, taught the savages that the chief agent of the Company was not a man to be trifled with.

The other incident has a pleasanter flavour. The great governor of the Company, Sir George Simpson, was about to pay his annual visit to the fort. For his reception Douglas staged a spectacle, partly because the Indians liked a show, and partly because the governor liked to be received ceremoniously. To the booming of cannon and the beating of drums, a company in brilliant uniforms, headed by Douglas, rode out of the fort. A mile or so away the governor, with a still more resplendent retinue, was received with due demonstration. Then to the skirl of the bagpipes the cavalcade wound its way in impressive procession back to the fort. The red-men were on hand in great numbers to see the parade and to participate in the festivities that followed. By such means the savages were impressed with the greatness and power of the Company of which Douglas was the representative.

Later, Douglas was located at Fort Vancouver on the Columbia River, which had become the most important post of the Company on the Pacific coast. From here he went to look for a suitable site on Vancouver Island for the erection of a fort to control the trade of that rich region. He chose a spot at the southern end of the island where stood an Indian village. Here he found a good harbour for ships, a plentiful supply of fresh water, and a mild and pleasant climate. The Indians were friendly, and gave willing assistance in the erection of the fort. Douglas, ever honest in his dealings with them, gave blankets in payment for their work. The timbers of the houses and fences were put together with wooden pegs, not a single nail being driven in the whole construction. By the end of the summer of 1843 the buildings and stockades were finished, and fifty men were living in the fort. Thus came into being Fort Victoria—named after the young queen who had a few years before ascended the throne of Britain. Fort Victoria soon became the most important post of the Company on the Pacific coast.

At this time there was a question as to the ownership of the wide region west of the Rockies in which the Hudson's Bay Company was operating. It was known as the Oregon

NEW BOUNDARY FIXED

territory, and it extended from the northern boundary of California in latitude 42° to the southern boundary of Alaska in latitude 54° 40′. Both Britain and the United States could properly make some pretensions to ownership on the score of exploration. Cook, Vancouver, Mackenzie, Fraser, and Thompson had made explorations in the northern part; while the Americans, Gray, Lewis, and Clark, had made explorations in the southern part. From the point of view of settlement the United States had rather the better claim to the region, for while thousands of Americans had poured across the mountains, few British, except the Hudson's Bay traders, had come into the territory.

Britain wished to divide the disputed territory at the Columbia River; the United States wanted the whole of it. The cry "Fifty-four-forty or fight" was raised by the Americans, and the president of the United States was anxious to go to war with Great Britain over the question. Fortunately, at the moment the United States became involved in a war with Mexico, and Britain did not believe that the territory was worth fighting for. So the storm blew over, and a compromise was reached upon the question in 1846. By the Oregon Treaty, the 49th parallel was to be the boundary from the Rockies to the Pacific, and the whole of Vancouver Island was to belong to Britain.

In 1849 the British government handed over the control of Vancouver Island to the Hudson's Bay Company on the condition that settlers were to be encouraged to take up the land. James Douglas was made governor. Soon there was trouble between the Indians and the colonists. One of the latter was murdered. Douglas compelled the immediate surrender of the murderers, who were hanged forthwith in the presence of their astonished tribesmen. This salutary lesson doubtless saved the colonists from extermination.

In 1851 the colonists petitioned for a representative government, a request which the home government readily granted. There were only a few voters in the colony, but they elected seven men to represent them in the legislature. Soon afterwards Governor Douglas opened the first Canadian parliament west of the Rockies, with a speech from the throne and some of the pomp that attends the opening of the mother of parliaments at Westminster.

In 1857 gold was discovered in the valley of the Fraser. At once there was a rush of gold-seekers from California, most of whom came by way of Victoria. The city was transformed in a few weeks by the resulting inflow of population. In 1858 nearly 30,000 people were living there, and Victoria had its first "boom." Speculators made fortunes in real estate. Over two hundred houses were built in a single month. Fifty-dollar lots sold for fifty times that price. Food became scarce, and flour brought fifty dollars a barrel. A gold stampede always brings together a great many lawless people, and to maintain order under such circumstances is a difficult task. But Governor Douglas was equal to the occasion. He upheld the dignity of the law with great firmness, and made life and property safe under most difficult conditions.

Naturally all the miners could not make rich strikes in the diggings. Many of them returned discouraged to California. Victoria became a city of empty houses. Real estate slumped and hundreds were ruined. Many of the miners who remained in the goldfields became rich. Half a million dollars' worth of gold was taken out the first year. A richer field was discovered in the Cariboo district farther north in the following year, and a similar rush took place to that region. Many of the miners remained permanently and formed the beginning of a colony.

Governor Douglas went into the goldfields and set up the machinery for maintaining law and order. He built up a system of roads so that goods could be transported in and out. This made it possible for the people to live at a reasonable cost. His commission as governor of Vancouver Island did not give him the authority to do all this; but, when the British government found out the good work he had accomplished, it proclaimed the territory a new colony under the name of British Columbia and made Douglas governor. A representative government was set up similar to that at Victoria, and a capital was established at New Westminster.

AN INTERNATIONAL FLURRY

All this was not accomplished without difficulty. The people were practically all Americans. The goods they bought, the newspapers they read, and the money they used were almost exclusively American. The Canadian provinces were two thousand miles away, and there was no means of communication with them except through the United States. Under such conditions the wonder is that the country did not become American. That Douglas was able to mould it into a loyal British colony is a tribute to his sagacity as a statesman.

In 1859 Douglas was one of the central figures in an international flurry over a trifling episode that might have had serious consequences. Near Vancouver is the little island of San Juan, the ownership of which was not settled by the Oregon Treaty of 1846. Both British and American citizens were living on the island. It happened one day that a British pig trespassed on an American garden and was killed by the owner of the garden. This started a quarrel in which citizens of both nations participated. It was reported that Governor Douglas was coming to seize the American offender and carry him off to Victoria for trial. A battalion of American soldiers was rushed to San Juan. A British squadron was lying in readiness at Victoria. Fortunately the governor remained cool in the face of an ugly situation. A sane American general arrived on the scene, and he and Douglas came to a peaceful understanding. It was agreed that the island should be jointly occupied until the rightful ownership could be determined by arbitration. And so two great nations were saved the humiliation of having to go to war over a dead pig. The possession of San Juan Island was not decided for several years. The question was finally referred to the Emperor of Germany as arbitrator. In 1872 he awarded the island to the United States.

Governor Douglas was knighted by Queen Victoria in 1863 in token of his great services as a pioneer statesman. He retired from the governorship the following year, and the people of all classes vied with each other in doing him honour. Two years later British Columbia and Vancouver Island were united under one government with Victoria as capital. Sir James Douglas was in retirement when British Columbia entered the Canadian confederation in 1871, but there can be no doubt that this step was largely due to the British sentiment that he had cultivated in the people of the province for so many years.

He died in Victoria in 1877 at the age of seventy-four.

XL

SIR JOHN A. MACDONALD

THE MASTER BUILDER

WHAT name stands highest in the roll of Canada's statesmen? This question would probably have but one answer from most Canadians, and the answer would be given without hesitation, "Sir John A. Macdonald." No other statesman has so captured the imagination of the Canadian people. Among those of his political faith he was ever a popular idol, and among his political opponents his greatness was unquestioned. His name is a symbol of Canadian loyalty to the Empire, and even yet serves as a rallying cry for the political party of which he was the head. He had his share of human weaknesses, but these are forgotten in the light of the great services that he rendered his country. When he began his political career Canada was weak and divided; when he ended that career nearly a half-century later Canada was strong and united. And during practically the whole of that long period he was the dominant figure in the political life of the country.

John Alexander Macdonald was born in Glasgow, Scotland, in 1815. His father was a cotton manufacturer, but his business was unsuccessful. In 1820 the family emigrated to Canada, and settled first at Kingston and later at Adolphustown, a United Empire Loyalist community. It is not surprising that the boy, growing up amid these surroundings, should have developed a deep feeling of loyalty to the Mother Country which remained one of his strongest characteristics till the end of his life.

For five years he attended a grammar school at Kingston, where he secured all the school education he ever had.

At the age of fifteen he began the study of law, and at twenty-one he was called to the bar. It is worthy of note that in the early years of his legal practice there came to study in his office two young men who, at a later time, also played important parts in the political life of Canada. These young men were Oliver Mowat and Alexander Campbell. The former became famous as the prime minister of Ontario for a long period; the latter was for many years a colleague of Macdonald and became lieutenant-governor of the province.

When the rebellion of 1837 broke out Macdonald enlisted, shouldered his musket, and marched and drilled with the militia. However, that was as far as his soldiering went, for the rising was over before he got into active service.

In 1844 the rising young lawyer was selected as a candidate for the legislature for Kingston. During the election campaign he issued a letter to the electors, in which among other things he said: "The prosperity of Canada depends upon its permanent connection with the Mother Country, and I shall resist to the utmost any attempt, from whatever quarter it may come, to weaken that union." In this statement he struck the keynote of his whole political career, unswerving devotion to British connection. He was victor in the contest, and was returned for Kingston in every successive election, with one exception, until his death.

During his first three years as a member of the legislature

Public Archives of Canada
SIR JOHN A. MACDONALD
(From a painting by Patterson)

DIFFICULT QUESTIONS SOLVED

he made few speeches, but devoted himself to mastering the methods of carrying on the business of the country. That he made rapid progress was shown by his entry into the cabinet of Mr. Draper in 1847. The government was, however, defeated the same year, and Macdonald spent some years in opposition. He spoke and voted against the Rebellion Losses Bill introduced in 1849 by the Baldwin-LaFontaine government. Many prominent Conservatives were so much incensed at Lord Elgin's assent to the bill that they drew up and signed a document advocating the annexation of Canada to the United States. Macdonald opposed this course with great energy and strength, and organized the British American League, which had for its objects the union of the British provinces in North America and the strengthening of the ties with the Mother Country. This organization did much at that time to enhance the loyalty of Canadians to Britain.

In 1854 Macdonald was again in the cabinet as attorney-general under the premiership of Sir Allan McNab. Two vexing problems had for many years perplexed the statesmen of Canada, but were now finally solved by this government. The first of these was the question of Clergy Reserves in Upper Canada,* and the second was that of Seigneurial Tenure in Lower Canada. A law was passed providing for the sale of all Clergy Reserve lands, and the division of the proceeds among the various municipalities of Upper Canada in proportion to population. Provision was made whereby the incumbents of churches already enjoying benefits from the Clergy Reserve lands should not during their lifetime be deprived of these. Thus the Clergy Reserves assisted in providing the various townships and villages of Upper Canada with schools, roads, drains, and bridges. The other question, that of Seigneurial Tenure, was settled by a law providing for the abolition of this method of holding land in Lower Canada and the establishment of Freehold

---

* Though Upper Canada and Lower Canada ceased to exist as separate provinces after the Act of Union, the names were retained and used for twenty-five years longer as a convenient means of designating the two fairly distinct parts of Canada.

Tenure, that is, the right of every man to own his land. Provision was made for the compensation of the seigneurs for any losses they might sustain by giving up their seigneuries. Thus a long-standing obstacle to the agricultural progress of Lower Canada was removed.

These two laws were not passed without great opposition in the legislature. Macdonald, seeing that he could not get them enacted with the help of his own party alone, secured the support of several moderate Liberals. This coalition he called Liberal-Conservative, a name that is still borne by one of the two great political parties of Canada.

The period between 1854 and 1864 was one of great political uncertainty in Canada. This was due largely to a question that was projected into the field of politics by George Brown, the editor of the *Globe*, an influential newspaper of Toronto. Brown contended that as Upper Canada had a larger population than Lower Canada, it should send more members to the legislature. He was elected to parliament and became one of the leaders of the Reform party in opposition to Macdonald. The principle of Representation by Population was opposed by a majority of the people in Lower Canada and supported by a majority in Upper Canada. So it came about that Macdonald had the support of a majority of the members from Lower Canada and a minority from Upper Canada. Ministry after ministry was formed, only to be defeated in a short time because it could not command the support of a majority of the members. Within a period of three years four ministries were defeated. Thus a "deadlock" was created, that is, a condition in which the business of the country could not be carried on because neither party in parliament was of sufficient strength to put through its measures.

At last Macdonald and Brown saw that the welfare of the country demanded that they should drop their differences and unite upon a plan to end the deadlock in the government. This plan was the confederation of all the provinces of British North America. The three maritime provinces had been discussing a union among themselves, and a conference on the question was arranged to take place in Charlottetown early in 1864. Canada asked for and obtained the privilege of sending delegates to this meeting. Macdonald, Brown, and several others attended the Charlottetown conference, and it was arranged that another meeting should take place later in the year at Quebec, when definite proposals for the union could be discussed.

And thus there was in October, 1864, at the ancient capital, one of the most famous gatherings in the history of Canada. Thirty-three delegates were there, representing all the provinces and Newfoundland as well. Macdonald and Brown were the leading members from Upper Canada, Cartier and Galt from Lower Canada, Tilley from New Brunswick, and Tupper from Nova Scotia. For several days they discussed the basis of the proposed union. There were sharp differences of opinion. At times it seemed as if the meeting must break up without coming to any agreement. Macdonald was the guiding spirit of the conference. His remarkable powers of harmonizing differences, of conciliating opposing forces, of inducing men to yield to the wishes of others, were never exercised to greater advantage. At length a basis of union was agreed upon and expressed in the form of seventy-two resolutions. The delegates departed to their several legislatures to get their consent to the union.

The feeling in favour of confederation was intensified by two occurrences in which the United States was concerned. In 1865 that country gave notice to Canada that the Reciprocity Treaty that had been agreed to in 1854 would not be renewed. For more than ten years there had been free trade in natural products between the two countries. This had been of considerable advantage to Canada, especially during the period of the American Civil War, when Canadian products had been in great demand in the United States. The cancellation of the agreement was regarded by Canada as an unfriendly act on the part of the neighbouring republic.

The ill-feeling of the Canadians was greatly increased in 1866 by armed invasions from over the American border. At several points bands of men hostile to Britain entered

Canada. The invaders were Fenians, members of a society that wished to compel Britain to give Home Rule to Ireland. Why the Fenians invaded Canada is not very clear, unless it was because they believed that in attacking this country they were thereby striking a blow against England. The Fenians were driven back by the Canadian militia wherever they set foot in Canada, the most serious engagement taking place at Ridgeway, on the Niagara frontier. The United States government made little effort to stop these raids, and this fact aroused in Canada considerable resentment against her neighbour.

These occurrences made the Canadians the more anxious to bring about a union among the provinces in order that they might be better prepared to repel a possible enemy.

In 1866 a committee of representatives of the interested provinces went to London to co-operate with the British government in drafting a bill for the union. Newfoundland and Prince Edward Island had in the meantime withdrawn from any part in negotiating the union, the terms proposed being unsatisfactory to them. In framing the bill Macdonald's was again the guiding hand. When finally the task was finished and the bill was presented to the British parliament, it was passed without opposition under the name of the "British North America Act." It came into force on July 1, 1867, a day that has ever since been designated as Canada's birthday. The united provinces were to be called the Dominion of Canada.

The British North America Act defined the government of Canada as it exists to-day. Its main principle was the union of the provinces for the control of matters of national concern, while leaving to each province the direction of its own local affairs. The principal features of the Act may be summarized as follows:—

1. Canada, New Brunswick, and Nova Scotia were united under one parliament. The first-named province was divided into two parts, called Ontario and Quebec, corresponding respectively to the Upper Canada and Lower Canada of the days before the Union. The federal parliament was to consist of a House of Commons and a Senate.

THE NEW DOMINION

The members of the former were to be elected by the people for five years. The number of members for Quebec was fixed at sixty-five, and each of the other provinces was to have such a number as its population in relation to that of Quebec warranted. Thus was solved the old question of Representation by Population. The members of the Senate were to be appointed by the governor-in-council for life. Ontario and Quebec were to have twenty-four senators each, and the two maritime provinces were to have twenty-four together.

2. Each province was to have a legislature consisting of a legislative assembly elected by the people for four years, and, if the province wished it, a legislative council appointed for life by the lieutenant-governor-in-council. Ontario was the only one of the four provinces to decide to do without a legislative council.

3. The matters to be controlled by the provincial parliaments were definitely assigned. These matters include education, the crown lands within the province, licenses, the control of the sale of liquor, and the establishment of courts of justice. All matters not specifically assigned to the provinces were to be controlled by the federal government. Among the most important are customs and excise duties, post offices, the militia, criminal law, and the appointment of judges.

The confederation of the four Canadian provinces was thus accomplished. The task had not been an easy one. The credit for bringing it about must be given mainly to Macdonald. True, he had not been the first to suggest it, nor could he have carried it out without assistance from political opponents as well as from his own supporters. But it was chiefly due to his persistence, tact, and qualities of leadership that the achievement was made possible. In recognition of his great services in bringing about confederation, Macdonald was knighted by the queen, and was chosen as the first prime minister. In the election that followed he carried the country by a large majority.

One of the first important acts of his government was the purchase in 1869 of the Hudson's Bay territory from the

Company that had for almost two hundred years held the lands of western Canada. The government agreed to give the Hudson's Bay Company the sum of £300,000 for the whole of this vast territory with the exception of one-twentieth of the fertile area and 45,000 acres adjacent to the trading-posts which the Company was allowed to retain. From the lands thus acquired the government, in 1870, carved out the Province of Manitoba. Thus a fifth province was added to the confederation.

The setting up of the new province was attended by a disturbing occurrence. The activities of the surveyors who came to lay out roads and townships were misunderstood by the Indians and half-breeds, who feared that they were to be deprived of their property by incoming white settlers. Unfortunately, nothing was done at first to relieve the fears thus aroused. Under Louis Riel the Indians and half-breeds seized Fort Garry and set up a provisional government. They refused to allow the newly appointed lieutenant-governor to enter the province, and kept the envoy of the government, Donald Smith, practically a prisoner for several months. The most serious occurrence of the rising was the shooting of Thomas Scott, a settler who refused to recognize the provisional government. The execution was ordered by Riel and carried out under very cruel circumstances. The government then despatched troops under Colonel Wolseley to the scene of the rising. When, after a toilsome journey, Wolseley reached Fort Garry, he found that Riel had fled to the United States and the rising was over.

In 1871 a conference was held at Washington between representatives of Great Britain and the United States in an effort to settle certain points in dispute between the two countries. As Canada was concerned in some of these matters, Sir John Macdonald was invited to take part in the conference as Canadian representative. One of the questions which Macdonald pressed was the claim against the United States for damages resulting from the Fenian raids. This claim, though very just and proper, the commission refused to consider, much to Macdonald's annoyance. There was

THE PACIFIC SCANDAL 243

also the question of the payment by the United States for the use of Canadian fisheries. This was not decided at the time, but was left to a board of arbitration, which some years later awarded five and a half million dollars to Canada. The Washington Treaty, in which the commission embodied the decisions reached upon the matters in dispute, was not very satisfactory from Canada's standpoint, but Macdonald advised parliament to accept its terms. The report of the fisheries arbitration, which came later, did much to allay the dissatisfaction of the Canadians.

In 1871 British Columbia entered the confederation upon the condition that a railway be built within ten years to connect it with the eastern provinces. Prince Edward Island, which had held aloof in 1867, changed its mind six years later, and asked admission upon the understanding that its means of communication with the mainland should be satisfactorily arranged. The Canadian confederation of seven provinces now extended from the Atlantic to the Pacific.

In the elections of 1872 Sir John Macdonald was returned to power, but by a greatly reduced majority. Early in the first session of parliament after the elections, serious accusations in connection with the building of the Canadian Pacific Railway were made against his government by Mr. L. S. Huntington, Liberal member for Shefford. It was charged that Sir Hugh Allan, a Montreal financier, had made large gifts of money to the government in order to secure, for a company of which he was the head, the charter to build the railway. Macdonald frankly acknowledged that his party had received the money, as political parties have always done from their friends, as a contribution to its campaign fund. He emphatically denied, however, that there was any corrupt bargain between his government and Sir Hugh Allan in connection with the granting of the charter to build the railway. For a time the charges were not generally regarded as damaging, but the publication of certain private correspondence belonging to Sir Hugh Allan and stolen from his office aroused suspicion throughout the country that there was something seriously wrong in the transaction. A bitter debate ensued in the house on a resolution of want of confidence in the government. The crisis came when Donald Smith (afterwards Lord Strathcona), at that time an influential supporter of Macdonald, made a speech strongly condemning the actions of the government. Macdonald, realizing that defeat in the House was inevitable, decided to resign rather than to allow the question to come to a vote. The "Pacific Scandal," as this episode is usually called, was a severe blow to the reputation of Macdonald as a statesman, though in the light of later events it probably does not loom to-day as a matter of such serious import as it did at the time. Without doubt Macdonald made a grave mistake in accepting a heavy subscription to the party election fund from a man who expected to receive benefits from the government. He paid the penalty for his indiscretion by incurring a storm of popular disapproval which swept his government out of office.

The Liberal leader, Hon. Alexander Mackenzie, a man of high integrity and strong character, was called upon to form a government. In the elections of 1874 he succeeded in securing a large majority, the Conservatives emerging with only forty-five members in a house of two hundred and six. Unfortunately for the new government, the country was then passing through a period of trade depression. Many factories closed their doors. Large numbers of men were thrown out of employment. Prices of farm products fell. Many Canadians emigrated to the United States. The government did nothing to relieve the situation except to urge the people to be content with conditions and wait for the coming of better times. Mackenzie refused to go on with the building of the Canadian Pacific Railway, much to the discontent of British Columbia, which threatened to withdraw from the confederation.

Sir John Macdonald began to repair his damaged reputation. He led his slender following in parliament with consummate skill, ably assisted by Tupper. His cheerful optimism and unfailing good-humour kept his party in the best of spirits and regained him many friends. With keen insight into the temper of the Canadian people, he

THE NATIONAL POLICY 245

knew that the pendulum of popular favour would soon swing in his direction again. In place of the inactivity of the government in the face of trade depression, he offered the country a constructive programme. This he called the "National Policy." It was a proposal to increase the duties on goods coming into the country so that Canadians could sell their own products in their own markets without undue competition from foreign countries. In this way, said Sir John, the Canadian producer would be *protected*, and a strong and prosperous country would be built up.

With much persuasiveness Macdonald preached his new doctrine through the country. He originated a new method of getting into contact with the people. This was the political picnic. During the summer days of 1876 he met thousands of people at open-air meetings in various parts of the country, and charmed them with his engaging personality and his humorous speeches. The people took kindly to his policy of Protection, and in the elections of 1878 the Conservatives were returned to power by almost as great a majority as that by which they had been defeated four years before. True to his promise, Macdonald put his Protection scheme into operation, and it is worthy of note that no government since his time, whether Conservative or Liberal, has seriously departed from this policy.

Under the new government, in 1880, a contract was made with the Canadian Pacific Railway Company for the construction of the railway to British Columbia in accordance with the agreement with that province on its entry into the confederation. The leading members of the company were Sir Donald Smith and Sir George Stephen. The company was assisted in its great undertaking by being given $25,000,000 and 25,000,000 acres of land along the route of the line. The railway was pushed rapidly through the rocks and forests of northern Ontario, across the prairies of the west, and over the mountains of British Columbia. The contract called for the completion of the line within ten years, but in spite of the tremendous difficulties it was actually finished in five. In 1885 the last spike was driven, and thus was completed what has proved to be the most important single work for the opening up of western Canada. The Canadian Pacific Railway is a lasting memorial to the faith of Sir John A. Macdonald and his colleagues in the immense possibilities of the great Canadian West.

With the opening of the railway and the incoming stream of settlers to the prairie lands, there came a repetition of what had occurred on the banks of the Red River fifteen years before. The Indians and half-breeds along the Saskatchewan saw their hunting-grounds being taken up by the hated whites. The government at Ottawa was slow in giving them assurances that their rights would not be violated. They brought back Louis Riel from exile in the United States and put him at their head. They attacked a body of mounted police at Duck Lake and killed fourteen men. They massacred two priests and several settlers at Frog Lake. The government hurried troops under General Middleton to the scene of the rising. Engagements took place at Cutknife Creek and Batoche, and the rebellion was soon over. Two hundred Canadian soldiers lost their lives, and there was grief in many Canadian homes. Riel and several other rebel leaders were captured. He was placed on trial for high treason, and being found guilty, was condemned to death. He was hanged at Regina, together with several Indians who had been convicted of murder during the rising. The Indians were thus given a stern warning that they could not hope to keep white settlers out of the West.

Sir John Macdonald was successful in the elections cf 1887 and again in 1891. The Liberals went into the latter campaign with the policy of unrestricted reciprocity with the United States. The Conservatives contended that such a policy meant eventually the severing of the ties with the Mother Country and annexation to the United States. They sounded the battle cry, "The old flag, the old policy, the old leader." In a campaign address to the electors Sir John reiterated his loyalty to the Empire in the famous phrase which since has been so often quoted in his honour: "A British subject I was born; a British subject I will die." The sentiment recalls that expressed in his first election address nearly fifty years before. The country reacted to the

AN ENDURING MONUMENT

patriotic appeal of the Conservative party in 1891 by returning the Macdonald government to power with a substantial majority.

Sir John was now an old man, seventy-six years of age. The campaign of 1891 had taken severe toll of his strength. In June he was suddenly stricken with paralysis, and in a few days he was dead. He was borne to his grave in Cataraqui cemetery, Kingston, to the accompaniment of a nation's grief. For twenty years he had directed the political destiny of his country as prime minister, and at the end of his life he was still first in the affections of the people.

Many monuments have been erected in Canada to the memory of Sir John A. Macdonald. One of the best known stands on Parliament Hill in Ottawa, and another at the entrance to Queen's Park, Toronto. The tall spare figure, with the clear-cut but homely features, still stirs the pulses of those Canadians who know the history of their country. But the most enduring monument to Macdonald's memory is a united Canada, strong, vigorous, and free.

XLI

JOSEPH HOWE

THE ORATOR-STATESMAN OF NOVA SCOTIA

"Boys, brag of your country. When I am abroad, I brag of everything that Nova Scotia is, has, or can produce; and when they beat me in everything else, I turn around on them and say, 'How high does your tide rise?'"

These were the words of Joseph Howe on one occasion to an audience in his native province. They contain the keynote of his career. He was above all else a patriot. He loved Nova Scotia, her rocky sea-girt coast, her lovely lakes and rivers, her fertile valleys, her splendid forests; but most of all he loved her rugged, honest people. He served his province with a lofty purpose and whole-hearted devotion that brought about great and far-reaching reforms. Nova Scotia is a better province to-day because Joseph Howe lived and worked and died there.

He was born in Halifax in 1804. His father was a United Empire Loyalist, a man of deeply religious nature, who taught his son to know and love the Bible. The elder Howe was a man of consequence in Halifax, for he held from the British government the offices of king's printer and postmaster-general for Nova Scotia, New Brunswick, Prince Edward Island, and the Bermudas. But in spite of these high-sounding titles, the family income was small. When Joseph was thirteen years old he had to be taken out of school and sent to work.

He found employment in a printing-office. When the work of the day was over he read a great deal and learned to write good prose and fair verse. It is largely due to this practice that he became in later years a great orator,

A POPULAR EDITOR

probably the best that Canada has ever produced. He found time also to engage in all forms of boyish sport, particularly swimming, rowing, skating, fishing, and spearing lobsters. He loved nature, and spent many joyous days by the seashore, in the forest, or on the lake or river. His poems and newspaper articles of a later period reflect the happiness that came to him from these excursions.

When he was twenty-three he formed a partnership with a companion and bought a newspaper called the *Acadian*. Not long afterwards he sold his share to his partner, and bought a larger and better equipped paper, the *Nova Scotian*. For eight years he devoted himself to editorial work and to making wide acquaintance among the people of the province. Having a free and easy manner, a ready wit, and a quick sympathy, he rapidly won popular confidence.

Public Archives of Canada

JOSEPH HOWE

He might have remained nothing more than a well-known newspaper editor had not an anonymous letter one day appeared in the *Nova Scotian*. This letter accused the magistrates of Halifax of incompetence, neglect, and corruption in administering the law. The magistrates were offended and charged Howe with criminal libel. He could not get a lawyer to take his case in court, so he resolved to defend himself. He spent two weeks in mastering the law of libel and looking up authorities on the question. At his trial he made his own defence in a brilliant speech, over six hours in length. It had so great an effect on the jury that he was soon acquitted. The people of Halifax were delighted at the outcome of the trial. Howe was carried from the courtroom on the shoulders of a cheering mob in triumphant procession. This incident established the liberty of the Press in Nova Scotia and won fame for Howe as an orator of great ability.

In the following year, 1836, he was chosen by the people of Halifax as member of the legislative assembly. He at once turned his attention to the reform of the government. At this time political conditions in Nova Scotia were much the same as those prevailing in Upper and Lower Canada. The governor, who was appointed by the British government, really administered the affairs of the province himself. He chose his advisers from the legislative council, which consisted of twelve members appointed for life by the crown. The legislative assembly, the representatives of the common people, had no means of checking the actions of the governor and his advisers, and had no control of the expenditure of public money or of the administration of the law. All the important public offices were filled by friends of the council, and, as was the case in Upper and Lower Canada, there grew up a Family Compact. That the officials were usually men of integrity and ability did not alter the fact that in their appointment or removal from office the representatives of the people had nothing to say.

The essential feature of responsible government is that the governor's advisers should come from the party having the majority in the assembly, and that they should continue in office only so long as they have the support of the assembly. This principle did not appeal to Howe at first; he feared that it would not work in Nova Scotia. But he demanded that the council should be elective like the assembly, or else that the executive council should be separated from the legislative council, and that both should contain representatives of all classes of the people. Appeals were made to the British government, and as a result Lord Falkland, the

RESPONSIBLE GOVERNMENT 251

governor, adopted a half-way measure, much the same as that employed by Lord Sydenham in Upper Canada. He invited two members of the assembly, of whom Howe was one, to join his executive council. There was, however, no prime minister, and the governor was still supreme. Howe soon found that he could not work under such conditions, and at length became wholly converted to the idea of responsible government. He attacked the existing system in speeches in the legislature and in articles in his newspaper, and at length the governor was recalled.

In the elections of 1847 the Reformers were successful on the issue of responsible government, largely through the efforts of Howe. The British government, seeing how matters stood, instructed the new governor to adopt the principle of ministerial responsibility. Accordingly, one of the leaders of the victorious party was called upon to form a ministry, and Howe was chosen as one of the principal members.

Thus responsible government was established in Nova Scotia by peaceful means, in contrast with the rebellion and bloodshed that preceded its adoption in Upper and Lower Canada. In his moment of triumph Howe wrote:—

> The blood of no brother in civil strife poured,
> In this hour of rejoicing encumbers our souls.

For several years his popularity made him the most influential member of the government. But presently a rival appeared on the scene in the person of Charles Tupper, a country doctor, who proved to be a foeman worthy of his steel. Howe became prime minister in 1860, but three years later he was beaten in the elections by Tupper. He retired from the legislature, and was appointed Fishery Commissioner by the British government.

Thus it happened that Howe had no part in the Charlottetown conference of 1864, nor was he present at Quebec when the basis of the confederation of the provinces was decided. As later events proved, this was unfortunate, for when Tupper returned to Halifax with the confederation proposals, Howe opposed them with all the vigour of which he was capable. This seemed to be at variance with his oft-expressed opinions, for he had made many speeches in which he had set before the people his vision of a great and united Canada extending from the Atlantic to the Pacific. When his inconsistency was pointed out, he maintained that he had meant a form of union different from that proposed by the confederation scheme. However, it looked as if his opposition sprang from wounded vanity; he had had no part in formulating the scheme, and therefore he would not support it. It is disappointing to find that a great man should have acted from such unworthy motives. "I will not play second fiddle to Tupper," he said to a friend. That doubtless explained his attitude.

Howe went to England in 1866, and did his best to persuade the British parliament not to pass the British North America Act. Failing in this, he threw himself into the campaign of 1867 in Nova Scotia and succeeded in turning the province against the confederation compact. "We are sold for the price of a sheepskin," he declared from every platform in the province, speaking of the subsidy of eighty cents per head of population that Nova Scotia was to receive from the Dominion government. In the elections Howe carried eighteen of the nineteen seats in the province, and Tupper was the only Conservative elected. Nova Scotia was nearly solid against confederation.

Howe then went again to England, this time to try to have the British North America Act repealed. Tupper followed, and persuaded Howe to meet him and talk over the situation. Later Tupper informed Sir John Macdonald that he thought that Howe might enter the Dominion cabinet. Sir John met Howe on his return to Canada, and, on the promise of "better terms" for Nova Scotia, the master-strategist won him over. When the news reached Halifax that he had entered Sir John Macdonald's cabinet, the cry went forth that Howe was a traitor and had sold himself for a portfolio. Deep resentment was aroused among his former supporters. Old friends turned their backs and refused to speak to him. To a man of Howe's sensitive nature this was a bitter experience. But, convinced as he was that further fight against carrying out the confederation scheme was futile, he saw

FINAL HONOURS

that it was better to sacrifice his own popularity than to endanger the peace of Canada.

Howe was never very successful in the larger field of Dominion politics. At Ottawa he was overshadowed by men of more commanding personality. He had the satisfaction, however, of carrying, with the help of Tupper, eighteen of the nineteen seats in Nova Scotia for Sir John Macdonald in the elections of 1872. The next year, in recognition of his distinguished political services, he was appointed lieutenant-governor of his native province. His old friends forgot their animosity of four years before and welcomed him with open arms. But within a month he was dead, and the people of Nova Scotia mourned the passing of their greatest statesman.

XLII

SIR GEORGES ÉTIENNE CARTIER

QUEBEC'S APOSTLE OF CONFEDERATION

WITH the possible exception of Sir Wilfrid Laurier at a later time, no other statesman has wielded such a powerful influence in Quebec as Sir Georges Étienne Cartier. As the leader of the Conservative party in that province for many years, he was very successful in moulding the opinions of the people in harmony with his own. His name is still one to conjure with in political contests in French-Canadian constituencies and, regardless of politics, is remembered with pride by all his compatriots.

He was born in the county of Verchères in 1814. He was descended from one of the nephews of Jacques Cartier, the adventurous Breton sailor, and in later life he showed all the qualities of energy, determination, and perseverance possessed by his illustrious namesake. He attended college for eight years, and then took up the study of law. He was called to the bar and began to practise in Montreal. Those were the days of the dominance of Papineau in Lower Canadian politics. Cartier as a young man of twenty-two fell under the spell of the fiery oratory of the rebel chief. He fought against the Loyalist troops at St. Denis, and found it advisable to escape to the United States, where he remained in hiding for a time. On being assured that he would not be arrested for his part in the rebellion, he returned to Montreal and resumed his practice of law. He repented his youthful folly, and ever afterwards remained a loyal subject with a strong attachment to British institutions. "An Englishman speaking French," he was wont to describe himself in his later years.

For ten years after the rebellion he took no part in political life. In 1848 he was elected member of parliament for Verchères and soon made rapid strides towards leadership. He was one of the strongest supporters of the proposal to abolish seigneurial tenure, believing that the slow progress of his province in agriculture was due to this method of holding land. He entered the cabinet, first as provincial secretary, and later as attorney-general for Lower Canada. In the latter capacity he brought about the codification of the laws of his province, that is, the systematic arrangement of the laws in their proper order and under their proper heads. This work was done by a committee under Cartier's direction, and was completed in four years. Cartier was very proud of this work, and said that he wanted no better epitaph after his death than that he had codified the laws of Lower Canada.

In 1857 he was joint prime minister with Sir John Macdonald in what was known as the Macdonald–Cartier administration. It was at this time that the question of the capital of Canada was settled. It will be remembered that after the burning of the parliament buildings at Montreal in 1849, parliament had met alternately at Toronto and Quebec four years at a time. Queen Victoria, on being asked to name the new capital, had selected Ottawa. Many members of the assembly were not pleased with the choice, and a resolution was introduced that Ottawa should not be the capital. This

Public Archives of Canada

SIR GEORGES ÉTIENNE CARTIER

was carried by a small majority, and the government resigned.

The Liberal leader, George Brown, was called to form a ministry. He accepted the task, but the new ministry was defeated in parliament in two days, and it also resigned. Cartier was next invited to take the helm, and what was called the Cartier-Macdonald administration was formed—really the same as had held power before Brown's brief reign. There was an Act of parliament that said that if a minister resigned office and accepted another within a month, he was not required to go back to his constituents for re-election. Now it was less than a month since Cartier's ministers had resigned office. So they adopted the expedient of taking different portfolios for a day or so, and then resigning these and taking again those that they had formerly held. So it was exactly the same ministry back again. This expedient was called "The Double Shuffle." The Conservatives were strongly blamed for what was regarded as a sharp trick. The law has since been changed so as to make a repetition of this impossible.

The Cartier-Macdonald ministry again brought up the resolution to make Ottawa the capital, and it was carried by a very small majority. The good queen's choice was confirmed, but Ottawa nearly missed the honour of being made the national capital. The administration that settled the question did not last long. In 1862 Macdonald introduced a Militia Bill which provided that 50,000 men should be drilled at military camps for a period of four weeks each year. The Lower Canadian members were much against the proposal, and Cartier could not hold their allegiance. The bill was defeated, and the government resigned. It was succeeded by a Liberal ministry, which also had a short life.

The events that followed have already been described in the story of Sir John A. Macdonald. Cartier was Macdonald's right-hand man in carrying though the confederation scheme. He was present at the Charlottetown and the Quebec conferences, and was a member of the committee that went to London to draft the British North America Act. The French people in Quebec were at first opposed to the scheme, as they feared that their rights might be endangered by the preponderance of the English in parliament. But when they realized that they would have control of their local affairs in their own legislature, they became enthusiastic for the plan. Cartier's influence was largely responsible for their change of attitude.

In recognition of the part he had played in bringing about the confederation of the provinces, Cartier was made a baronet by the queen. In the first federal cabinet he was minister of defence. Strangely enough, he suffered a personal defeat in his own constituency of Montreal East in the elections of 1872, but speedily found a seat for a Manitoba constituency. Death came suddenly, and cut short a career of splendid public service in 1873.

XLIII

HON. GEORGE BROWN

JOURNALIST AND REFORMER

THREE questions have probably caused more acrimonious debate and bitter strife in Canada than any others. They were the questions of responsible government, the Clergy Reserves, and representation by population. With all three the name of George Brown was associated. For responsible government he fought valiantly in the ranks of Robert Baldwin. Over the Clergy Reserves difficulty he crossed swords with Bishop Strachan and others. But the cause of representation by population was peculiarly his own, and for it he waged a strenuous and unceasing battle until success was attained. It is due in no small degree to the vigour and determination of George Brown that these three problems were eventually solved in a satisfactory way.

George Brown was born in 1818 in Edinburgh—a Scotsman like his great rival Macdonald. At the age of twenty he emigrated to America with his father. They landed in New York, and four years later were joint owners of a religious newspaper, which had a large circulation among the Scottish population of the United States. In 1843 the son came to Canada with the object of extending the circulation of their newspaper. At that time Kingston was the seat of the government, and while visiting that city Brown made the acquaintance of the leading members of the Baldwin government. They were so much impressed with the young man's grasp of Canadian affairs and his sympathy with their cause, that they suggested to him the plan of starting a newspaper in Canada. The outcome of this was the establishment of the *Globe* at Toronto as a political newspaper supporting the Liberal cause, with George Brown as founder, editor, and proprietor. The *Globe* appeared first in 1844 as a weekly, and rapidly gained in circulation and influence. Soon it was issued twice a week, and then three times, and finally in 1853 it became a daily.

George Brown was a man of strong opinions and indomitable will. He was intolerant of ideas that were not in harmony with his own, and was much given to sweeping denunciation of those who disagreed with him. He expressed his opinions in very forcible language. He was wont to call a spade a spade. If a politician made a misstatement, he was likely to be told, not that he was inaccurate, but that he lied. Thus Brown came to exercise an almost tyrannical influence upon public opinion in Canada. Nevertheless, at heart he was a kindly man. He got into close touch with the common people of the province.

Public Archives of Canada
HON. GEORGE BROWN

He met them in their homes, he visited their schools, he talked with them about their crops and stock, he discussed with them the political questions of the day. He spoke, wrote, and fought for the rights of the people, and this in part accounts for his hold upon their affections.

He supported with great vigour, on the platform and in the columns of the *Globe*, the demand for responsible government until this principle was finally recognized. He assailed with equal force the establishment of separate schools, but was unable to prevent this. He vehemently supported the proposal to secularize the Clergy Reserves, and it was to some extent due to his emphatic demands that this was finally accomplished.

But it was to the principle of representation by population, or "Rep. by Pop." as it was familiarly called, that he gave his most constant and unwearied support. As the term suggests, it means that the number of members of parliament should be proportionate to population. At the time of the union of Upper and Lower Canada it was arranged that each province should send forty-two members to the legislative assembly. Later this number was increased to sixty-five. Upper Canada grew in population more rapidly than Lower Canada, and Brown maintained that this fact should be recognized by giving Upper Canada a larger number of representatives in the assembly.

Against this the Lower Canadian members maintained that the understanding at the union was that the provinces should have equal representation. It would be a breach of faith if that equality were disturbed. Moreover, at the time of the union Lower Canada had had a considerably larger population, but had made little objection to the equality of representation.

The question wrecked more than one administration, for the parties were so nearly equally divided that neither could carry on the government for any length of time. This "deadlock" was one of the causes that led to confederation. Brown won his fight in the end by seeing to it that one of the clauses of the British North America Act provided for representation by population. In accordance with this provision, Quebec sends sixty-five members to the House of Commons, and the other provinces a proportionate number according to their population.

Brown entered parliament in 1851, and by reason of his dominating personality he forged rapidly to the front and soon became the leader of the Reformers. The story of his brief premiership in 1857, which came about over the selection of the Canadian capital, has already been told in the sketch of Sir Georges Cartier. It was characteristic of Brown's impetuous nature that he readily accepted the

FIGHT FOR CONFEDERATION 261

task of forming a government, though he must have known that he could not long command the confidence of the assembly. He was unsparing in his denunciation of the Cartier-Macdonald administration, which succeeded his own, for its action in the "Double-Shuffle" episode.

Hon. George Brown was one of the earliest advocates of the confederation of the provinces. In 1859, at a Liberal convention in Toronto, he proposed what he called a "joint authority" for the control of matters of common concern, and local legislatures for the control of matters peculiar to each province. He moved a resolution to this effect in parliament the following year, but it was defeated. However, within the next two or three years the leaders of both parties became convinced that the plan was a good one.

Brown's unselfish action in dropping party differences and uniting with his personal and political enemy, Sir John Macdonald, to carry through the confederation scheme will always be remembered to his credit. He took into Macdonald's coalition cabinet two of his own supporters, Oliver Mowat and William McDougall. He worked loyally with Macdonald till the accomplishment of the scheme was assured, and then resigned his portfolio in 1865.

With his withdrawal from the cabinet Brown's political career practically ended. He was defeated in the elections of 1867 and retired to his editorial chair. He was appointed a member of the Senate in 1873, but seldom took part in debate. He twice declined a knighthood as a reward for his services. In 1875 he refused the lieutenant-governorship of Ontario, believing that if he accepted it he would have to withdraw from the editorship of the *Globe*, a possibility that he would not entertain. He died in 1880, as the result of a wound from a pistol in the hands of a printer whom he had discharged.

XLIV

HON. ALEXANDER MACKENZIE

THE STONE-MASON WHO BECAME PRIME MINISTER

THE pages of the political history of Canada are generously besprinkled with Scottish names. Indeed, as one looks back over the history of this country, one cannot but be struck by the large number of important political achievements that are associated with the names of Scotsmen. William Lyon Mackenzie, John Strachan, James Douglas, John A. Macdonald, George Brown, Donald Smith, Alexander Mackenzie —to mention only those whose careers are sketched in this book—were all Scots who left the indelible impress of their character and ideals upon our history. Not the least among these famous Scottish Canadians was Alexander Mackenzie, who came to Canada in 1842 as an immigrant boy, and thirty-one years later was prime minister. The reader should be careful to distinguish this man from the famous explorer of an earlier age who bore the same name.

Mackenzie was born in Perthshire, Scotland, in 1822. His father was a stone-mason, and the family lived in humble circumstances. The young lad received only a common school education, and at an early age was apprenticed in his father's trade. He emigrated to Canada at the age of twenty, and settled first at Kingston. He had no resources except capable hands, a keen intelligence, an honest heart, and an indomitable will. Little did the youth of twenty think that these were the qualities that would eventually carry him to the highest position in the gift of the people of his adopted country.

He completed his apprenticeship at Kingston and became an efficient stone-mason. He was a serious-minded youth, and, realizing that he had obtained too meagre an education, he employed his leisure moments in reading and study. As a result of untiring persistence, he obtained a command of the English language and a knowledge of public affairs excelled by few men in the country.

After several years in Kingston, Mackenzie decided to go farther west. He settled at Sarnia, where he became a contractor on a large scale and acquired considerable wealth. He became interested in political matters and bought a newspaper, the *Lambton Shield*, which he conducted as a Liberal organ supporting the policies of Hon. George Brown. He steadily grew in influence in his community and the surrounding country. The people respected and admired him because of his moral earnestness and his vigorous expression of his political opinions. He was elected in 1861 as member of the Canadian parliament and allied himself heartily with Brown in his demands for reform.

Public Archives of Canada
HON. ALEXANDER MACKENZIE

When Brown resigned from the coalition ministry that had arranged the details leading to confederation, John A. Macdonald recognized Mackenzie's worth by inviting him to take the vacant place. However, Mackenzie declined the position out of loyalty to his leader.

Mackenzie was elected as member for Lambton in the first parliament following confederation, and soon became the leader of the Opposition at Ottawa. For two years he was also member of the Ontario legislature, and was for some months in the cabinet as provincial treasurer under the premiership of Hon. Edward Blake. At that time a man might hold membership in both the federal and the provincial parliaments, a principle known as "dual representation." However, in 1872 the privilege of dual representation was abolished, and both Blake and Mackenzie sacrificed their important provincial posts to devote themselves to the affairs of the Opposition in the federal parliament at Ottawa.

Mackenzie led the attack against the government of Sir John Macdonald in connection with the Pacific Railway charter, and was the mover of the want of confidence motion which compelled the government to resign in 1873. When called upon to form a ministry to succeed Macdonald's he hesitated. He would have preferred to serve under Blake, as he had done in the provincial arena, but Blake declined the premiership. Mackenzie formed a strong government, and in the elections of 1874 he profited by the wave of popular indignation against the former ministry. He carried the country by a tremendous majority.

The new government began its administration under happy auspices. Not only was it supported by an overwhelming volume of public opinion, but it was faced in the House of Commons by an opposition that was crushed and dispirited. Nevertheless, clouds soon began to appear on the political horizon. Mackenzie, though a keen debater and an able administrator, disdained the arts that attract popular support. In this respect he stood in marked contrast to his opponent, Sir John Macdonald, whose geniality won friends among the members of the House, sometimes at Mackenzie's expense. Mackenzie undertook to administer the affairs of the public works department in addition to the duties of the premiership. He did this with characteristic thoroughness, becoming so immersed in the details of his department that he forgot the voters in the constituencies and neglected the important work of cultivating public opinion. His government gradually lost popularity, a condition that so skilful a tactician as Macdonald was quick to appreciate and turn to his own advantage.

The government's method of carrying forward the Canadian

Pacific Railway project did little to win popular approval. The Allan Company gave up its charter to build the road, and for a time Mackenzie tried to persuade other capitalists to undertake the task. Failing in this, he decided that the government itself should construct the road, and work was begun on certain sections. But it was carried on so slowly that British Columbia grew restive, with the growing certainty that the project would not be completed within the ten years stipulated at its entrance into confederation in 1871. Mackenzie himself declared that the railway could not be completed within ten years even if all the resources of the British Empire were used. Edward Blake asserted that nothing could justify the pouring of the people's hard-earned money down the gorges of British Columbia. As a consequence of what it regarded as a breach of faith, the western province was on the verge of secession from the union, a disaster that was averted largely by the tact of the governor-general, Lord Dufferin.

The legislative record of the Mackenzie government was very creditable. The Ballot Act of 1874 abolished open voting and introduced voting by a secret ballot. This measure very greatly reduced bribery and intimidation at elections. When an elector could record his vote without anybody else knowing how he did so, he was much less likely to be bought or frightened into voting contrary to his judgment. The government did much to restrict the sale of intoxicants by passing the Canada Temperance Act, better known as the Scott Act. The government established the Royal Military College at Kingston for the training of officers for the Canadian militia. It also established the Supreme Court of Canada, to which appeals from the judgments of lower courts might be carried.

Mackenzie was unfortunate in the time at which it was his lot to assume power. A wave of commercial depression had just begun to spread over the world, and included Canada in its embrace. The people began to experience hard times. For this condition the Conservatives laid the blame upon the policy of the government. They declared that the duties on goods entering Canada were so low that foreign countries were able to undersell Canadian producers in their own market. This condition, said the Conservatives, was compelling Canadian factories to cease operation and to throw people out of work. The Liberals retorted that the hard times were the result of world-wide conditions over which the government had no more control than "the fly on the wheel." The latter phrase was taken up by their opponents and used against them with telling effect upon public opinion.

At this time the Conservatives began to proclaim the National Policy, the policy of Protection, described in the biography of Sir John Macdonald. Mackenzie hesitated for a time as to the policy to be announced by the Liberals. It is probable that Blake and Laurier, his two chief lieutenants, urged him to adopt the policy of Protection also, but he was too stanch a free-trader to give his consent. Finally he declared that the tariff must remain as it was, and that the people must patiently wait the return of better times, which would occur sooner or later in the natural course of events.

In the election campaign of 1878 Mackenzie was confident that he would be returned to power. He could not believe that the people would turn out a ministry that had given the country such efficient, economical, and honest government. The result of the elections was to him as astonishing as it was unexpected. He suffered a defeat as overwhelming as his victory had been four years before. There are few examples in Canadian history of such a striking change in public opinion within so short a period.

Mackenzie remained as leader of the Liberal party for a short time after its rejection at the polls, but in 1880 he was forced to resign on account of ill-health. He was succeeded by Hon. Edward Blake, who continued as leader till 1887. Mackenzie, however, retained his seat in parliament until his death in 1892.

From a humble origin, without initial advantages of wealth or education, Alexander Mackenzie rose by native ability and hard work to the highest position that this country offers. Yet he always remained at heart a thorough democrat. This was shown in a remarkable way in 1875, when he declined the honour of knighthood offered to him by Queen Victoria. He elevated public life to a higher plane of purity, and during four difficult years he gave the country a government against which there was never a hint of scandal. He will be remembered in Canada as a statesman and prime minister of tireless industry, of dauntless courage, and of stainless honour.

XLV

SIR CHARLES TUPPER

THE FIGHTER FROM NOVA SCOTIA

THE little province of Nova Scotia has probably produced, in proportion to its size and population, more noted statesmen than any other province in the Dominion. Since confederation it has supplied Canada with three prime ministers and many outstanding members of cabinets. Second only to Hon. Joseph Howe among famous public men in Nova Scotia stands Sir Charles Tupper. He was of British-American origin, the family emigrating from New England to Nova Scotia before the Revolution. He was born in Amherst in 1821. His father was principal of a Baptist college, editor of a church paper, and an author of some repute. The boy had thus the advantage of growing up in an intellectual atmosphere. He attended public and private schools in his native town, and later was sent to Acadia College, where he secured the degree of Master of Arts. He then proceeded to the University of Edinburgh, where he had a distinguished career and graduated in medicine. He began the practice of his profession in Amherst, and devoted the next twelve years to it exclusively. Having accumulated considerable wealth in that period, he could afford to turn his attention to politics.

In 1855, when Joseph Howe was at the crest of his popularity and influence in Nova Scotia, Dr. Tupper had the temerity to oppose him in the elections as the Conservative candidate in Cumberland. Howe at first thought he would have no trouble in defeating his opponent, and was rather patronizing towards him. As time went on, however, he found that he had a real contest on his hands. The young country doctor developed surprising fighting qualities and considerable persuasiveness of speech. When the votes were counted it was found that Tupper was elected, and from that moment he was an outstanding figure in the political life of the province. Howe himself said that he had been beaten by the future leader of the Conservative party.

Within a year Tupper was provincial secretary and the most aggressive member of the Conservative government. He was sent to England to secure assistance in the building of the proposed intercolonial railway. While there he discussed the proposal of the confederation of the provinces. In the next election the Conservatives were beaten; Howe returned as prime minister, and Tupper spent the next four years as the leading member of the opposition. However, in the following election the Conservatives were again returned to power, and in 1864 Tupper became prime minister.

Public Archives of Canada
SIR CHARLES TUPPER

The most important achievement of the new administration was the establishment of a public school system for the province. In its essential features this system was similar to that set up in Upper Canada under the direction of Dr. Ryerson —a free system supported by local taxation and assisted by government grants. It required no small degree of courage to carry through a scheme of this kind, for in Nova Scotia, as in Upper Canada, the idea that the state owed an education to every child was slow to take hold. The prospect of helping to pay for the education of other people's children did not appeal to many hard-headed Nova Scotians. That Tupper's educational policy was justified by the results is shown by the fact that within ten years the attendance in the schools of Nova Scotia increased threefold. Notwithstanding Tupper's great services to his native province at a later time, the establishment of a free system of education is regarded by many as the crowning act of a great career.

Dr. Tupper was active in promoting the scheme of uniting the three maritime provinces. He was the leading spirit in arranging the Charlottetown conference in 1864, to which Upper and Lower Canada asked to be permitted to send representatives. He was favourable to the larger scheme of confederating all the British provinces, and at the Quebec conference later in the year was a strong supporter of Sir John Macdonald in his proposals. He and the Canadian premier made an agreement at this time that they would stand together after the scheme was put into operation, an agreement that was later carried out to the letter.

Notwithstanding very strong and bitter opposition aroused by Howe in Nova Scotia against the confederation scheme, Tupper carried through the legislature a motion to send delegates to London to settle the basis of union, and later went to the London conference to assist in framing the British North America Act. In the first federal election following confederation he had the keen disappointment of finding his province almost a unit against the plan. In all the nineteen constituencies he himself was the only Conservative elected. Howe had done his work thoroughly.

When Howe went to London to persuade the British parliament to repeal the Confederation Act, Tupper, with resolute courage, followed. With some difficulty he arranged a private conference with Howe, and with consummate tact and skill he brought about the conversion of his great antagonist.

"Howe," said he, "what are you going to do when you find that the British government will not repeal the Confederation Act?"

"I shall see that Nova Scotia does not pay a cent of taxes

to the Dominion government," replied Howe. "I have eight hundred voters in every constituency who will support me in my refusal."

"Where are you going to get the money for your roads, bridges, and schools?" asked Tupper. "You have no power of taxation, and, if the people disobey the law, the federal subs'dy will be cut off."

"We will risk the consequences," returned Howe.

"If you will cease your opposition and enter the federal cabinet," Tupper continued, "I shall support you as strongly as I have hitherto opposed you."

After two hours of free and frank discussion, Howe saw the uselessness and the danger of further opposition. Much against his personal inclination he agreed to Tupper's suggestion. That same night Tupper wrote to Sir John Macdonald that Howe would accept a portfolio if it were offered to him. The conversion of his great opponent was a remarkable triumph for Tupper.

If any man from Nova Scotia deserved a seat in the first federal cabinet following the confederation, that man was Tupper. But in order to make it easier for Sir John Macdonald to form the first Canadian ministry he unselfishly stood aside, and asked that another Nova Scotian be selected in his place. With equal unselfishness he declined the position of chairman of the board of commissioners that was appointed to build the intercolonial railway. He did not enter the cabinet till 1870. In the elections of 1872 he had the satisfaction of seeing a complete reversal of public opinion in Nova Scotia, the government carrying every seat but one. He was minister of customs when the Macdonald government resigned in 1873 following the "Pacific Scandal."

He was a strong critic of the Mackenzie administration during its term of office. His fighting qualities revived the drooping spirits of his party during the dark days of opposition, and were to a considerable extent responsible for the triumphant return of the Conservatives to power in the next parliament. He took up Sir John Macdonald's "National Policy" with enthusiasm, and carried the elections of 1878 in Nova Scotia for the Conservatives by a large majority.

SIR CHARLES TUPPER

Tupper remained in the Macdonald cabinet till 1884. It was due in no small degree to his unwavering support that the Canadian Pacific Railway was carried to successful completion. In the face of strong opposition in parliament, he carried through loan after loan for the company constructing the railway. His opponents declared that the road led across "a sea of mountains," and "would never pay for its axle-grease." But Tupper exhibited an optimism that admitted no possibility of failure, a courage that recognized no obstacle, and a determination that overcame all difficulties.

Years later, when the railway was in successful operation and had opened up the great Canadian West for settlement, it must have been a source of great satisfaction to him that his most glowing predictions for the future of the road had been abundantly fulfilled.

THE C.P.R. PIERCES THE ROCKIES

In 1884 Tupper was appointed to the important office of Canadian High Commissioner at London, having charge of the business of the Dominion with the Imperial government, with particular reference to trade relations and immigration. In this office he rendered distinguished service, and was honoured by Queen Victoria by being made a baronet.

When the Conservative government in 1896, after a reign of eighteen years, showed signs of breaking up, as all old governments eventually do, Sir Charles Tupper was called back to Canada to take the premiership. The attitude of the Bowell government on the Manitoba School question, discussed in the sketch of Sir Wilfrid Laurier, had aroused great dissatisfaction in the ranks of its supporters. If anyone

RETIREMENT

could have stemmed the tide and saved the situation for the Conservatives, it was this doughty old warrior of Nova Scotia, now seventy-five years of age. He plunged into the battle with all the vigour of youth and fought valiantly. But the task was too much for even his superb fighting qualities. The people were tired of the old government and wanted a change. The Conservatives went down to defeat, and the Liberals under Sir Wilfrid Laurier reigned in their stead. Writing of this election, Sir John Willison said concerning Tupper: "No braver man ever led a party to battle, and no more gallant fight was ever made to save a field than his in 1896."

Sir Charles remained as leader of the opposition in parliament for four years. In the elections of 1900 the Conservatives were again badly beaten, and their old battle-scarred leader was outvoted in his own constituency, suffering his first personal defeat in forty years of public life. His advancing years made it advisable to give up the leadership of the party. He resigned, and was succeeded by Mr. R. L. Borden. He retired to private life, and lived to the splendid old age of ninety-four—the last survivor of the Fathers of Confederation.

XLVI

SIR LEONARD TILLEY

THE FAVOURITE SON OF NEW BRUNSWICK

The most famous and best loved statesman of New Brunswick was Sir Leonard Tilley. That he was held in high regard in his native province requires no other proof than that he filled at various times all the important public offices in the gift of the people. In the course of a long public career of over forty years, he held in succession the posts of member of the legislature, provincial prime minister, member of the federal parliament, federal cabinet minister, and lieutenant-governor of the province. He was also one of the outstanding Fathers of Confederation, and did more than any other man to popularize the union in his own province.

He was born in 1818 of United Empire Loyalist parents. One of his ancestors had come out to America in the *Mayflower*. At an early age he went into business in St. John and was very successful. At the age of thirty-two he was elected as one of the representatives for St. John in the legislature. He was a strong advocate of temperance, and succeeded in persuading the government to pass in 1855 a prohibition law for the province. The law was later repealed because the people were not ready for it, but Tilley ever afterwards retained the loyal support of the temperance forces of the province. He rose rapidly to the front rank in the legislature, and was prime minister from 1860 to 1865.

Tilley was an early supporter of the idea of maritime union. In 1863, during the visit of the Hon. D'Arcy McGee to New Brunswick, he was impressed by the eloquent arguments of the distinguished Canadian in favour of the confederation

AT THE CONFEDERATION CONFERENCES

of all the British provinces; and when in 1864 a large delegation of leading Canadians came to the maritime provinces, he became wholly convinced of the advantages of such a union. He went to the Charlottetown conference in 1864 to discuss with the other maritime delegates the union of the three provinces. On the arrival of the eight Canadian representatives who had requested to be heard, two days were spent in considering the possibilities of the larger union. The conference then adjourned, to reassemble in Quebec in October.

The Canadian delegates in the meantime visited Halifax and St. John, and, by their public addresses, did much to arouse a favourable sentiment towards the confederation of the five provinces.

At the Quebec conference Tilley was one of the most active members in drafting the basis of the union. One of the difficult questions was the provision of money for the provincial legislatures to keep up those services which were to be entrusted to the provinces. At length

Public Archives of Canada
SIR LEONARD TILLEY

it was arranged that each province should receive from the federal government an annual subsidy of eighty cents per head of population. The results of the deliberations of the conference were embodied in seventy-two resolutions, which were to be the basis of the Act confederating the provinces.

The elections in New Brunswick were due about this time, and it was agreed to make the confederation proposals the issue of the campaign. It was thought that public opinion upon the question could thus be fairly tested. This election was very bitterly fought. The opponents of confederation raised the cry that the scheme would greatly increase taxation. The people were told that their land, their horses, cattle, and sheep would all be taxed for the benefit of the Canadians. The latter were pictured as tricksters trying to inveigle the unsuspecting New Brunswickers into a disadvantageous bargain. The merits of the question were lost sight of, and a few catch-phrases turned the tide of popular feeling against Tilley and his government. One example of the type of argument used in the campaign may be given. A speaker at a public meeting told of a little boy who asked, "Father, what country do we belong to?" "My son," replied the father, "we have no country, for Mr. Tilley has sold us all to the Canadians for eighty cents a head." This referred, of course, to the method of calculating the subsidy payable to each of the provinces. So the phrase "Sold to the Canadians at eighty cents a head" became an election cry which was used to good effect as a campaign argument. When the smoke of battle had lifted it was found that Tilley had been overwhelmingly defeated. Out of forty-one seats he had won only six. It looked as if the confederation scheme had been smashed in New Brunswick.

The new government that succeeded Tilley's was composed of men who were politically opposed on almost every question save that of confederation. It lasted scarcely a year, and then resigned. In the meantime Tilley had gone up and down the province addressing the people at public meetings and laying before them the advantages of confederation. The threat of a Fenian invasion from the United States brought home to them the necessity of union for the sake of protection. When a new election took place in 1866 it was found that the people had completely reversed their decision of the year before. Out of forty-one seats Tilley's party won thirty-three. There are few instances in Canadian history of such a complete transformation in public opinion in so short a period.

Tilley and five other representatives from New Brunswick were members of the committee which met in London in 1866 to draft the bill for confederation. He watched carefully the interests of New Brunswick in all the discussions. He secured assurances that the intercolonial railway would be carried to completion at an early date. He also arranged that the province should retain for its own use the export duty on lumber.

There is a story that, when a name for the united provinces was being considered, it was Tilley who proposed the name which was finally adopted, the Dominion of Canada. It is said that he obtained the suggestion from the scriptural passage, Zechariah ix. 10: "His dominion shall be from sea even to sea, and from the river even to the ends of the earth."

Tilley was made minister of customs in the first Dominion cabinet after confederation. Later he became minister of finance. He was regarded as one of the strongest members of the government—keen and clear-headed in business, lucid and forceful in speech, kindly and courteous in manner. Shortly before the resignation of Sir John Macdonald's government, following the Pacific Scandal, Mr. Tilley was appointed lieutenant-governor of New Brunswick. He spent five years in that office, but resigned during the momentous election campaign of 1878, to re-enter political life at the request of Macdonald. When Sir John returned to power after the elections, he again selected Tilley as his finance minister. It was Tilley's task to put into operation the Conservative policy of Protection, a policy that has been maintained ever since by both political parties in Canada. Tilley was knighted by the queen for his distinguished services. In 1885 he was once more appointed lieutenant-governor of New Brunswick, and remained in office till 1893, when he retired from political life. He died in 1896.

Sir Leonard Tilley was a man of many amiable qualities, admired and respected alike by political friends and political opponents. He had a great capacity for making friends, owing largely to his sterling honesty, his kindly consideration of the opinions of others, and his unfailing courtesy even in the heat of political debate. His memory will live long in the history of the province whose destinies he did so much to mould and in the history of the Dominion which he did so much to create.

T

XLVII

THOMAS D'ARCY McGEE

THE IRISH-CANADIAN PATRIOT

A CONSPIRATOR, a rebel, and a leader of an Irish revolution against Britain, a fugitive from British justice, an exile in a foreign land, an editor of three bitterly anti-British newspapers—all these D'Arcy McGee had been before he was thirty years of age. A British patriot, an honoured member of the Canadian parliament, a minister of the crown, one of the Fathers of Confederation—all these he was during the last ten years of his life. Seldom has a man's career shown such striking contrasts in attitude and ideals. Seldom, too, has a man exhibited such numerous and varied powers. A vigorous writer, a pleasing poet, an inspiring orator, a high-minded statesman, he exerted a powerful influence upon Canadian life during the short period that he lived in this country. Unfortunately for Canada, his life was cut short by an assassin's hand ere he had reached the summit of his powers.

Thomas D'Arcy McGee was born in Ireland in 1825. From his mother he learned the legendary lore of his country, and imbibed a love of history and literature. Though she died when he was quite young, the impress of her influence was deeply stamped upon his character. At seventeen he emigrated to the United States with his sister, and landed in Boston penniless. An oration on liberty that he made from a cart on the street one Fourth of July attracted the attention of a newspaper editor. A few days later he was offered a position on this newspaper, and so brilliant was his work that within three years he was joint-editor. He returned to the land of his birth, and shortly afterwards

A YOUNG REVOLUTIONIST 279

was appointed parliamentary correspondent at London for two Irish newspapers. Here he became interested in the Young Ireland party, which had for its purpose the redress of the wrongs of Ireland by freeing her from the rule of England. A revolution was planned with McGee as one of the leaders. A cargo of arms was to be sent from Scotland

Public Archives of Canada
THOMAS D'ARCY McGEE

to Ireland for the use of the rebels. The British authorities got word of the projected rising. The cargo of arms was never landed. The insurrection was over before it was fairly begun. Disguised as a priest, McGee escaped arrest, and took ship at Londonderry for the United States once more.

During the next few years McGee was editor of two newspapers in turn, both of which were devoted to the interests of the Irish citizens of the Republic. He seems suddenly to have become convinced that his revolutionary ideas were all wrong, and that the best safeguard of Irish liberty lay in continuance under the British flag. Where he had formerly been fiercely anti-British, he now became ardently pro-British. Migrating to Canada in 1857, he again became a citizen of the Empire against which he had conspired. In Montreal he established his fourth newspaper, and through its columns and on the public platform he began to advocate the union of the British provinces. His enthusiasm was transferred from the cause of Irish freedom to the cause of colonial union.

In less than a year after his arrival in Canada he was elected to parliament as one of the members for Montreal. At first he allied himself with the Reformers under George Brown, though he did not agree with all Brown's policies, particularly that of representation by population. In the debate in 1860 on Brown's resolution for the federal union of the two provinces, McGee made an eloquent speech in support of the idea of including all the British provinces in the union. He pointed out the advantages that would follow such a step. There would be a removal of all tariff walls and a stimulation to inter-provincial trade. There would therefore be wider markets for the products of each colony. Further, there would be greater strength through union. This McGee illustrated by reference to Æsop's fable of the bundle of sticks. Singly, the sticks could be easily broken; in a bundle, they resisted all efforts to break them. Similarly, as an independent colony, each province was in constant danger of absorption by the United States; united, they would be strong enough to resist absorption. McGee even had a prophetic vision of the great West included in the union, thus combining under one government a vast territory extending from ocean to ocean.

From the first McGee insisted that a federal union was the ideal arrangement, that is, a central government for the control of matters of common interest, and local legislatures for the management of matters of particular concern to each province. Macdonald and many other statesmen were at first inclined to support the principle of legislative union,

A BRILLIANT STATESMAN

that is, the setting up of a single central parliament, in which all the provinces would be represented and which would control the affairs of the united provinces without the assistance of local legislatures. In time, however, all the leading statesmen accepted McGee's view.

In 1862, on the defeat of the Cartier-Macdonald administration, McGee entered the Reform cabinet which succeeded it. Next year this cabinet was reorganized, and McGee was dropped without any apparent reason. He resented this and went over to the Conservatives, whose policy at this time was more in harmony with his own. The following year he was in the Taché-Macdonald cabinet as minister of agriculture. His progress had been rapid. A member of parliament within a year of his arrival in Canada, and a cabinet minister within five years! Moreover, he was on all sides acknowledged as an able debater and the most finished orator in the House. Whether in his place in parliament or on the public platform, he could hold his listeners spellbound by the mellow richness of his voice, the poetic eloquence of his language, his mastery of pathos and humour, his ready wit, and his biting sarcasm.

From 1859 to 1863 McGee paid yearly visits to the maritime provinces, making frequent speeches and always pleading the cause of union with Canada. "Your destiny and ours," said he, speaking at St. John in 1863, "are as inseparable as are the waters which pour into the Bay of Chaleur, rising though they do on the one hand in the Canadian and on the other in the New Brunswick highlands. Geographically we are bound up beyond the power of extinction." In 1864 he organized an excursion of a hundred leading men of Canada to the maritime provinces. They visited Halifax, St. John, and Fredericton, and were royally feasted and entertained. At a banquet in their honour in Fredericton, McGee made an unusually fine speech in support of confederation. In the course of this he said: "If the colonies remain long as fragments, we shall be lost; but let us be united, and we shall be as a rock, which, unmoved itself, flings back the waves that may be dashed upon it by the storm." By campaigning in this eloquent manner, and by bringing together in social intercourse the people of Canada and the people of the maritime provinces, McGee probably did more than any other man to develop the confederation sentiment.

D'Arcy McGee was one of the eight members of the Canadian cabinet who met the maritime representatives at Charlottetown in 1864. Later in the same year he attended the Quebec conference, and was active in framing the resolutions that formed the basis of confederation. He was not a member of the committee that proceeded to London in 1866 to frame the British North America Act, having been in that year appointed as the Canadian representative at the international exposition at Paris.

During the last three years of his life McGee was actively fighting a new menace to the peace of Ireland, the Fenian society. This organization took its name from that given to the soldiers who fought for Ireland during the early days of her history. The Fenians had for their purpose the liberation of Ireland from the rule of England. The society became very active in Ireland and in the United States, which contained a large number of Irish immigrants. The close of the Civil War in the United States set free a great many Irish soldiers who were ready for adventure. The Fenians formed a plan of invading Canada and the maritime provinces, thus striking at Britain through her colonies. Under Colonel O'Neill a body of a thousand crossed the Niagara frontier and engaged in a brief skirmish with the Canadian militia at Ridgeway in 1866. The raiders did not try to advance farther, however, and withdrew to their own side of the river. Canadians sprang to arms to repel the invaders, and no other serious raids were attempted.

McGee was hostile to Fenianism from the first. In a speech in Montreal in 1865 he referred to the members as "a seditious Irish society originating in New York, whose founders have chosen to go behind the long Christian record of their ancestors to find in days of pagan darkness and blindness an appropriate name for themselves." He advised his compatriots in Canada to shun the organization. "Establish a committee which will purge your ranks of this political leprosy. Weed out and cast off these rotten members, who, without a single governmental grievance to complain of in Canada, would yet weaken and divide us in these days of danger and anxiety." In this strong language he threw down the gage of battle to the Fenians, and from that moment he was a marked man.

Of those who deserved a place in the first cabinet after confederation because of services they had rendered in accomplishing the union of the provinces, D'Arcy McGee undoubtedly stood among the first. But he unselfishly stood aside to make it easier for Sir John Macdonald to form a cabinet representing all elements of the people. Macdonald made it plain that it was only a temporary exclusion, and that he would be taken into the cabinet in the near future. McGee, however, was tired of political life and hoped to be appointed to a commissionership which would leave him some leisure for literary work.

His last speech in the House of Commons was made on the night of April 6, 1868. It was in defence of the appointment of Dr. Tupper to go to England to oppose Joseph Howe's attempt to break up the confederation. He closed his speech with an expression of his confidence in the success of confederation and a prophecy that the people of Canada would cherish it in their hearts as one of their greatest blessings. Who shall say that both his hope and his prophecy have not been abundantly fulfilled?

He finished his speech at midnight, and left the House with a friend. He was happy in the thought that on the morrow he would return to Montreal to celebrate his forty-third birthday with his family. He parted with his friend at the corner of Sparks and Metcalfe Streets. As he turned to enter the door of his lodgings on Sparks Street, an assassin stepped out of the shadows behind him and shot him dead. Later a man named Whelan, a member of the Fenian society, was arrested for the murder, and was tried, convicted, and executed.

D'Arcy McGee was a man of remarkable powers. He was a journalist, who wielded great influence upon public opinion; an historian, who left behind him several important works; a poet, who, though not great, was always musical; an orator, who was without peer in Canada; and a statesman, who did much to bring about the greatest achievement in Canadian history. In the discussion of the confederation question, other statesmen of his time appealed to the intelligence and reason of the people; he appealed to their hearts and emotions. He may therefore justly be called the great inspirer of the confederation movement. Before it was time the stirring voice was stilled, and all too soon, as Sir Charles Tupper said, "the grave closed over the most eloquent man in Canada."

XLVIII

LORD STRATHCONA

TRADER, RAILWAY BUILDER, AND STATESMAN

PERHAPS the most remarkable example of the poor boy who has come to Canada to seek fame and fortune and who has actually achieved these by rising to the highest rung of the ladder in both the commercial and the political world is Donald Alexander Smith, later Sir Donald Smith, and still later Baron Strathcona and Mount Royal. Like many other famous Canadians, he came from Scotland, richly endowed with the characteristics of the people of that country—industry, determination, persistence, integrity, and moral strength—qualities that in a large measure account for his success as a builder of Canada.

Donald Alexander Smith was born in 1820 at Forres, the place at which, according to Shakespeare, the witches of Macbeth had sung their weird incantations. He received a fair education, and was, in accordance with the wishes of his mother, about to take up the study of law, when an incident occurred that changed the whole current of his life. This was a visit to his home by his mother's brother, a fur-trader of the Hudson's Bay Company The young lad fell under the spell of his uncle's tales of adventure in the wilds of Canada. Law books were thrown to the winds, the prospect of becoming a lawyer was abandoned, and the youthful Scotsman made preparations to embark upon a career of romance among the wastes of northern America. His uncle procured for him a junior clerkship in the Hudson's Bay Company. He set out for Canada, and, after a stormy passage of fifty days, landed in Montreal, a youth of eighteen, with little to recommend him except a strong body, a courageous spirit, and the will to succeed.

He at once found himself a humble employee of a great trading company at a salary of £20 a year, with food and clothing provided. He laboured for some years in the Company's interests at its posts north of the St. Lawrence. One winter he had serious trouble with his eyes, arising from long journeys over the sunlit snow. Fearing that he might become blind, he started for Montreal to have an examination made. Reaching headquarters, he was met by Sir George Simpson, the governor of the Company.

"Why are you here?" sternly asked the governor.

"I came to have my eyes examined," meekly replied the young clerk.

"Who gave you leave to come?" inquired Sir George with still greater sternness.

"Nobody," returned Smith; "I am afraid that I am going blind, and I thought it might be dangerous to wait till I got permission to come."

"Eyes or no eyes, blind or not, it makes no difference to me," stormed the unsympathetic governor. "You came without leave, and you must be taught a lesson."

"Call the doctor to look at his eyes," he continued to an attendant, showing that he was not wholly inhuman.

The examination was quickly over, and the doctor declared that there was nothing seriously wrong.

"You have been guilty of a grave breach of discipline,"

A FAITHFUL SERVANT

said the governor, again addressing the young man, "and such an act must not be repeated. You will leave within half an hour for Hamilton Inlet."

Hamilton Inlet was one of the Company's posts on the bleak and desolate shore of Labrador. To reach it meant a journey of more than a thousand miles through pathless forests, over snow-covered wastes, and across rocky hills, plunging rivers, and frozen lakes. Smith, obedient to the governor's order, immediately set out with two Indian guides. This arduous journey began in midwinter and ended in early spring. In its difficulties and hardships it recalls the journeys of Hearne and Franklin at an earlier time across north-western Canada. It was due to his endurance, strength, and courage that Smith at length reached his destination in safety.

For thirteen years he remained at this lonely northern post, steadily increasing the Company's fur-trade and constantly rising in the estimation of the officials. He acted as physician to the Indians, attended to their spiritual welfare, and even on occasion performed the marriage ceremony when some trader took an Indian wife. He experimented in the cultivation of vegetables, and proved that they could be grown quite successfully in that northern latitude. He wrote his mother lengthy letters which could be mailed only at long intervals, on the arrival of the Company's ship at the post.

At length Smith was transferred to posts on Hudson Bay, and step by step he rose to the office of chief trader, and later to chief factor. In the discharge of his duties he travelled very widely over the north-west and gained an intimate knowledge of and great influence over the various Indian tribes. Finally, after thirty years of faithful and valuable service, he was made resident governor of the Company in Canada, with headquarters at Montreal.

When the Hudson's Bay Company in 1870 surrendered to the Dominion government its rights to the lands of western Canada, many of the English shareholders believed that its trading days were over, and were willing to part with their shares at low prices. Smith, knowing that the future trade of the Company was quite safe, quietly bought up large blocks of shares until he had obtained a controlling interest. Thus he laid the foundation for his large fortune. In 1889 he reached the highest office in the great organization, and became governor of the Hudson's Bay Company.

When the trouble with the Indians and half-breeds over the establishment of the Province of Manitoba arose in 1870, Sir John Macdonald looked about for an influential man who knew the situation thoroughly to send to quiet the rebels. He selected Donald Smith, and persuaded him to accept the task. He was instructed "to report on the best method of quieting and removing the dissatisfaction" among the malcontents.

When Smith reached Fort Garry he found that the rebels had seized the Company's stores, had set up a "provisional government," and had made political prisoners of several English settlers. Smith kept cool in this critical situation. A single false step would have precipitated a massacre of the English settlers. By his steadiness and tact he succeeded in outwitting Riel, the rebel leader. He persuaded Riel to call a great meeting in the courtyard of the fort. Over a thousand people gathered, and Smith made a speech setting forth the proposals of the government in establishing the new province. He induced the people to select twenty English and twenty French delegates who would form a convention to consider the proposals. After lengthy consideration, this convention decided to send a delegation of three to Ottawa to negotiate with the government. Riel was furious at Smith's success. In his rage he decided, by a display of force, to secure recognition of and respect for his "provisional government." Accordingly he condemned Thomas Scott, one of the prisoners, to be shot. The execution was carried out under conditions of great barbarity. But Riel's influence was gradually disappearing; the majority of the people refused longer to support him. Smith reached Ottawa, presented his report, and advised that a military force should be sent to impress and overawe the Indians. Such a force was prepared and sent under Colonel Wolseley, but when it reached Fort Garry everything was quiet. Riel had fled to the United States and the rebellion was over. The establishment of the Province of Manitoba and its inclusion in the confederation was thus brought about through the diplomacy of Donald Smith without serious bloodshed beyond the wanton execution of Thomas Scott.

Having proved his worth in commerce and diplomacy, Donald Smith now entered political life. In 1870 he was elected to the first legislature of Manitoba as the member for Winnipeg. The following year he was sent to the House of Commons at Ottawa as the representative of Selkirk in support of Sir John Macdonald. It was in this year that British Columbia entered the Canadian confederation upon the condition that a railway should immediately be begun to connect it with the eastern provinces. Mr. Smith, knowing the possibilities of the West, was warmly in favour of the construction of such a railway, but at first wanted it done as a government enterprise. When Sir John Macdonald proposed that it should be built by a private company, Mr. Smith was opposed to the scheme; and when later the Pacific Scandal was aired in parliament, he broke away from Sir John, much to the latter's indignation. His powerful speech in condemnation of the government had not a little to do in bringing about its resignation. In the next parliament he was a supporter of the new administration of Hon. Alexander Mackenzie.

In the meantime Mr. Smith had become seriously interested in railway construction on his own account. With two partners, he had bought an American line, the St. Paul and Pacific Railway, which had become bankrupt. The new management soon made the railway a paying concern. When Sir John Macdonald returned to power in 1878, Mr. Smith rejoined the Conservatives. His experience with the St. Paul and Pacific had convinced him that railways could best be put through by private companies. When the government proposed to give a new contract to a private company for the construction of the Canadian Pacific, he gave the scheme his cordial support. He formed a company, of which he himself and his cousin George Stephen were the principal members, and entered into a contract with the government to build the railway. The enterprise was not carried through without great difficulties. The company was compelled to borrow from the government large sums of money, which, however, were paid back within a year after the opening of the road. Sir Charles Tupper assisted greatly by pushing the loans through parliament in the face of much opposition. The construction was rapidly pressed forward, and in 1885, just five years after the contract was given, the railway was completed and connected up with the parts already built by the government, forming a continuous line from Montreal to Vancouver, a distance of more than three thousand miles. Donald Smith drove the last spike at Craigellachie in the Rocky Mountains.

During the period of construction of the Canadian Pacific Mr. Smith was out of parliament. He returned, however, in 1887 as member for Montreal West, and retained his seat till 1896. He had been knighted in the meantime, and was now Sir Donald Smith. He was appointed Canadian High Commissioner, succeeding Sir Charles Tupper, who had been recalled to Canada to bolster up the tottering Conservative government. Though he was now seventy-six years of age, Sir Donald still retained the bodily vigour and mental alertness of youth. His tall, erect figure, with snowy hair and beard, was a familiar sight in the Canadian offices and on the streets of London for many years. He held the respect and confidence of the statesmen of the Empire during the whole period of his office as High Commissioner. In 1897 he was raised to the peerage with the title Baron Strathcona and Mount Royal.

During the South African War Lord Strathcona became convinced that the British army needed the assistance of specially trained men to cope with the Boer scouts on the southern veldts. He accordingly recruited a body of men from the western plains of Canada and fitted them out at his own expense. They were known as the Strathcona Horse, and they gave an excellent account of themselves during the war.

Lord Strathcona died in 1914 at the splendid old age of ninety-four. It is safe to say that few Canadians have rendered more distinguished service to this country and to the Empire. As a business man and as a railroad builder he did much to promote the material prosperity of the Dominion, and as a statesman he did even more to strengthen the ties which bind Canada to the Motherland.

XLIX

SIR OLIVER MOWAT

ONTARIO'S GREAT REFORM PREMIER

ONE of the most outstanding of the prime ministers of Ontario was Sir Oliver Mowat. He held the post as head of the government for twenty-four years without a break. No other man in any part of the British Empire has held a similar position for so long a continuous period. That fact alone indicates the confidence which the people of the province reposed in him. He might have remained as prime minister for many years longer had he not resigned to accept a portfolio in the federal cabinet.

Oliver Mowat was born in Kingston in 1820 of Scottish parents. Very early he showed signs of unusual ability. It is said that at the age of five he used to sit on a high stool in his father's office and read the newspapers to the clerks. At sixteen he began the study of law in the office of John A. Macdonald. The coincidence of this association of two brilliant political leaders of a future time has already been commented upon in another connection. There was formed between the two men at this time a personal friendship which the political controversies of later years failed to disturb. When Mowat was called to the bar, he began the practice of his profession in Toronto. He was a keen and clever lawyer, and soon built up an excellent legal business.

Though his early political affiliations had been Conservative, Mowat entered parliament as a Reformer, and rapidly made his way to the front ranks of his party. He was an active supporter of George Brown in the effort to secure representation by population. He was a member of Brown's short-lived administration in 1857, following the controversy over the location of the Dominion capital at Ottawa. In 1864 he was one of the three Reformers who entered Macdonald's coalition cabinet to end the "deadlock" in parliament. He took a leading part in the Quebec conference to consider the confederation proposals, and had a great deal to do with the drafting of the resolutions passed at that assembly. At one of the sessions of the conference Macdonald passed a note to him across the table, offering him the position of vice-chancellor of Upper Canada, an important judgeship which had just become vacant. When the work of the confederation conference was completed, Mowat resigned from the government and accepted the post thus offered. He continued a judge for eight years, and discharged his important duties with distinguished ability. In 1872, when Hon. Edward Blake resigned the premiership of Ontario, Mr. Mowat was chosen as his successor. So he left the bench to re-enter political life.

Public Archives of Canada
SIR OLIVER MOWAT

Shortly after he became prime minister Mr. Mowat was able to perform a great service to many of the municipalities of Ontario. In 1852, twenty years before he took office, the government had passed the Municipal Loan Fund Act. Under the terms of this Act the government was empowered to borrow money and lend it to municipalities to enable them to provide schools, roads, bridges, and drains. Many municipalities took advantage of this arrangement and became deeply involved in debt. When the time for payment came some municipalities would not or could not repay these loans. Successive governments were unwilling to compel repayment for fear of losing the political support of the municipalities concerned. In 1873 Mr. Mowat's government found itself in possession of a large surplus. It determined to use this in helping to clear up these municipal debts, which by this time amounted to twelve million dollars, and were a very serious burden. The richer municipalities were compelled to pay up their debts in full, others were required to pay part, and those that were too poor to pay were let off altogether.

Mr. Mowat had several disputes with the Dominion government. The most important was in connection with the boundary of Ontario. Naturally he wanted Ontario to be as large as possible, for the larger the province the greater the provincial revenue would be. Naturally, too, the Dominion government did not wish the province to be any larger than necessary, for all the territory not included in the provinces belonged to the Dominion, and would be a source of revenue to the federal government. The Quebec Act of 1774 had fixed the western boundary of Canada as a line from the junction of the Ohio and Mississippi Rivers north to the territory held by the Hudson's Bay Company. Sir John Macdonald claimed that this line should be drawn "due north" from the mouth of the Ohio, which would bring the boundary a few miles west of Port Arthur. Mr. Mowat claimed that the line should be drawn "in a northerly direction" along the Mississippi to its source and thence due north. This would bring the western boundary to the Lake of the Woods. Moreover, Macdonald maintained that the northern boundary of the province should be the height of land north of the Great Lakes; Mowat maintained that it should be three hundred miles farther north along the English and Albany Rivers. The matter was referred to three arbitrators, who decided in favour of Mowat's claim. Later, in order that there should be no doubt as to the justice of the decision, the Dominion government laid the question before the British Privy Council, which upheld the finding of the arbitrators. So the Province of Ontario secured an area more than twice as large as the Dominion government proposed to allot to her.

Other disputes between Mr. Mowat and Sir John Macdonald concerned the rights of the province over several matters that were not clearly assigned to either the Dominion or the province in the British North America Act. In all these disputes the provincial premier's claims were upheld by the Privy Council. He succeeded in establishing the principle that the provincial legislatures are co-ordinate with and not subordinate to the federal parliament. Mr. Mowat's success in having his contentions confirmed contributed not a little to his long hold upon the confidence of the people of Ontario. He was returned to power in election after election, until it began to look as if the Conservative opposition in the legislature could never win.

Though Mr. Mowat may have been at variance with Sir John Macdonald on almost every other political question, he was at one with him in his unswerving loyalty to Britain. During the years of industrial depression between 1886 and 1896, a movement, fathered by Mr. Goldwin Smith and supported by some Canadian politicians, was launched for the establishment of commercial union between Canada and the United States. It was proposed that the two countries should set up free trade between themselves and maintain a common tariff against the rest of the world. Mr. Mowat opposed this proposal with great vigour. In letters to the Press and in speeches from the public platform, he denounced the project as "veiled annexation," and his uncompromising attitude had no small influence in putting an end to the movement.

In 1896, when Sir Wilfrid Laurier won the Dominion elections, he appointed Sir Oliver Mowat to the Senate, and gave him a seat in the cabinet as minister of justice. In the following year he resigned his portfolio and was appointed lieutenant-governor of Ontario, a position which he held till his death in 1903. He will be remembered by the people of his province as a political leader of shrewd judgment, a statesman of stainless honour, and a determined champion of "provincial rights."

L

SIR WILFRID LAURIER

THE SILVER-TONGUED CHIEFTAIN OF LIBERALISM

THE place in the Conservative party held so long by Sir John Macdonald, was held in the Liberal party by Sir Wilfrid Laurier. The two great chieftains were contemporaries, and sat opposite to each other in parliament for a long period, though Sir John was the senior in age by more than twenty years. Though opposed politically, each respected and admired the other. Sir Wilfrid learned from his great rival many lessons in political leadership that were useful to him in later years. One of the finest speeches ever made in the Canadian parliament was that delivered by the Liberal leader in eulogy of the Conservative chieftain upon the death of the latter in 1891.

Sir Wilfrid Laurier was leader of the Liberal party of Canada for more than thirty years, during fifteen of which he was prime minister. For the whole of that long period he held the affection of his followers and the respect of his opponents. This was largely due to his stainless character, his unfailing courtesy, his kindly sympathy, his fairness to opponents, and his brilliant gifts of speech. His name still serves, and doubtless will serve for years to come, as a rallying cry in party conflict to those of his political faith.

Wilfrid Laurier was born in the little village of St. Lin, in Quebec, in 1841. His father was a land surveyor and farmer. His mother was a cultured Frenchwoman, and, though she died when the boy was five years of age, he always retained the tenderest recollection of the lessons he learned at her knee. He attended the parish school with the other French lads at St. Lin, but at the age of ten he was

EARLY POLITICAL CAREER

sent by his father to an English school. For two years he was taught by a Scotch schoolmaster, and for part of that time lived with a Presbyterian family. Thus the French Roman Catholic boy learned the lesson of religious tolerance, the effect of which he never lost in his subsequent career.

At the age of twelve he entered L'Assomption College, where he spent seven years. Upon his graduation he took the law course at McGill University. On the completion of this he started the practice of law in Montreal. His health, never robust during his early years, began to cause alarm. In the hope of regaining it he left the city and went to the village of Arthabaskaville as the editor of a country newspaper. This proved an unsuccessful venture, and in a few months the newspaper ceased publication. He resumed his legal practice, and soon became recognized as one of the most successful lawyers in the district.

Public Archives of Canada
SIR WILFRID LAURIER

In 1871 the brilliant young lawyer entered upon his political career as member of the legislature of Quebec. Three years later the constituency of Drummond-Arthabaska sent him to the House of Commons in the election that brought defeat to the Macdonald administration and elevated the Liberals to power under the premiership of Hon. Alexander Mackenzie. He soon won recognition as the leader of the French Liberals, and in 1877 was offered a seat in the cabinet as minister of inland revenue. To the surprise of everybody, he was defeated n his constituency in the by-election that followed, but speedily found a seat in Quebec East. He did not have much opportunity at this time to show his ability as an administrator, for the Mackenzie government was defeated the next year in the election that restored Sir John Macdonald to office.

For the next eighteen years Mr. Laurier was in opposition, and had the disappointment of seeing his party defeated at the hands of Macdonald in three successive elections. He served as Quebec lieutenant first under Mackenzie and later under Blake. During this period his most notable accomplishment was a famous speech that he made in 1885 in defence of Riel after the Saskatchewan rebellion. He took the ground that Riel was insane, and that the government should intervene to prevent the carrying out of the sentence of the courts. The speech was regarded as a brilliant effort, and produced a profound effect upon parliament and the country, especially upon his compatriots in Quebec.

In 1887, on the resignation of Hon. Edward Blake as leader of the Liberal party, Mr. Laurier was chosen as his successor. In the election of 1891 his party was beaten on the question of unrestricted reciprocity with the United States. In the same year Sir John Macdonald died, and from that moment the fortunes of the Liberal party began to rise. The Conservative government had been a long time in office and began to show signs of breaking up. Within five years after Macdonald's death there were four Conservative prime ministers. Sir John Abbott and Sir Mackenzie Bowell resigned after brief periods of leadership; Sir John Thompson died after a premiership of less than two years; and Sir Charles Tupper was defeated in the election of 1896.

The occasion of the defeat of the Conservatives after their many years of power was a dispute over the schools of Manitoba. When this province was established its government had set up two sets of schools, Protestant and Roman Catholic. In 1890 the provincial government decided to abolish this system and to set up instead a single system without any religious distinction. The Roman Catholics protested against being deprived of what they regarded as their rights, and appealed to the Dominion government.

ACCESSION TO THE PREMIERSHIP

Requests to the Manitoba government to restore the rights of the minority proved unavailing. Sir Mackenzie Bowell, the prime minister, then introduced in parliament what was called the Remedial Bill, which proposed to establish separate schools for Roman Catholics in Manitoba. Mr. Laurier was in a difficult position. He found himself faced with two alternatives. Either he must unite with the Conservatives and help to force an undesired school system upon the province, or he must offend those of his own church by denying them the schools they desired. He chose the latter course. He declared his policy to be one of conciliation and not of coercion. He proposed to discuss the question in a friendly way with the Manitoba government in the hope of reaching some settlement that would be acceptable to all parties. There was so much opposition to the Remedial Bill that the government asked for the dissolution of parliament. Sir Mackenzie Bowell resigned, and Sir Charles Tupper came from England to lead the Conservatives in a forlorn hope. He fought gallantly, but the battle cry "Hands off Manitoba!" carried the Liberals to victory in the election.

Mr. Laurier succeeded to the premiership in 1896 under very favourable circumstances. He was supported by a great popular majority in the country, and by a large following in the House of Commons. The Opposition was disorganized and discouraged. The country itself had entered upon a period of great material expansion. Everything pointed to the probability of a long lease of power for the Liberals. Mr. Laurier selected for his cabinet a group of strong administrators, probably the most capable, as a whole, that Canada has ever had. So high was their acknowledged ability that their opponents, somewhat enviously, no doubt, called them the "Ministry of all the Talents." Three provincial premiers (Sir Oliver Mowat from Ontario, Hon. A. G. Blair from New Brunswick, Hon. W. S. Fielding from Nova Scotia), the Attorney-General of Manitoba (Hon. Clifford Sifton), and several outstanding Liberals from the parliamentary ranks formed a cabinet that commanded confidence throughout the country.

In 1897 Mr. Laurier went to England to be present at the ceremonies in connection with the Diamond Jubilee of the coronation of Queen Victoria. At the same time he attended the Imperial Conference, a meeting of the statesmen of the Empire to discuss affairs that affected the Dominions in common. The Canadian prime minister was greeted with enthusiasm wherever he went. His striking appearance, his graceful manners, his eloquent speeches, and, most of all, his assurances of Canadian loyalty to the Motherland produced a splendid impression upon the people of England. He accepted knighthood at the hands of his sovereign, and returned to Canada as Sir Wilfrid Laurier.

The loyalty of the Canadian people soon had an opportunity to express itself. In 1899 Britain was plunged into a war in South Africa. President Kruger of the Transvaal Republic, angered at the demand of the British government that English residents in his country should be fairly treated, determined to drive them out of South Africa. He declared war and invaded Natal. The Canadian government was quick to offer assistance in the Empire's defence. Within a few weeks a contingent of 1,000 men was equipped and despatched to South Africa. Later contingents brought the number of Canadians in active service up to 7,000. They fought bravely, and showed that they were able to hold their own with the sharpshooters of the African veldts. The most important engagement in which they took part was at Paardeberg in February, 1900. Here they charged the Boer trenches, and, though at first driven back with heavy loss, they made a second attack, during which the Boers were routed and their leader, Cronje, was captured. In these charges the Canadians lost over one hundred men in killed and wounded. The grief of Canada in the loss of her sons was mingled with pride that they had borne themselves gallantly in a far country and had shed their blood in proof of their devotion to the old Motherland across the seas.

The Boer war, which had so greatly strengthened the bonds of Empire, had scarcely ended when an event occurred which caused in Canada no small annoyance with Britain. The

ALASKA BOUNDARY

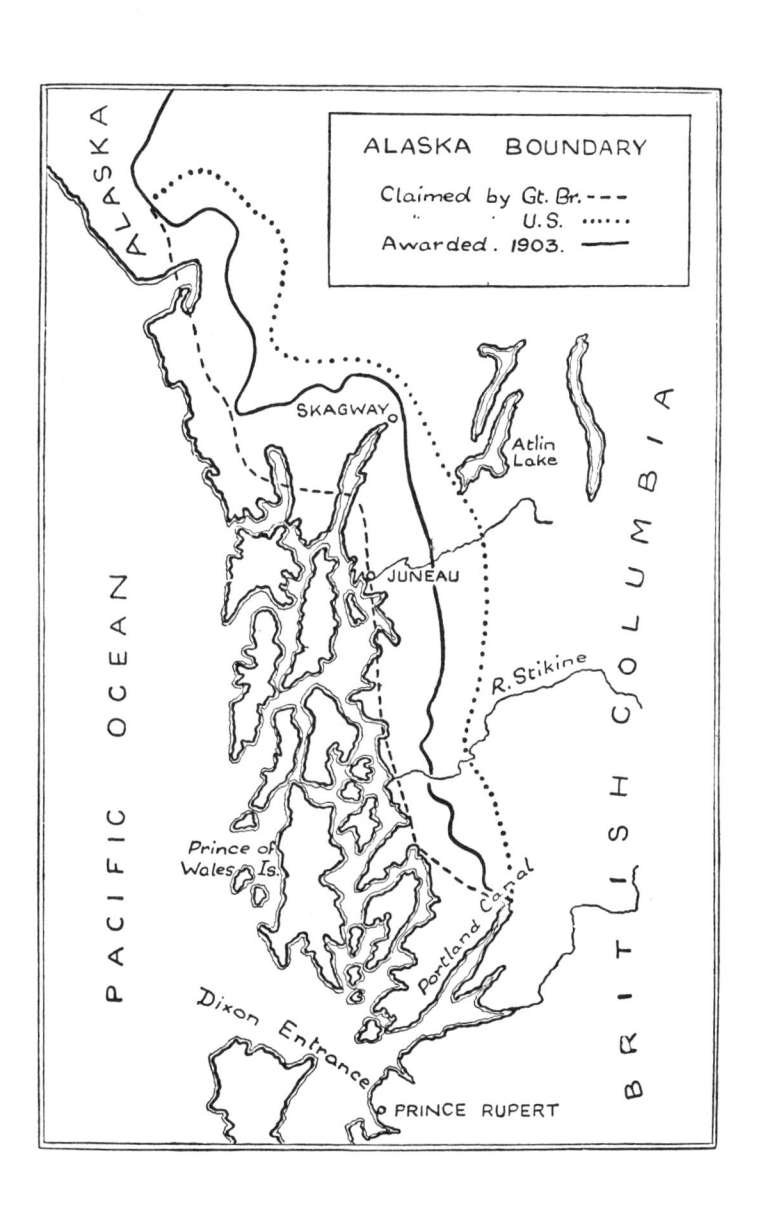

Claimed by Gt. Br. - - -
" U.S. ....
Awarded. 1903. ———

occasion was the settlement of the boundary between Alaska
and Canada. It is necessary to go back in history for many
years to understand this question aright. In early times
Russian sailors used to visit the western coasts of America
in quest of seals and whales, and Alaska was regarded as a
Russian possession. When trading-posts of the Hudson's Bay
Company began to be set up along these coasts, it became
necessary to define the boundary between British and Russian
America. By a treaty made in 1825 between Great Britain
and Russia, the latter country was given, in addition to
the great Alaskan peninsula, a strip of land along the
western coast, extending from the 141st meridian south-
eastward to Portland Channel. The eastern limit of this
"panhandle" was not clearly defined. In 1867 the United
States bought Alaska from Russia. After this several attempts
to settle the boundary were futile. The discovery of gold in
the Klondike in 1897 made it necessary to come to some
conclusion on the question.

In 1903 a board of arbitration to decide the matter was
agreed upon. On this board the United States had three
representatives, Canada two, and Great Britain one. Lord
Alverstone, the chief justice of England, was the British
representative and the chairman of the board, and the two
Canadian representatives were Sir Louis Jetté, chief justice
of Quebec, and Mr. A. B. (afterwards Sir Allen) Aylesworth,
a prominent lawyer of Ontario.

The main point of difficulty lay in the statement of the
treaty of 1825 that, from the head of Portland Channel,
the boundary should follow the summits of the mountains
parallel to the coast, but at no point was it to extend more
than thirty-five miles inland. The coast is very much indented
by deep channels cutting many miles into the land. The
Americans claimed that the boundary should follow the
windings of the coast and at thirty-five miles' distance,
except where this was cut shorter by the presence of a
mountain range. The Canadians claimed that the line should
be located at a distance thirty-five miles from the general
trend of the coast. It is probable that the American contention was more nearly borne out by the terms of the

A RAILWAY ERA

treaty than the Canadian. The decision of the arbitration board was a compromise between the two claims, though rather more favourable to the United States. The two Canadian representatives were so much displeased that they refused to sign the award. Many people in this country believed that Britain had sacrificed the interests of Canada for the sake of gaining favour with the United States. Even Sir Wilfrid Laurier spoke hotly in parliament about the right of Canada to direct her own affairs and make her own bargains. But in the light of sober thought most people have come to believe that the decision was not unfair, and that Canada did not suffer any serious injustice. The momentary irritation over an adverse decision was only a ripple on the placid surface of the deep and abiding affection that Canada has for Britain.

The early years of this century brought rapid development to the Canadian West. During the fifteen years of Sir Wilfrid Laurier's premiership, large numbers of immigrants came from Great Britain and other European countries and from the United States. They spread over the fertile prairie lands of western Canada, taking up farms and producing wheat and live stock in great abundance.

Though the Canadian Pacific Railway had been very active in building branch lines, it could not keep up with the demands for transportation. The government felt that another transcontinental railway was needed. In 1903 it gave a charter to the Grand Trunk Railway to build a line from Winnipeg to Prince Rupert, guaranteeing its bonds and giving it cash subsidies. The government itself built the National Transcontinental from Moncton to Winnipeg through the timber and clay belt of northern Quebec and Ontario, and agreed to rent it to the Grand Trunk for a nominal sum yearly. The two lines were pushed forward rapidly, and by 1915 trains were running across Canada on a second transcontinental line.

In the meantime a third line was making its way across the continent. The Canadian Northern Railway Company was busy buying railways and building new ones until it, too, had a line from Montreal to Vancouver. This company was also assisted by large subsidies from the Dominion and the provincial governments.

The large inflow of population to the West made the organization of new provinces desirable. In 1905 the Laurier government divided the region that had been known as the North-West Territories into two provinces called Alberta and Saskatchewan, each comprising about a quarter of a million square miles. Thus the confederation of the present nine provinces of the Dominion was complete, forming an unbroken line from the Atlantic to the Pacific.

The question of the defence of the Empire was much to the fore in the Imperial Conference in 1907, and again at the special Defence Conference of 1909. Great Britain was becoming alarmed at the activity shown by Germany in building up its fleet. Realizing that her existence depended upon her supremacy on the seas, Britain sought the best means of strengthening her defences, and made it known to her overseas Dominions that she needed help. She was compelled to recall the Halifax and Esquimalt squadrons of her navy from Canadian waters for service nearer home. Sir Wilfrid Laurier was always an intensely loyal British subject. "When Britain is at war, Canada is at war," he said. He was willing that Canada should help the Mother Country, but disagreed with her statesmen as to the form that this assistance should take. Some of the other Dominions made direct contributions to the British navy. It was never Sir Wilfrid's policy to contribute directly to the support of the navy; he proposed rather to assist the Empire by setting up measures of defence at home. Accordingly, in 1909 he introduced in the Canadian parliament his proposals for home defence. A naval college was to be established at Halifax. Two vessels, the *Niobe* and the *Rainbow*, were to be bought from the British government for coast defence. Nine other vessels were to be built at a cost of about ten million dollars as the beginning of a Canadian navy. These proposals were not very popular in Canada. Sir Wilfrid's opponents spoke contemptuously of his "tin-pot" navy. In Quebec he was attacked by his French compatriots for acknowledging that Canada was bound to take part in Britain's foreign wars.

THE RECIPROCITY AGREEMENT

His naval policy had not a little to do with his defeat in the elections of 1911.

One of the features of Sir Wilfrid Laurier's regime was a growing friendliness with the United States. In 1911 the government thought that it would be a good thing for Canada to secure closer trade relations with the neighbouring republic. Accordingly Hon. W. S. Fielding, the minister of finance, went to Washington and negotiated a Reciprocity agreement between the two countries. This agreement provided for a large measure of free trade, larger in fact than that provided by the Reciprocity Treaty of 1854. There was to be free trade in grain, fruits, vegetables, live stock, dairy products, and fish; and reduced duties on meats, flour, and coal. The agreement was vigorously debated in the House of Commons for some weeks, and at length Sir Wilfrid decided to dissolve parliament and appeal to the country. A hot election campaign followed. The Conservatives urged that the Reciprocity agreement would mean that the trade avenues in Canada would be largely north and south. In view of the fact that the country had recently built at a great cost a transcontinental railway for the trade east and west, this appeared to them a very bad policy. At any rate, said the Conservatives, there was a danger that commercial union with the United States would eventually lead to political union, and no loyal Canadian desired that. On the other hand the Liberals asserted that the disasters feared by their opponents were quite impossible, and dwelt upon the material advantages to be gained under the agreement. In the elections of September, 1911, the Liberals, much to the surprise of Sir Wilfrid, were defeated, and the Conservatives, under the leadership of Mr. R. L. Borden, came into power.

Sir Wilfrid Laurier had directed the government of Canada for a longer continuous period than any previous prime minister. Under his rule Canada enjoyed an era of unexampled prosperity and made rapid material progress. His great aims appeared to be to promote religious and racial harmony among the people, and to make Canada a nation within the Empire. In these worthy aims he succeeded to a very large degree, and Canada has reason to hold him in grateful remembrance.

After his defeat in 1911, he continued as leader of the Liberal opposition in Parliament for several years. Though patriotically assisting the government in its measures during the early period of the Great War, he found himself unable to support the policy of conscription adopted by the coalition government in 1917. In the elections of that year he was deserted by many of his parliamentary followers, and as a result his party was badly defeated. He died suddenly during the parliamentary session of 1919, and the nation mourned the passing of a much-loved statesman and a great Canadian.

LI

SIR JAMES WHITNEY

ONTARIO'S GREAT CONSERVATIVE PREMIER

The people of the Province of Ontario have good reason for the high estimation in which they hold the memory of Sir James Whitney. More than any other prime minister, he is associated in their minds with the qualities of straightforwardness and honesty. His opinions were always given with a directness, clearness, and force that never left any doubt as to his meaning. However much opponents might disagree with his ideas, they never questioned the sincerity of his desire to promote the good of the province.

James Pliny Whitney was born in Williamsburg, Dundas county, in 1843. He attended the Cornwall Grammar School, and later entered upon the study of law. He was called to the bar in 1876. He was elected to the legislature as the representative of Dundas county in 1888. His industry, energy, and force of character soon brought him recognition as an outstanding member. In 1896 he was chosen leader of the Conservative party in the provincial parliament. At that time the Liberals were strongly entrenched in power, for they had given the province a long period of efficient and economical government. However, after thirty-three years of continuous rule the Liberals were finally defeated in the election of 1905, and Mr. Whitney succeeded to the premiership.

The years of the Whitney administration, from 1905-1914, form a period of great material advancement in the province. This was due in no small degree to the vigorous activity of the government. Mr. Whitney carried through many wise measures, the most important of which may be summarized under five headings: (1) extension of educational facilities; (2) improvement in the method of controlling the liquor traffic; (3) development of the water powers of the province; (4) opening up of New Ontario; (5) reform of provincial prisons and asylums. These five topics will be briefly considered in order.

(1) *Extension of Educational Facilities*

One of the first educational improvements undertaken by Mr. Whitney was the reorganization of the methods of training teachers. The great majority of the teachers in the elementary schools had received only a few months of training in county Model Schools. Only a small proportion had been trained in the three existing Normal Schools. In 1907 Mr. Whitney abolished all but a few of the county Model Schools, and built four new Normal Schools. He raised the standard of scholarship required for entrance into these schools, and extended the course of training to one year. The result of this policy was to increase the efficiency of the elementary schools through the provision of better-trained teachers.

Public Archives of Canada
SIR JAMES P. WHITNEY

Another educational measure was the establishment of continuation schools. These were designed to extend the work of the elementary schools by providing courses of study suited to local needs. They became very popular, and were rapidly established in towns and villages in all parts of the province. To-day there are more than two hundred continuation schools in operation. They have brought a secondary school education to the doors of the people of the smaller urban centres and of the rural communities.

One of the most remarkable features of Mr. Whitney's educational policy was the initiation of a scheme of technical education. Educational experts were sent to the United States and Europe to study and report upon the methods of technical education in operation there. A scheme was developed for Ontario, including some of the best features of foreign systems, but in the main embodying original features adapted to conditions in this province. As a result of the operation of this scheme, practically every city and large town has now either a technical school or a vocational department in its high school. In these schools young men and women are given, in addition to a general education, special training fitting them for the trades and industries. Students can now acquire, in a comparatively short time in a technical or vocational department, a training for a particular trade or industry formerly requiring years under an apprenticeship system. These schools provide not only full-time courses, but also part-time and night courses, which are attended by tens of thousands of students.

Still another educational reform brought about by Mr. Whitney was the improvement and the cheapening of textbooks used in the schools. A great deal of money has been saved by the parents of the children through the provision of good textbooks at a low price. In giving this advantage to the people the government has had, however, to bear a portion of the cost of the textbooks through the payment of considerable sums to the publishers.

(2) *Method of Controlling the Liquor Traffic*

The control of the sale of intoxicating liquor has always been a difficult problem for the provincial government. In the earlier days statesmen sought to regulate it by a license system, that is, by putting the sale exclusively in the hands of those who paid the government for a license. This license was subject to certain restrictions. The hours for the sale of liquor were limited, and severe penalties were provided for violation of the regulations. Mr. Whitney continued this plan, but added provisions whereby municipalities might banish the sale of liquor within their boundaries. By a system known as "Local Option," the electors might by a three-fifths vote require the municipal council to pass a by-law to prevent the issue of licenses within the municipality. Mr. Whitney always insisted that such a law must have the support of a large body of public opinion, and hence required that at least three-fifths of the voters should support it. Similarly, to repeal a local option by-law a three-fifths majority was essential. By means of this measure intoxicating liquor was excluded from a large number of the municipalities of Ontario.

(3) *Development of Water Powers*

One of the outstanding achievements of Mr. Whitney's administration was the development of the great water powers of the province in the production of electricity for industrial and domestic purposes. In 1906 the government established the Hydro-Electric Power Commission, the function of which is to co-operate with the municipalities of the province in securing electric power at a lower rate than that at which it could be obtained from private companies. The Commission consists of three members, one of whom must be a member of the provincial cabinet, and one of whom must represent the co-operating municipalities. The first chairman of the Commission was Mr. (afterwards Sir) Adam Beck, the member of the legislature for London. He was a man of remarkable vision and determination. He carried out the enterprises of the Commission with good judgment and tireless energy. To him more than to anybody else is due the rapid advance in the general use of electricity in the province.

Under the plan at present in operation, the government supplies the Commission with money to make contracts for the supply of power, to purchase existing power plants, and to construct new power plants. The money thus borrowed, together with interest, will eventually be paid back to the government by the Commission. The Commission undertakes to supply power to any municipality desiring it at

HYDRO-ELECTRIC POWER

rates agreed upon, and to convey the power over its own transmission lines. The rates charged cover the municipality's share of the cost of producing the electricity and its share in providing a sinking fund for the repayment of the capital cost to the government in thirty or forty years. The municipality then conveys the power over its own distributing lines to its patrons. The rates charged to the consumers by the municipality cover the sum paid to the Hydro-Electric Power Commission and a sum sufficient to provide a sinking fund to repay the investment of the municipality in thirty or forty years. The scheme is a great co-operative enterprise. The co-operating municipalities in reality own the power plants and main transmission lines operated by the Hydro-Electric Power Commission. The latter is the agency through which the co-operation is given effect.

The operations of the Commission have extended very greatly during the thirty years of its existence. During the first year it supplied 3,500 horse-power to eight municipalities; during 1936 it supplied 1,650,000 horse-power to nearly eight hundred municipalities. It has power plants at many points in the province, one of them, the Queenston–Chippawa plant below Niagara Falls, being the largest in the world. The Commission is constantly investigating new sources of power supply and extending its facilities to more and more of the people of the province. The advantages in affording cheap power to turn the wheels of industry and to increase the comfort and convenience of the homes of the people are beyond calculation.

(4) *Opening Up of New Ontario*

The Liberal government which preceded that of Mr. Whitney began the construction of the Timiskaming and Northern Ontario Railway from North Bay to connect the rich agricultural lands of the north with southern Ontario. Mr. Whitney continued the railway to Cochrane, where it forms a junction with the National Transcontinental lines. During the construction of this railway silver was discovered at Cobalt, and later gold at Porcupine. This railway has thus opened up a rich mining region, as well as a fine agricultural area with large resources of timber and pulpwood. Northern Ontario, with its valuable mineral deposits, its fertile lands, its widespread forests, and its extensive water powers, is a source of unlimited wealth to the people and of ever-increasing revenue to the government of Ontario.

Under Sir James Whitney the province secured a large addition to its territory. In 1912, by negotiation with the Dominion and with the Province of Manitoba, the district of Patricia, comprising an area of nearly 150,000 square miles, was added, making a total area for the province of over 400,000 square miles.

(5) *Prison and Hospital Reform*

One of the prominent members of Sir James Whitney's cabinet during the whole period of his administration was Hon. W. J. Hanna, who held the portfolio of provincial secretary. Mr. Hanna was a very able lawyer of Sarnia, with a large and lucrative practice, which he willingly sacrificed in order to serve the province. Under his supervision fell the provincial prisons and asylums. In these he set up reforms which have placed Ontario in the forefront of the world in the humanitarian treatment of prisoners. To Mr. Hanna, a criminal was not an outcast but a man who might, by proper treatment, be transformed into a good citizen. Accordingly, he instituted the plan of treating prisoners kindly, teaching them useful trades, placing them on their honour with regard to conduct, and giving them privileges as a reward of merit. As a result of these methods, many prisoners who might otherwise have become hardened criminals have been rehabilitated and restored as useful members of society. The Ontario prison farm at Guelph embodies Mr. Hanna's advanced ideas of a reformatory institution. In the asylums, or mental hospitals as he renamed them, he established the scientific study and treatment of patients with the view of restoring them to a normal condition or fitting them for some sort of useful service.

Sir James Whitney died in 1914. The best tribute to his statesmanship lies in the fact that his successors in office

"HONEST AND BOLD"

have continued the policies that he laid down, viz. the provision of better educational facilities for the people, the stricter regulation of the liquor traffic, the extension of the hydro-electric power system, and the development of the resources of New Ontario. A striking statue in Queen's Park, Toronto, in front of the legislative buildings, perpetuates the memory of the prime minister who was "bold enough to be honest, and honest enough to be bold."

LII

SIR ROBERT BORDEN

CANADA'S WAR PREMIER

SIR ROBERT BORDEN will be remembered in history as Canada's "war premier." In all the British Empire he was the only prime minister who retained the confidence of the people during the whole period of the Great War. He had been in office for three years when it began; he bore the burden of government during the four years of its duration; and he remained at his post for two years after its close. He proved himself a dependable leader of the people during that terrible period of storm and stress. His quiet firmness of purpose steadied their determination; his unswerving loyalty fired them with patriotic zeal; his unremitting industry inspired them to continuous effort. Canada has reason to hold Sir Robert Borden in grateful remembrance for his wise direction of national affairs in her hour of peril.

Robert Laird Borden was born at Grand Pré in Nova Scotia in 1854. He studied law, was called to the bar, and became one of the outstanding lawyers in his native province. He entered the federal parliament in 1896 as a Conservative member for Halifax after the election that brought a crushing defeat to the Conservative government at the hands of the Liberal forces under Sir Wilfrid Laurier. Mr. Borden rapidly made his way to the front ranks of his party, and, after the resignation of Sir Charles Tupper in 1901, he was chosen leader. He lost two general elections, but eventually, in 1911, he was successful on the issue of Reciprocity with the United States. He was the third prime minister since confederation that came out of Nova Scotia.

THE GREAT WAR

In 1913, believing that war in Europe was near, Mr. Borden proposed that Canada should contribute three Dreadnoughts to the British navy, "the best ships of war that science could devise and that money could buy." Thus he believed Canada might share in the defence of the Empire of which she formed a part. The estimated cost of the three warships was $35,000,000, which parliament was asked to vote. The question provoked a long and bitter debate in the House of Commons. The opposition under Sir Wilfrid Laurier fought vigorously against the proposal, and supported instead the scheme of a Canadian navy. At length, amid scenes of great disorder on the floor of the House, the debate was cut short by "closure." The Dreadnought scheme was carried in the Commons by a large majority, but was defeated in the Senate, and so had to be dropped.

Public Archives of Canada
SIR ROBERT BORDEN

During those fateful days of August, 1914, when war clouds suddenly appeared on the European horizon, and conflict between Britain and Germany seemed certain, Mr. Borden cabled the British government as follows: "If unhappily war should ensue, the Canadian people will be united in a common resolve to put forth every effort and to make every sacrifice necessary to ensure the integrity and to maintain the honour of our Empire." Thus did the prime minister pledge the loyalty of Canada to the Empire, and, as events proved, he had gauged aright the sentiment of her people.

Six weeks later, at a special war session of parliament, Sir

Wilfrid Laurier, in a finely patriotic speech, assured the government of the hearty support of the opposition in all necessary war measures. He said: "We are British subjects, and to-day we are faced with the consequences which are involved in that proud fact. Long have we enjoyed the benefits of our British citizenship; to-day it is our duty and our privilege to accept its responsibilities—yes, and its sacrifices."

At the close of his speech in the same debate Mr. Borden said: "As to our duty all are agreed, east and west, and we stand shoulder to shoulder with Britain and the other British possessions in this quarrel. And that duty we shall not fail to fulfil as the honour of Canada demands. Not for love of battle, not for lust of conquest, not for greed of possessions, but for the cause of honour, to maintain solemn pledges, to uphold the principle of liberty, to withstand forces that would convert the world into an armed camp—yes, in the name of the very peace that we sought at any cost save that of dishonour, we have entered into this war; and, while gravely conscious of the tremendous issues involved, and of all the sacrifices that they may entail, we do not shrink from them, but with firm hearts we abide the event."

Thus splendidly did Canada's two great statesmen speak in the name of Canadians, and splendidly did Canadians respond. Within six weeks of the declaration of war, 33,000 men were equipped and ready for transportation overseas. For every man required, five offered to go. The fine energy of the minister of militia, General Sir Sam Hughes, had much to do with the swift preparation. Early in October, 1914, the first division embarked at Quebec for England. After three months' training there, the men were transferred to France, and early in 1915 they were on the fighting front. During the next two years three other divisions were recruited and sent across. After that, the four divisions were kept up to full strength by a constant stream of recruits. Altogether more than half a million soldiers, the flower of the manhood of Canada, enlisted, nearly all of them voluntarily. Of that number more than 400,000 went overseas. And when the war was over, after four years of

OUTSTANDING ENGAGEMENTS 317

unparalleled struggle, more than 50,000 of Canada's finest sons were dead and lay in many a nameless grave in France and Flanders. Of those who survived over 150,000 were wounded, and many of them permanently disabled. Thus did Canada prove not only her stanch loyalty to the old Mother across the seas, but also her determination that honour and justice should not perish from the earth.

The Great War was such a tremendous thing that its complete story would require many volumes to tell. In a brief sketch it is impossible to give an adequate account of even the comparatively small part that Canada played in the vast arena of the war. There were, however, some events in which our soldiers showed such noble heroism and endurance that every Canadian should remember them with pride.

(1) *St. Julien*

The first of these outstanding engagements was at St. Julien, near the town of Ypres, in Flanders, in April, 1915. The Canadians occupied trenches on a three-mile front. At their left French colonial soldiers occupied a four-mile line. One afternoon a cloud of yellowish-green vapour slowly poured across "No Man's Land" from the German lines. It was chlorine gas, an inhuman weapon of warfare never before used by a civilized nation. The deadly vapour choked and blinded the soldiers, and many died in agony. A gap was made in the French line, and through it the Germans poured. The Canadians dropped back to head them off. Two thousand Canadians attacked seven thousand Germans and drove them from their position. In the days that followed the Germans made other gas attacks and tried desperately to break through, but the line held. The cost was great, for over seven hundred Canadians were killed and two thousand wounded. By all the rules of warfare the Canadians were defeated. But they did not know it, and so stood firm. Had the Germans succeeded in breaking through, they would probably have taken the port of Calais, from which they could have dominated the Strait of Dover and crippled the operations of the British fleet. "The gallant work of the Canadians saved the situation," reported the

British commander. And the British prime minister, Mr. Lloyd George, generously said: "Just as the Rocky Mountains hurl back the storms of the West, so did these heroes break the hurricane of the German fury amid the flames and poison fumes of Gehenna; they held high the honour of Canada, and saved the British army." It was a proud yet tragic day for Canada.

(2) *Courcelette*

Some of the most dreadful fighting of the war occurred in 1916 along the Somme River. The battle began in July and continued for six months. The purpose was not so much to gain ground as to wear down the German resistance to the point of collapse. Tremendous artillery bombardments and gas attacks caused fearful slaughter on both sides. The Canadians were not engaged in the Battle of the Somme until September. They were then under the command of General Sir Julian Byng, who was later to become governor-general of Canada. On September 15th the Canadians were sent "over the top" to capture the village of Courcelette. Assisted by a strong artillery "barrage" and by "tanks," they carried out the task, and took 1,200 prisoners. This success was largely due to a French-Canadian battalion from Quebec. The enemy made several counter-attacks during the following week, but were unable to wrest the village from its captors.

(3) *Vimy Ridge*

One of the greatest events of the war was the capture of Vimy Ridge in 1917, an achievement in which the Canadians bore a distinguished part. Vimy Ridge was an elevation six miles long by two miles wide between Arras and Lens. It was a strategic point from which the Germans commanded the mining region surrounding Lens. Along the western slope of the ridge they had constructed several lines of trenches, parallel with each other. From these trenches deep tunnels were burrowed into the hillside, forming "dugouts," which were fitted up very comfortably as shelters for the soldiers. Evidently the Germans expected to stay there a long time. Large guns were hidden at various points on the slope. The British made careful preparations for the attack. Great quantities of ammunition and many large guns were brought up. For two weeks the slope was bombarded. Then in the early hours of Easter Monday, April 9th, the order was given to charge with bayonets. The Canadians formed part of the attacking army. Crossing "No Man's Land," they reached a maze of trenches containing only broken guns and dead men, so well had the artillery done its work. There was severe fighting at the top of the ridge, but the machine-gun positions were quickly captured. The last point to be taken was Hill 145, where the Germans maintained a stubborn resistance. In the evening it fell to the Canadians, who swept over the crest and down the eastern slope in pursuit of the fleeing enemy. Four thousand prisoners were taken, besides immense quantities of ammunition, machine-guns, and cannon. The capture of Vimy Ridge was indeed, as Sir Douglas Haig described it, "an achievement of the highest order."

(4) *Lens*

One of the most intense struggles of the war was fought at Hill 70, a slight elevation which dominates Lens from the north. The British desired to capture it, and the Germans wished to retain it, because of its strategic importance. One night in August, 1917, the British guns poured a torrent of shells into the German trenches. In the early morning the Canadians went "over the top," and, protected by a barrage from the artillery, swept to the crest of the hill. There was bloody fighting among the dumps and shafts of the mines, and many of our men fell before the fire of the machine-guns of the enemy. But the Canadians penetrated the line and drove the Germans out of their strongholds. In spite of counter-attacks for several days, the Canadians held what they had won.

(5) *Passchendaele*

The Canadians were once more back at Ypres in October, 1917. North-east of the city, behind the German line, the little village of Passchendaele was perched on a ridge. It was a strategic point commanding the plain to the east. To the Canadians was assigned the task of capturing it. The attack was preceded by the usual bombardment by the heavy guns. On the night of October 25th rain fell heavily. At daylight the Canadians, protected by a heavy barrage, began to move forward over ground of indescribable difficulty. They floundered forward, now up to the knees in mud, now up to the armpits in the slime and water of shell-holes. They were sprayed by bullets from machine-guns and by shrapnel from bursting shells. They stumbled over broken and deserted German trenches and over masses of twisted barbed wire. All day they fought desperately, storming position after position. By night they had reached and occupied a line near the crest of the ridge. For many days the battle continued, artillery duels alternating with infantry attacks. At length on November 7th the capture of the ridge and of the ruined town was completed. The Canadians had attained their objective, but at terrific cost in lives and blood.

(6) *Amiens, Arras, Cambrai, Mons*

It will suffice to pass in rapid review the main engagements in which the Canadians participated during the last year of the war. General Sir Arthur Currie, a Canadian-bred soldier, was then in command, and skilfully directed their operations. When the German advance in the early months of 1918 was checked and the tide began to roll backward, our men were in the thickest of the fight. At the Battle of Amiens early in August they were in the centre of the British line, and advanced eight miles on the first day, the largest gain made in a single day during the war. By the end of August the Germans had been pushed back to the Hindenburg Line, which they fondly deemed impregnable. In the Battle of Arras early in September the Canadians broke through this vaunted line on a six-mile front, and the Germans began to realize that they had lost the war. Some of the severest fighting during the whole period of the war took place about Cambrai, which the Canadians captured on October 9th, after a two weeks' struggle. Then on

AID BY CANADIANS AT HOME 321

November 11th, the day on which the armistice was signed, our men entered Mons, the place from which four years before the British had begun their famous retreat before the German hosts.

During the whole period of the war the Canadian forces captured 45,000 prisoners, 850 artillery guns, 4,200 machine-guns, and liberated from enemy control 130 towns and villages. This surely is a record of accomplishment in which all Canadians may feel a justifiable pride.

It was not only on the fighting lines in France and Flanders that Canada helped to win the Great War. Canadians who could not go to fight on the battlefields put forth extraordinary efforts and made unusual sacrifices to support the soldiers in the trenches. A few of the ways in which the people at home assisted should be pointed out.

The total outlay for war purposes to the end of 1918 was considerably over a billion dollars. To meet this enormous expense the government was compelled to borrow money from the people themselves. This it did by giving an opportunity to subscribe to war loans. Altogether the government raised nearly a billion and a half dollars in this way—an average of nearly two hundred dollars for every man, woman, and child in the country. The people did not give this money to the government, but lent it at a fair rate of interest.

In order to pay the interest on the large loans and to meet the increased expenditures, the government found it necessary to secure new sources of revenue. The customs and excise duties on luxuries, such as tea, coffee, tobacco, and liquors, were greatly increased. Special war taxes were levied on automobiles and jewellery. A graded scale of taxation was adopted for incomes and business profits. Taxes were placed upon railway tickets, telegrams, money orders, cheques, letters, and patent medicines. Some of these taxes have since been removed or reduced, but the bulk of them still remain. It is probable that they will have to be continued for many years. The national debt is about two and a half billions of dollars, and the interest charges on this huge sum must be met year by year through the revenues that the government obtains by taxation.

The voluntary contributions of the Canadian people for relief purposes growing out of the war were very generous. Towards the Patriotic Fund they contributed nearly fifty million dollars. This fund was devoted to the assistance of the dependent relatives of the soldiers overseas. To the Canadian Red Cross the people contributed over twenty million dollars to aid in providing for the sick and wounded, equipping hospitals, and caring for prisoners and refugees. Generous contributions were also made to the British Red Cross, the Belgian Relief Fund, and to the Y.M.C.A. for war work. Provincial governments contributed largely. Ontario gave a million bags of flour, Quebec four million pounds of cheese, Alberta a half million bushels of oats, Nova Scotia machine-guns, and other provinces similar gifts. Ontario built, equipped, and maintained a large military hospital in England. In addition to all this, numberless organizations and individuals were constantly at work in providing field comforts for the soldiers overseas.

A scheme of food control was placed in operation by the Canadian government. The purpose was to prevent waste and to increase the quantity of food products available for export to feed the armies in the field and the people of the allied nations. Certain restrictions were placed upon the serving of beef and bacon in hotels and restaurants, and the people generally were requested to abstain from eating meat on certain days. The use of substitutes was encouraged. The making of highly refined flour was stopped, and manufacturers were required to use a larger percentage of the whole wheat in the production of flour. Restrictions were also placed on the use of sugar in public eating-places. The result of these regulations was that the exports of food were immensely increased without causing the Canadian people any undue inconvenience.

One of the remarkable features of the war was the noble response of Canadian women to the call of duty. Nearly three thousand served as nurses overseas in base hospitals, clearing stations, and hospital ships, and in endurance and

COALITION OF PARTIES

heroism they were not inferior to the men on the fighting lines. In Canada women took the place of the men who were called to the front in munition factories, in business offices, and in agriculture. In recognition of the great services of the women of Canada during the war, the Dominion government in 1918 gave women the right to vote in federal affairs on the same conditions as men. Several of the provinces have extended to them a similar right in provincial affairs.

Early in 1917 Sir Robert Borden saw that the four Canadian divisions in France could not be kept up to strength by voluntary enlistment. It became necessary to obtain the requisite recruits by conscription. He announced that a Military Service Act would be passed, calling out by classes all the men between eighteen and forty-five years of age who had not enlisted. Sir Robert believed, however, that such an Act should not be a partisan measure, but should have the support of both political parties. He therefore proposed that a Union government should be established, including men of both parties, in order that the war might be carried forward with the support of the whole of the Canadian people, regardless of party. The idea of conscription was distasteful to many, but most people felt that it must be adopted if the soldiers in the trenches were to be fairly supported. A Union government was accordingly formed, and an election was called on the issue of the Military Service Act. Sir Wilfrid Laurier found himself unable to support the principle of conscription, believing that voluntary enlistment would still secure a sufficient number of recruits. In the election of December, 1917, the Union government emerged with a very large majority. Shortly afterwards the Military Service Act was put into force. Over eighty thousand men were secured in this way, including many who reported voluntarily. Thus Canada showed that she wished her men to be adequately supported on the firing-line.

At the end of the war, the government was confronted with the serious problem of absorbing nearly 400,000 men in civil life once more. In the majority of cases the returned men dropped back into their former work. In the case of the disabled the problem was more difficult. The government set up the Department of Soldiers' Civil Re-establishment, which arranged for the medical care of those requiring it and for the re-training of those whose disability made it impossible for them to resume their former work. A Soldier Settlement Board was also established, which arranged for loans to those returned men who wished to take up land. Pensions were provided for the dependents of those who lost their lives, and for disabled soldiers in proportion to the degree of their disability.

When the war was over, representatives of the Allied Powers met in conference at Versailles, near Paris, to decide the terms of peace. The sums of money that Germany should be required to pay and the territory that she should surrender as reparation for damages were determined. But the most important work of the peace conference was the establishment of the League of Nations. This was the outgrowth of a proposal of President Wilson of the United States, who believed that the best safeguard against the recurrence of war was some form of organization among the nations of the world which might provide for the settlement of international disputes without recourse to arms. At present (1938) nearly sixty states, including all the important self-governing nations of the world, except Brazil, Japan, Germany, Italy, Chile, and the United States, are members of a great organization which has for its purpose the abolition of war. President Wilson was unable to induce his own country to accept membership in the League. The United States has stood aloof, fearing that its participation might result in its entanglement in international controversies in Europe in which it has no desire to engage.

The League of Nations has its headquarters at Geneva in Switzerland. It has three branches, the Secretariat, the Council, and the Assembly. The Secretariat consists of the permanent officials, who give their full time to the business of the League. The Council, which meets three times a year, consists at present of three permanent members representing the three Great Powers who are members of the League (Great Britain, France, and Russia), and

LEAGUE OF NATIONS 325

eleven temporary members elected by the Assembly. The Assembly, which meets once a year, consists of not more than three representatives from each of the states constituting the membership of the League.

There is no division of authority between the Assembly and the Council. Each may deal with any matter within the sphere of the League, but both bodies must be in agreement upon any action that is taken in international matters. In practice the Assembly has devoted itself largely to the promotion of good will among the nations, and to the furtherance of humanitarian projects, such as the control of the drug traffic, the combating of disease, and the improvement of labour conditions; while the Council has been concerned mainly with the settlement of disputes between rival states. The Assembly is the "parliament" of the League, and the Council is the "cabinet" or committee through which the decisions of the League are carried out.

One of the most important achievements of the League of Nations was the establishment in 1922 of a Permanent Court of International Justice, consisting of fifteen judges of outstanding repute, elected for a period of nine years by the Assembly and the Council. This Court is given power to hear and decide upon matters of dispute between states, and to give advice upon international questions referred to it by the League. It has its permanent quarters at The Hague, the capital of Holland, and meets at least once a year. Already the Court has settled many matters of contention between nations, and has proved its usefulness in the promotion of international harmony.

From the first Canada has had representatives in the Assembly of the League. A Canadian, Senator Dandurand, was president of the Assembly in 1925, and the following year he was elected as a member of the Council. This may rightly be taken as a recognition of the importance that Canada has assumed in the eyes of the world.

In recent years the League has lost some of its earlier prestige and influence owing to the withdrawal of powerful states which have declined to be bound by its decisions. It has been unable to prevent Italy's conquest of Ethiopia,

Y

Japan's attack upon China, the civil war in Spain, or Germany's absorption of Austria. The opinion that the League is no longer an effective agency for peace or for curbing the encroachments of aggressive nations upon weaker peoples is at present (1938) quite widely held. This is a pessimistic view which, it is hoped, future events may prove unjustified. It would be sad indeed if an organization, founded with such high hopes and with such lofty aims, should fail to accomplish its splendid purpose.

Sir Robert Borden was one of the leading members of the conference of Versailles which decided the terms of the treaty of peace that closed the war. He signed the treaty as the representative of Canada on terms of equality with the other allied nations. He was later a leading figure at Geneva when the League of Nations was launched. His health was broken as a result of the tremendous strain that he endured during the war and the period of readjustment that followed. In 1920 the man who had so wisely guided the destinies of Canada during the most trying period of her history gave up the reins of power to other hands and retired to private life. He was succeeded in the premiership by Hon. Arthur Meighen, who had been one of the leading members of the Union Ministry.

Sir Robert had the good fortune, denied to other prime ministers of Canada, to withdraw from public life at the height of his popularity and power, and to be permitted for many years to watch from the quiet haven of his home the tide of events sweep by without feeling any responsibility for their course. He died in June, 1937, at the age of eighty-three, and Canadians felt that a great man had been called to his reward.

Sir Robert Borden disdained the arts of the petty politician and never sought the plaudits of the multitude. Never a narrow partisan, he seldom antagonized those who opposed him. Invariably courteous, considerate, and tolerant, he was nevertheless a stern antagonist when occasion demanded. He had a judicial mind which was not swayed by passion or prejudice nor subject to hasty decision. By political friends and foes alike, he was respected and admired for his sterling integrity and his high qualities of mind and heart. He was a keen debater, an able parliamentarian, a constructive statesman, and an honest administrator. His wise guidance during the Great War enhanced the prestige of Canada in the eyes of all the world. He made this country completely autonomous without disturbing in the least her sentimental attachment to Britain. His name will always occupy a proud place in Canada's scroll of fame.

The lesson that the Great War brought is written deep upon the heart of Canada. Her sons fought bravely side by side with those of the Motherland and of the sister overseas Dominions in defence of honour, justice, and humanity. The fifty thousand graves in Flanders' fields are mournful tokens of her deep devotion to the lofty aims for which the Empire stands. In tens of thousands of Canadian homes there is grief for those who lie at rest beneath the skies of foreign lands, but there is pride and thankfulness as well in the knowledge that they died for noble ends. In our hospitals and streets the scarred and broken forms of men who strove and bled remind us daily of unselfish sacrifice for high ideals. The names of those who gave their lives are graven deep in brass and stone in church and public square in every town and hamlet, and will serve in years to come to keep before the minds of generations yet to be the glorious cause for which our country fought.

INDEX

Abercrombie, General, 89
Alaska Boundary, 302
Alberta, 304
Algonquin Indians, 26, 35
Allan, Sir Hugh, 243
Alverstone, Lord, 302
Amherst, General, 93, 95, 103
Amiens, 320
Amundsen, 188
Anticosti Island, 14
Arkansas River, 58
Arnold, General, 114
Arras, 320
Ashburton, Lord, 207
Ashburton Treaty, 207
Aylesworth, Sir Allen, 302

Back, Lieutenant, 184, 186
Bagot, Sir Charles, 210, 216
Baldoon Settlement, 177
Baldwin, Robert, 209–213, 216, 221
Ballot Act, 265
Batoche, 246
Beaver Dams, 173
Beck, Sir Adam, 310
Belle Isle, Strait of, 13
Bigot, 87
Blake, Hon. Edward, 264, 265, 266, 293, 298
Borden, Sir Robert, 305, 314–326
Boscawen, Admiral, 94
Bougainville, 90, 95
Bouquet, Colonel, 111
Bowell, Sir Mackenzie, 298
Braddock, General, 86
Brant, Joseph, 120–124
Brébeuf, Father Jean, 35–40

British Columbia, 232, 243
British North America Act, 240, 252, 270, 294
Brock, Sir Isaac, 159–165, 168
Brown, Hon. George, 238, 258–261, 263
Byng, General Sir Julian, 318

Cabot, John, 8–11
Cabot, Sebastian, 9
Cambrai, 320
Campbell, Sir Alexander, 236
Canada Temperance Act, 265
Canadian Northern Railway, 303
Canadian Pacific Railway, 243, 265, 272, 289
Canadian Red Cross, 322
Cariboo District, 232
Carleton, Sir Guy, 112–119
Cartier, Jacques, 12–20
Cartier, Sir Georges Étienne, 254–257
Cataraqui, 61, 69
Chaleur, Bay of, 14
Champlain, Samuel de, 21–29
Charlesbourg Royal, 20
Charlottetown Conference, 239, 270, 275
Chipewyan, Fort, 137, 140, 184
Christian Guardian, The, 224
Churchill, Fort, 131
Clergy Reserves, 118, 190, 206, 221, 225
Colborne, Sir John, 198, 202
Colonial Advocate, 190
Columbia River, 143, 148
Columbus, Christopher, 1–7
Constitutional Act, 118, 189

328

INDEX 329

Cook, Captain James, 125–130
Coppermine River, 131, 184
Courcelette, 318
Coureurs de bois, 51
Court of International Justice, 325
Crèvecœur, Fort, 64
Cronje, General, 300
Currie, General Sir Arthur, 320
Cutknife Creek, 246

Dalhousie, Lord, 196
Dalyell, Captain, 109
Dandurand, Senator, 325
Daniel, Father, 37
Daulac (Dollard), Adam, 41–45
Dearborn, General, 163, 220
De Levis, 101
De Monts, 22
Denonville, 70
Department of Soldiers' Civil Re-establishment, 324
Detroit, 107, 162, 169
Donnacona, 16
Dorchester, Lord, 112–119, 157
"Double Shuffle," 256
Douglas, Sir James, 228–234
Drucour, 94
Duchesneau, 70
Duck Lake, 246
Dundas Street, 157
Du Quesne, Fort, 86
Durham, Lord, 198

Elgin, Earl of, 211
Enterprise, Fort, 184
Etherington, Captain, 109
Extradition, 208

Family Compact, 190, 250
Fenians, 240, 282
Fielding, Hon. W. S., 305
Fitzgibbon, Lieutenant, 173, 193
Franklin, Sir John, 183–188
Fraser River, 140, 232
Freehold Tenure, 237
Frog Lake, 246
Frontenac, Count, 67–73
Frontenac, Fort, 61

Garry, Fort, 242, 288
Gaspé Bay, 14
George, Fort, 87, 164
Gladwyn, Major, 108
Globe, The, 238, 258
Grand River, 122
"Great Administration, The," 211
Great Slave Lake, 135
Great War, The, 315
Griffon, 62
Groseilliers, 52

Habitants, 49
Halifax, 22
Hanna, Hon. W. J., 312
Harrison, General, 168
Head, Sir Francis Bond, 192
Hearne, Samuel, 131–136
Henry VII, King, 9
Hochelaga, 17
Hood, Lieutenant, 184, 185
Howe, Joseph 248–253, 268, 269
Hudson, Henry, 30–34
Hudson's Bay Company, 54, 177, 242, 285
Hughes, General Sir Sam, 316
Hull, General, 162
Huntington, Mr. L. S., 243
Huron Indians, 26, 35
Hydro-Electric Power Commission, 310
Imperial Conference, 300
Imperial Defence Proposals, 304, 315
Iroquois Indians, 26, 35, 41
Isabella, Queen of Spain, 3

James Bay, 32
Jesuit Mission, 37
Jetté, Sir Louis, 302
Jogues, Father, 40
Johnson, Sir William, 106, 111, 120
Joliet, Louis, 57

King's College, 221
Kingston, 204, 236
King William's Island, 188

INDEX

Kirke, David, 28
Klondike, 302
Kruger, President, 300

La Barre, 70
Lachine, 60, 71
LaFontaine, Sir Louis, 214-217
Lalement, Father, 37
La Salle, Sieur de, 60-66
Laurier, Sir Wilfrid, 296-306, 314, 316, 323
Laval, Bishop, 50, 69
La Vérendrye, 78-84
League of Nations, 324
Le Caron, Father, 37
Lens, 319
Liquor, Control of, 50, 69, 309
Local Option, 310
Long Sault Rapids, 42
Louisbourg, Fort, 93
Louisiana, 65
Lount, Samuel, 193

McClintock, 188
Macdonald, Sir John A., 235-247, 261, 264, 270
Macdonell, Captain Miles, 179
Macdonell, Colonel, 165
Macdougall, Hon. William, 261
McGee, Thomas D'Arcy, 274, 278-284
Mackenzie, Hon. Alexander, 262-267, 297,
Mackenzie, Sir Alexander, 137-141
Mackenzie River, 138, 186
Mackenzie, William Lyon, 189-194, 195, 209
McNab, Colonel Sir Allan, 193, 237
Magdalen Islands, 13
Maine Boundary, 207
Malden, Fort, 162, 168
Mandan Indians, 82
Manitoba, 242
Manitoba School Question, 272, 298
Marquette, Father Jacques, 56-59

Matthews, Peter, 193
Meares, Captain James, 142
Meighen, Hon. Arthur, 326
Metcalfe, Sir Charles, 210
Michilimackinac, 65, 109, 162
Middleton, General, 246
Military Service Act, 323
Mississippi River, 56, 62, 148
Mohawk Migration, 122
Monckton, General, 95
Mons, 320
Montcalm, Marquis de, 85-91, 95
Montgomery, General, 114
Montgomery's Tavern, 192
Montmorency River, 90, 96
Montreal, 17, 101, 114, 212
Moraviantown, 170
Mowat, Sir Oliver, 236, 261, 292-295
Municipal Government, 206, 211
Municipal Loan Fund Act, 293
Murray, General James, 101-105

Napierville, 200
National Policy, 245, 266
National Transcontinental Railway, 303
Navy Island, 193
Nelson, Dr. Wolfred, 198
Newark, 156
New Brunswick, 13, 240, 274
Newfoundland, 10, 13, 240
Nootka Sound, 129, 142
North-West Company, 147, 178
North-West Passage, 10, 30, 129, 186
Nova Scotia, 240, 268
Nova Scotian, The, 249

One Hundred Associates, Company of, 28, 46
Ontario, 240, 292, 305
Ontario School System, 225, 308
Order of Good Cheer, 24
Oregon Question, 231
Oswego, Fort, 87
Ottawa, 212, 256

INDEX 331

Paardeberg, 300
Pacific Scandal, 243
Papineau, Louis Joseph, 195-200, 214
Paris, Treaty of, 104
Passchendaele, 319
Patricia, District of, 312
Patriotic Fund, 322
" Patriots," 197
Peace River, 140
Phips, Sir William, 71
Pitt, Fort, 110
Plains of Abraham, 91, 99
Pontiac, 106-111
Port Royal, 24
Poutrincourt, 22
Prevost, Sir George, 162
Prince Edward Island, 13, 177, 243
Prince Rupert, 53
Procter, General, 170
"Protection," 245, 266
Providence, Fort, 184

Quebec, 25, 240, 254
Quebec Act, 113, 294
Quebec Conference, 239, 270, 275, 282, 293
Quebec, Sieges of, 28, 71, 90, 95, 101, 115
Queenston Heights, 164

Radisson, Pierre, 51-55
Rae, Dr., 187
Rebellion Losses Bill, 211
Rebellion of 1837, 192, 197
Rebellion of 1838, 199
Reciprocity Proposals, 305
Reciprocity Treaty, 239
Récollet Mission, 37
Red River Colony, 178
Red River Rebellion, 242, 288
Remedial Bill, 299
"Representation by Population," 238, 241, 260
Responsible Government, 190, 210, 250
Revolutionary War, 114, 121

Richardson, Dr., 184, 185
Ridgeway, 240, 282
Riel, Louis, 242, 246, 298
Robertson, Colin, 180
Roberval, Sieur de, 19
Rocky Mountains, 84, 140, 148
Royal Military College, 265
Ryerson, Dr. Egerton, 223-224

St. Charles River, 17, 95
St. Croix Island, 22
St. Croix River, 206
St. Denis, 197
St. Eustache, 198
St. Foy, 102
St. James' Cathedral, 222
St. James, Fort, 228
St. Julien, 317
St. Lawrence River, 16
Sandwich, 162, 169
San Juan, 233
San Salvador, 6
Saskatchewan, 304
Saskatchewan Rebellion, 246
Saunders, Admiral, 95
Schoodic River, 207
Scott Act, 265
Scott, Sir Walter, 176, 182
Scott, Thomas, 242, 288
Secord, Laura, 172-175
Seigneurial System, 49, 237
Selkirk, Earl of, 176-182
Semple, Robert, 180
Seven Oaks, 180
Seven Years' War, 93, 113
Sheaffe, General, 164
Simcoe, Sir John Graves, 152-158
Simpson, Sir George, 230, 286
Smith, Donald (Lord Strathcona), 242, 244, 285-291
Soldier Settlement Board, 324
South African War, 290, 300
Sovereign Council, 46
Stadacona, 16
Strachan, Dr. John, 218-222
Strathcona Horse, 290
Strathcona, Lord, 285-291

INDEX

Supreme Court of Canada, 265
Sydenham, Lord, 201–208, 210, 215

Taché, Étienne P., 197
Talon, Jean, 46–50
Tecumseh, 162, 166–171
Thompson, David, 145–151
Thomson, Charles Poulett, 201–208
Ticonderoga, Fort, 89
Tilley, Sir Leonard, 274–277
Timiskaming and Northern Ontario Railway, 311
Tonty, Henry de, 64
Toronto, 157
Townshend, General, 95
Tracy, Marquis de, 47
Trinity University, 221
Tupper, Sir Charles, 251, 268–273

Union, Act of, 203
Union Government, 323
United Empire Loyalists, 116, 153
University of Toronto, 221

Vancouver, Captain George, 142–144
Vancouver, Colony, 231

Vancouver, Fort, 230
Van Rensselaer, General, 164
Vaudreuil, 86, 95, 98, 103
Verchères, Madeleine de, 74–77
Versailles, Conference of, 324
Victoria, Fort, 230
Victoria University, 225
Vignau, Nicolas, 27
Vimy Ridge, 318
Vincent, General, 173

War of 1812, 161
Washington Treaty, 242
Webster, Daniel, 207
Weir, Lieutenant, 197
Whitney, Sir James, 307–313
William Henry, Fort, 87
Wilson, President, 324
Windermere, Lake, 149
Winnipeg, 182
Wolfe, General James, 92–100
Wolseley, General, 242
Women's Franchise, 323
Wool, Captain, 164, 173

Yonge Street, 157
York, 157, 161
York Factory, 146, 179